1 MONTH OF
FREE
READING

at

www.ForgottenBooks.com

By purchasing this book you are eligible for one month membership to ForgottenBooks.com, giving you unlimited access to our entire collection of over 700,000 titles via our web site and mobile apps.

To claim your free month visit:

www.forgottenbooks.com/free225476

* Offer is valid for 45 days from date of purchase. Terms and conditions apply.

ISBN 978-0-365-12275-3
PIBN 10225476

This book is a reproduction of an important historical work. Forgotten Books uses state-of-the-art technology to digitally reconstruct the work, preserving the original format whilst repairing imperfections present in the aged copy. In rare cases, an imperfection in the original, such as a blemish or missing page, may be replicated in our edition. We do, however, repair the vast majority of imperfections successfully; any imperfections that remain are intentionally left to preserve the state of such historical works.

Forgotten Books is a registered trademark of FB &c Ltd.
Copyright © 2017 FB &c Ltd.
FB &c Ltd, Dalton House, 60 Windsor Avenue, London, SW19 2RR.
Company number 08720141. Registered in England and Wales.

For support please visit www.forgottenbooks.com

MEMOIRS

OF

CHARLES MATHEWS,

COMEDIAN.

BY MRS. MATHEWS.

"A man so various, that he seemed to be
Not one, but all mankind's epitome."—DRYDEN.

"Proteus for shape, and mocking-bird for tongue."

SECOND EDITION.

VOL. I.

LONDON:
RICHARD BENTLEY, NEW BURLINGTON STREET,
Publisher in Ordinary to Her Majesty.

1839.

Mathews

MEMOIRS

OF

CHARLES MATHEWS,

COMEDIAN.

BY MRS. MATHEWS.

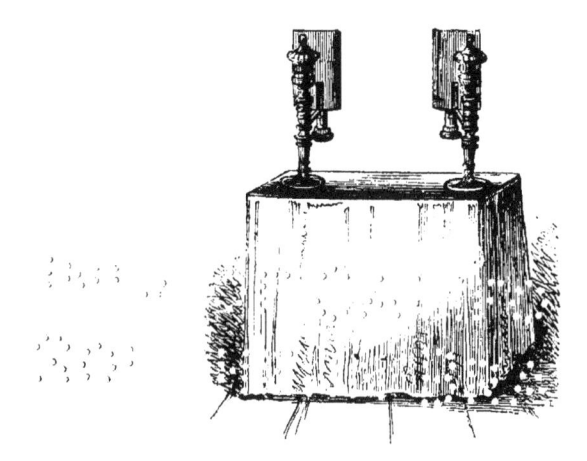

"A man so various, that he seemed to be
Not one, but all mankind's epitome."—DRYDEN.

"Proteus for shape, and mocking-bird for tongue."

SECOND EDITION.

VOL. I.

LONDON:
RICHARD BENTLEY, NEW BURLINGTON STREET,
Publisher in Ordinary to Her Majesty.

1839.

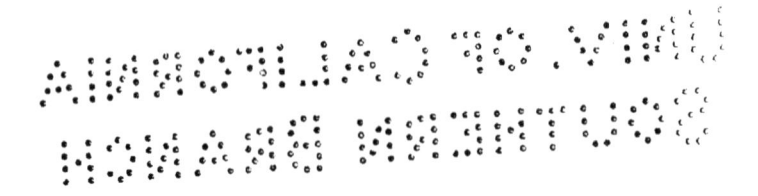

LONDON:
PRINTED BY SAMUEL BENTLEY,
Bangor House, Shoe Lane

LIST OF PLATES.

VOL. I.

Portrait of Charles Mathews	*to face Title.*
Mr. Mathews as *Lenitive* in " The Prize "	*page* 168
Portrait of George Colman, Esq.	. 340

VOL. II.

Mr. Mathews studying four celebrated Characters, by Harlowe	*to face Title.*
Portrait of Thomas Hill, Esq.	*page* 69
Mr. Mathews as the Spanish Ambassador	. 76
Mr. Mathews as the Coachman, " Prime Bang-up," in " Hit or Miss "	. 113
Mr. Mathews as the " Old Scotch Lady "	. 452

CONTENTS

OF THE FIRST VOLUME.

CHAPTER I.

My determination to write my Life.— Birth, parentage, and education; life, character, and behaviour.—My retentive memory. —My birth-place.—My Grandfather and father.—Family Disputes.—Fanatic Visiters.—My face and figure when a Child.— Hannah Moore and Garrick.—My school-days.—The school-master and usher.—My precocious attempts at mimicry.—A perambulating Fishmonger. — My imitation of his queer cry, and his revenge. . . . . . . Page 1

CHAPTER II.

Methodist Preachers: Brothers Hill, Durrant, Huntington, Berridge. — Fanatics' Tabernacle in Tottenham Court Road. — "The Oven."—Early Bigotry. — "Wrestling."—First Love.— Musical Mania. — Incipient yearnings after popular applause. — Enfield Races. 18

CHAPTER III.

Merchant Tailors' School.—Flogging.—Serjeant Pell.—William Mathews. — Religious experience. — Saintly Epistles. — Religious Fanaticism. — Pious Tracts with odd titles. — Huntingdon the Coalheaver, and his miracles.—Rowland Hill.—Popular preaching. 32

CHAPTER IV.

French School.—Private Theatricals.—Master Elliston.—First Visit to a Theatre, and its effect.—Literary attempt.—Mr. John Litchfield.—Major Topham.—William Mathews.—The Thespian Magazine.—Editorship.—Death of Edwin the Comedian.—Correspondence with Mr. Thomas Harris, the proprietor of Covent Garden Theatre.—Apprenticeship to his father.—Macklin.—First appearance on a public stage with Mr. John Litchfield.—Richmond *at* Richmond.—The Duke of Clarence and Mrs. Jordan.—Second appearance in public.—Canterbury.—Last appearance in the character of a Bookseller.—Introduction to the Agent of the Dublin Theatre.—Engagement, and departure from home. . Page 50

CHAPTER V.

Early Letters to his friend Mr. John Litchfield.—Departure from Home.—Journey to Ireland.—Dublin.—Introduction to Daly the Manager.—Mrs. Wells (afterwards Mrs. Sumbel).—Owenson.—Miss Campion (afterwards Mrs. Pope).—Miss Farren.—Holman.—Honourable Mrs. Twiselton.—Dishonourable conduct of Daly.—First appearance on the Dublin Stage.—His Salary.—" Fontainville Forest."—Cherry.—John Palmer.—Captain Wathen.—Mathews's Cast of Characters in Dublin, and his quick study.—Mr. Boaden the author.—Mr. and Mrs. Davenport. . . 80

CHAPTER VI.

Study in the fields.—In danger of being drowned.—An Irish *humane society.*—Virtues of Whiskey.—Mrs. Bateman and the Chevalier D'Eon; their fencing.—Mathews's prospects.—Buck, the Artist.—Daly's engagements.—Mathews's first appearance on the stage as a dancer.—Mathews's characters.—Cooke's performances in Dublin.—Supper with Cooke, and *a scene,* principal characters by Cooke and Mathews, and Mrs. Byrn.—Whiskey Punch and the Passions. . . . . . Page 112

CHAPTER VII.

Leaf out of Cooke's Common-place book.—His talents as an actor.—Death of Parsons, the comedian.—Captain Wathen's kindness.—Cherry.—Miss Wallis.—Holman.—Imitations.—Theatrical perplexity.—Quarrel between Cooke and Daly.—Cooke withdraws from the Theatre.—Miss Campion.—Mathews's distress in Dublin. —Kemble's appearance in Hamlet.—His recognition of Mathews. —Incledon and Miss Poole.—Cooke enlists as a common soldier.— Anecdote.—Incledon.—Mathews's characters.—His performance of Clown in a pantomime. — Resolves to quit the profession of an actor, and return to London.—Mr. Montague, Talbot, and Henry Ireland.—The Shakspeare Forgeries.—Voyage from Ireland.—Arrival in Swansea.—The theatre of that town.—Talbot's dismay at sea.—His finikin manners.—Anecdote. . . . 136

CHAPTER VIII.

Mr. Mathews at the Swansea Theatre.—Memoranda of his performances there.— His success.— Engaged for the season.— Mr. Mathews appears as Clown.—The Shakspeare Forgeries.—" Vortigern and Rowena" condemned. — Dr. Parr deceived. — Ireland ruined.—Mr. Mathews performs at Carmarthen with Mr. Nash, afterwards the architect, and Mr. Pugin, the architectural draughtsman.—Lee Sugg, the ventriloquist.—His dislike of Mr. Mathews, and murderous attack upon him.—An entertainment by Lee Sugg described.—His scheme to outwit the Welsh, and its failure.—His tricks and annoyances to obtain money from Mr. Mathews.—His death. 161

CHAPTER IX.

Wynne, the leader of the Swansea band.—His romantic and melancholy history.—His irritable temperament.—His peculiarities.—Wynne at a musical rehearsal, and the tricks played on him by the wags of the theatre.—His antipathy to dogs, and unintentional cruelty.—Ludicrous mistakes by Wynne.—Mr. Mathews's successful imitation of his peculiarities. . . Page 181

CHAPTER X.

Mr. Mathews and Miss Strong.—His engagement to her, and his Father's letter to him on the subject.—His marriage with Miss Strong.—Increasing Ambition.—Application to Tate Wilkinson, the York Patentee.—The Manager's letters in reply.—Mr. Mathews's visit to his family in London.—His reception.—Mr. and Mrs. John Litchfield.—Mr. Mathews's engagement with Tate Wilkinson, and journey into Yorkshire. . . 194

CHAPTER XI.

Arrival at Pontefract.—First interview with Tate Wilkinson.—The Manager's habit of confusing names.—Mr. Mathews's first appearance announced.—His début.—The result.—Emery.—Personal identity.—York.—Mr. Mathews's first appearance there.—Messrs. Melvin and Denman.—Mr. Rock.—Mr. T. Knight. 209

CHAPTER XII.

Dispiriting treatment.—Ill health.—Emery's departure to fulfil his engagement at Covent Garden Theatre.—Mr. Mathews's letter introducing him to Mr. Litchfield.—Hull.—Mr. Mathews's opening character. — Fresh mortifications. — Mr. Hatton's arrival. — Another disappointment.—The consequences.—Mr. Mathews's letter of remonstrance to the Manager.—Tate Wilkinson's reply.— Increasing success of Mr. Mathews.—His letter to Mr. Litchfield announcing Hatton's discharge.—Triumph of industry and integrity. —Letter to Mr. Litchfield from Doncaster. . . Page 225

CHAPTER XIII.

Haunted room. — Eccentrics of Tate Wilkinson's company.— Johnny Winter, the wardrobe-keeper and tailor. — Kemble and Shakspeare.—Dress for a Bishop.—Johnny and a dramatic aspirant.—Mr. Mathews in *Caleb Quotem*.—" Charlie Wood's" benefit. —Winter's ambition for a horse.—Johnny and the manager.— Marriage of Johnny's daughter.—Stephen Kemble's new dress.— Mrs. Siddons. 243

CHAPTER XIV.

Leeds.—Prejudice entertained there against actors.—Rudeness to female performers.—Outrage upon Mr. Holman, and upon Miss Gough.—Feeling towards actors in Hull.—Anecdote.—Denman and the landlady.—Johnny Winter and Dwyer.—Winter's disdain of " mock modesty."—Lady W—ne and her brother.—Miss Topham. — Major Topham.—Mrs. Townend. — Idiots.—Tommy Myers.—Journey from York to London and back for a shilling.— " Fond Barney." 271

CHAPTER XV.

Unpopularity of the Income-tax.— Mr. Mathews's whimsical remonstrance to the Commissioners.—Anecdote of Quick.—Letter of Mr. Litchfield to Mr. Mathews.—Mrs. Litchfield as *Lady Mac-*

beth.—Cooke's success at Covent Garden.—Mrs. Mathews a novelist.—Straitened circumstances of Mr. Mathews.—Mrs. Mathews's literary projects for defraying the claims upon her husband.—Letter to Mr. Litchfield.—Tate Wilkinson's opinion of Mr. Mathews.—Mr. William Mathews's departure for the West Indies, and letter to his brother.—Letter to Mr. Litchfield.—Tate Wilkinson's opinion of Murphy's Life of Garrick. — Mr. Mathews's success at York.— His fondness for attending trials. — Action for killing a donkey.—Witness interrogated by Counsellors Raine and Cockle. —Humour of the witness.—Letter of Mr. William Mathews to his brother. . . . . . Page 299

CHAPTER XVI.

Mr. Mathews's accident while performing at York.—Death of his brother.—Letter to Mr. Litchfield. — Mrs. Mathews's illness and dying wishes.—Letter to Mr. Litchfield.—Death of Mrs. Mathews.—A remarkable dream.—Letter from Mr. Colman, offering Mr. Mathews an engagement in London.—Correspondence on the subject. 323

CHAPTER XVII.

George Colman at York.—Tate Wilkinson's reception of him.— The York performers.—Mr. Colman's dramatic reading.—" Little Knight."—Mr. Liston.—Tate Wilkinson's letters to him. — Mr. Mathews's second marriage.—Wedding incidents.—Miss De Camp. —Mr. Colman's letter to Mr. Mathews.—The Yorkshire tailor and the mis-fit. — Parting interview between Mr. Mathews and Tate Wilkinson. 349

CHAPTER XVIII.

Anecdotes of Tate Wilkinson. 366

CHAPTER XIX.

Arrival in London of Mr. Mathews and his young wife. — Their reception at the paternal home. — Gloom of the house. — Removal to Manchester-street. — Old Mr. Mathews listening to his son's songs and stories.—Mr. Mathews's first appearance in London.—Anecdote of Mr. Cumberland.—Letter from Tate Wilkinson.—Letter from a York actor.—Mr. Liston.—Death of Tate Wilkinson. . . . . . Page 402

CHAPTER XX.

Mr. Mathews's success in " Love Laughs at Locksmiths."—His *Mr. Wiggins*.—His engagement at Liverpool.—Letter from Mr. Lewis.—His prediction.—Letter from Mr. Mathews to Mr. Litchfield.—Serious accident to Mr. Mathews.—Mr. Young the actor. —His talent in mimicry.—Letter respecting him from Mr. Colman.—Birth of Mr. Mathews's son.— Letter from Mr. Colman.— Letter to Mr. Litchfield.— Letter from Mr. Emery. . 415

AUTOBIOGRAPHY

OF

CHARLES MATHEWS.

CHAPTER I.

My determination to write my Life.—Birth, parentage, and education; life, character, and behaviour.—My retentive memory.—My birth-place.—My Grandfather and Father.—Family Disputes.—Fanatic Visiters.—My face and figure when a child.—Hannah More and Garrick.—My school-days.—The school-master and usher.—My precocious attempts at mimicry.—A perambulating fishmonger.—My imitation of his queer cry, and his revenge.

"HE who pleads his own cause has a fool for his client," say the lawyers. I am afraid the writer of his own life is liable to the same imputation. I should have begun to write mine years ago, if I had had the courage. "On their own merits modest men are dumb,"—on their demerits they are not likely to dwell. What then is a poor fellow to do, who, with the terrors of the press before his eyes, feels it a sort of duty to himself to put on record a few remarkable events, anecdotes of celebrated men, hair-breadth escapes by flood and field, opinions of contemporaries, and various scenes in the drama of life in which he has been a principal actor?

It is not merely a record of my own adventures and mishaps — my life and opinions, that I am vain enough to think amusing; but some of those singular events which, contrary to all probability or my own expectation, mingled me with remarkable men. Few individuals have had greater opportunities afforded them than myself of associating or coming in contact with persons of every class of society, as I trust I shall be able to show. The original causes of such heterogeneous associations it will be my business to depict—but, from one chance or another, "they lay in my way," and I have known, visited, corresponded, or conversed with kings, lords, commons, merchants, traders; all from the cobbler's stall to the palace, I have, like Asmodeus, contrived to enter—and, therefore, think I have at least the wherewithal to furnish an amusing work.

Well, then, for some years I have hoped the day would arrive when I should have the courage to "attempt my own life." I *really* have to plead the excuse of publishing "at the desire of too partial friends." I have been coaxed, wheedled, urged, tempted, bribed, goaded almost, to — begin. "Make a commencement at all events.

Try; 'tis a shame — such stores of anecdotes — you will only have to copy, and instead of the dazzling white paper before you, you can shut your lids, while the eyes are turned within, and have only the labour of remembering, while others are battering their brains for invention." "Yes," said I, "true—but then the plan, the construction, the language! The public has been fed with such high dishes, that"—"They are more likely to be pleased with simple fare," said a good-natured, round, dimple-faced friend. "Ah! there indeed!" said I; "if I believed that!" "Believe it then from me; write fearlessly—nay, carelessly if you like." "What! with the terrors of the Quarterly and Edinburgh, *cum multis aliis*, before my eyes?" "You have nothing to fear from them, if you do not 'attempt' too much. Flowery writing, or metaphorical description, will 'confound you,' not the deed of writing as you speak."

"Well!" said I, "seriously, I am thinking of it. Begin I will, my—my—what? 'Apology?' —I hear a hiss at the word. 'Records?'—already done. 'Reminiscences?'—stale. Well, then,— Birth, parentage, and education—Life, character, and behaviour, of Charles Mathews, Comedian, who was—Hang it! I have heard those words before, and precisely so arranged; but no matter—I will pursue that style of biography to the letter: it has sold many a sheet-list of all 'the unfortunate malefactors,' and perhaps it is not yet so damaged in the service but that it may be of service to me. I will begin with the birth, and pursue it to — nay, not quite to the last scene — I must leave that to somebody more alive to the subject than myself."

I have never written with a view to publication since I was sixteen, and have considerable doubt whether I am qualified for the task. I have resolved to put down rapidly the matter which my memory is charged withal, and shall risk the reading just as I should a letter written in a hurry to an indulgent friend, of which I had preserved no copy. I have never kept a journal or diary, or made a memorandum of a conversation in my life; but I have an excellent—nay, an extraordinary memory, (an invaluable gift to one of my profession,) and, having given public proof of this, I may venture to make the remark. I fearlessly pledge myself to the declaration, that I can perfectly recollect and repeat most of the anecdotes and conversations of remarkable persons whom I have met in early life, with as much facility as I related them at the time they happened.

Addison remarks, " that no one peruses a book with so much content, if he be unacquainted with the author, as when he is informed of his situation in life, his connexions, his disposition, and, above all, of his person." Now, knowing the misery of ungratified curiosity, I feel it my duty to proceed upon this hint, and shall therefore endeavour to afford every facility in my power to those who may do me the honour to read my life and experience, towards their full enjoyment of these volumes, by satisfying the most insatiable propensity for prying that ever afflicted the most curious and inquisitive of the human race.

I shall commence this narrative with " those early years wherein the human mind receives its first bias,—when the seeds of all our future actions are sown in the heart, and when causes, in themselves so trifling as almost to be imperceptible, chain us to good or bad, to fortune or misfortune;" and, with this object in view, I hope I shall be excused if, in the outset, I dwell for some time on the situation in life, connexions, and disposition of others,—I mean, of that excellent man my father, and of the peculiar society in which he moved.

To begin at the beginning, then, I shall commence with my first birthday.*

---

* On a fly-leaf of the huge Family Bible, the following memoranda may be found in his father's writing:—

After the heading of—

"James Mathews, his Book,
1765,

was born the 20th of July 1742, and married to Elizabeth Manly the 21st of July 1765, who was born in the month of June 1744—

Heirs together of the grace of life!"—

may then be seen, in regular succession, the dates of the births of fourteen children, seven daughters and seven sons. Of the latter,

" Charles Mathews, the seventh son of James and Elizabeth

I was born on the 28th of June 1776, at half-past two o'clock " and a cloudy morning," at No. 18, Strand, London. The house, I regret to say, no longer exists; for, in the summer of 1833, I had the mortification to see the venerable residence of my forefathers, the interesting birthplace of the hero of these pages, destroyed piecemeal by unhallowed hands, who, regardless of all its classical, poetical, and histrionic associations, demolished, brick by brick, every vestige of its former appearance, and "left not a rack behind,"—for what? Oh, bathos! to open to the public—a view of Hungerford Market!

My grandfather was a native of Glamorganshire, and the real family name was Matthew, which he changed, for an estate, to Mathews with one T. He died, leaving this property in litigation; and my father thereby lost a T and a Chancery suit. The estate was worth 200*l.* a year, and cost him about 210*l.* annually in law and repairs; so that its loss became a gain,*—a fact, I take it, of no small importance to the world.

Mathews, was born on June the 28th, 1776, at a quarter before three o'clock in the morning."

For the consideration of those who are disposed to regard as portentous, and who are apt to draw conclusions from such facts, it may be added, that my husband was the *seventh son* of a *seventh son.* Out of the fourteen children born, the latest survivors (and for more than thirty years) were the seventh daughter and the seventh son.—A. M.

* This resembles an " *endowment*" in Scotland, which is there called a " *mortification.*"—A. M.

My father was a respectable, and what was called a "serious," bookseller. Indeed he was himself so rigid a sectarian as to have been selected to be prime minister at one of her chapels by no less a personage than Lady Huntingdon herself; so that it will be easily imagined I was not indebted to him for any of my theatrical propensities. He, good man, assured me that he had never seen a play in his life. His father, also a bookseller, was one of those persons who thought it sinful to enjoy innocent amusement, and his son was forbidden to be gay or mirthful. *My* father was obedient, (my son cannot say as much of his father,) and I have not yet sufficiently repented of my disobedience to add, " Alas! would that I had been obedient too!" " Just as the twig is bent," they say, " the tree's inclined;" but had I been so inclined, I might have been at this moment a " serious bookseller" also, for my father had designed me for his successor. But, as it happens in the best-regulated families, the husband and wife did not chance to agree — that is, upon religious points.

My excellent mother was strict in her adherence to the tenets of the Church of England ; my father was a rigid Calvinist. Yet these differences of opinion, I must do them the justice to say, were conducted with such good breeding, that I do not recollect ever witnessing any unpleasant controversies. My father was satisfied with sincerity in any one; he allowed my mother to think for herself, without opposing, still less persecuting, her for her opinions; and she, with most dignified church-pride, as some of the sectarians designated it, satisfied her mind by thoroughly, in her heart, despising the ignorant fanatics by whom he was surrounded—for surrounded I may call it—to the destruction of the well-being of his family. Had he been a professed gambler, we could not have felt more alarm at the entrance of a black-leg into the family circle than the arrival of a newly-acquired *brother*. Yet he, the sincerest of the sincere—the most guileless, the most intrinsically honest and moral man, I believe now in my heart, that ever passed sixty-four summers in this sublunary globe, remained a liberal Christian amongst wretched fanatics—moderate in a crowd of raving enthusiasts,—the mildest of preachers—the kindest of advisers; himself an example to the wholesale dealers in brimstone,—the pawnbrokers, hosiers, butchers, shoemakers, travelling tinkers—no matter how low, how ignorant—(blasphemers, I then and now consider many of them)—to whose tender mercies I was constantly subject. A regular set of technical cant phrases pervaded the discourse of them all. I and you, my gentle readers, were damned, and they were saved; they had "had a call," or were "of the elect," and little other qualification was necessary to start as expounders of the word, and to spout nonsense by the hour.

Such were those by whom my father was hemmed in. Had he not been bitten by one of these rabid animals very early in life, his naturally cheerful mind and kindly benevolent disposition, would have admirably qualified him for a contented, quiet, and happy member of the real, true mode of worship, as *I* think, and trust ever shall think.

But I have dwelt so long upon my parentage, that I have nearly forgotten the advice of the great Spectator, and the necessity of relieving the minds of the curious in minutiæ—" Above all, his person."

For a more exact description of this, I have referred to my nurse, who was alive to tell the tale within ten years of the date hereof. She assured me that I was a long, thin, skewer of a child; of a restless, fidgety temperament, and by no means regular features—quite the contrary; and, as if Nature herself suspected she had not formed me in one of her happiest moments, the Fates combined with her to render me more remarkable, and, finding there was not the least chance of my being a beauty, conspired to make me comical.

The agreeable twist of my would-be features was occasioned, as the above-named lady assured me,—indeed, I have heard my mother with great tenderness and delicacy confirm it,—by a species of hysteric fits to which I was subject in infancy, one of which distorted my mouth and eyebrows to such a degree as to render me almost hideous for a time; though my partial nurse declared my "eyes made up for all, they were so bright and lively." Be this as it may, certain it is that, after the recovery from this attack, folks laughed the moment they saw me, and said, "Bless the dear little dear! it is not a beauty, to be sure; but what a funny face it has!" The "off-side" of my mouth, as a coachman would say, took such an affection for my ear, that it seemed to make a perpetual struggle to form a closer communication with it; and one eyebrow became fixed as a rusty weathercock, while the other popped up an inch apparently beyond its proper position. The effects remain to this day, though moderated. "Wrymouth" was a nickname applied to me when at school; and, for the first seven years of my life, I was in the habit of holding my hand to my cheek to hide the blemish. What good or evil "was here wrapt up in countenance," or how far this may have interfered to direct my future pursuits, I do not attempt to say.

I am now about to relate a circumstance which properly belongs to one of the "seven ages," namely, the first; but as my talent is not quite equal to that of the Irishman who said, "There's not a man in the four provinces has such a memory as me—I never heard that story yet but I could repeat it fifty years afterwards," I do not pretend to recollect what happened to me in infancy, yet am I correctly clear as to the description of the scene by my father. It was no less than the justly-celebrated Hannah More's introducing Garrick to him in his own shop. He had never seen him act, and therefore could not feel any of that glow that I feel in relating the incident—he had never witnessed, therefore could not appreciate his talents.

Reader! do you not, as I do, pity from the bottom of your heart the unfortunate victim of prejudice, who could voluntarily deprive himself of the effects of that resplendent genius, the admiration not only of England, but of Europe! What reward would you accept to be deprived of the reminiscence of the gratification afforded you by a Kemble,—a Siddons,—a Talma? Nay, had you been a play-goer till lately, and as suddenly converted as some of these would-be saints have been, would you not say—now be candid, " Well, I am glad I saw Mrs. Siddons first?"—But whither am I wandering?

Well,—notwithstanding this sacrifice of pleasure to principle, my father's pride was gratified that the introduction took place; and when the testimony to that great man's private worth as well as splendid talents was given, at the ceremony of depositing his honoured remains in Westminster Abbey, by the long procession of Lords and Commons that followed, an impression was made on the mind of a trader, that must have staggered his senses, and, in spite of the sentiments his misleaders had implanted in him, he used ever after to erect his crest when he related that he had had the honour of the great Garrick's acquaintance.

As soon as my ears were susceptible of having the delicious fact instilled into them, I heard that on the occasion of the introduction — *credat!* — Reader, take breath,—he, Garrick, took me in his arms! Yes, I was touched, embraced, fondled by the immortal David! That I cannot describe my sensations, will easily be believed when I state that I could not by possibility have been three years old, inasmuch as I was born on the 28th of June, he having made his final bow to the Public on the 10th in that same year—(a fact I would impress on the numerous persons who during my life have pestered me with the question, "Do you remember Garrick, Mr. Mathews?" my answer having always been, " No, sir, I can prove an *alibi.*")—Well, he took me in his arms, and, like the near-sighted lady who said, when a coal-scuttle entered the room in place of an expected infant, "Dear! how like its father!" no doubt made some common-place observation; but my father often declared that he burst into a fit of laughter, and said, "Why, his face laughs all over, but certainly on the wrong side of his mouth!"

I do not go so far as to say this did or did not

affect my future destiny; that my father in his serious moods alluded to it with such a feeling, there can be no doubt: it *may* have been ominous.

Hannah More was at that time of a serious cast, as it is called, but did not quite believe that the association with little Davy endangered the soul. Whether she was of my father's principles or not, I cannot tell; for to this hour I do not know what these Wesleyans, and Whitfieldites, and Huntingtonians were disputing, nay, quarrelling about; nor why two human beings, believing in one God, should condemn each other to everlasting punishment, because their leaders gave different interpretations to the same text in Scripture. Miss Hannah, at all events, submitted some of her small religious tracts to my father, who published them; and I may presume from this, that, as he was so employed by her, he declined putting his name to what she called her Sacred Dramas. He held himself in such a situation personally responsible, though he did not carry his prejudices so far as to exclude from his shelves the works of our great English dramatists.

In due course of time I was sent to school—St. Martin's Free School was, I believe, the first. In the indiscriminate selection of a first school, there are very few who reflect on its consequent effects in after life. Had I twenty sons, I would never send one to the school of a man fond of punishment. I say fond, for I am convinced that my first pompous pedagogue had no gratification equal to the superintending a flagellation. " Let this little gentleman feel the rod!" I have the sound in my ears at this moment. Had flogging given knowledge, I might have been a dangerous rival to the seven Greek sages. But, alas! I did not flourish, though my master did! Often have I cast an eye to the little cherubs that clung on the corner of the organ at the end of the schoolroom, and wished I had been shaped like them, —only head and wings!

Our master, Pownall, was a remarkably handsome man, but pomposity itself. His usher, Shaw, a lank bony Scotchman,—how can I describe him?—squinted " more than a gentleman ought." He had a barbarous accent, and therefore, I suppose, was selected to teach the " Breetish languitch in its oreeginal peurity" to us cockneys. He was a quaint man—thin as a pitchfork. He used to shamble up and down the school by slow fits, rubbing his gamboge chin with his burnt-umber fingers, and directing little bits of broken unintelligible advice to the leering, sheepish, idle little animals who sat in rows up the room, walking before them like Aaron with his rod.

I was at that time particularly fond of carrying a bit of broken looking-glass, to dazzle " Shaw's queer optics" with. Many were the convulsive, painfully-smothered laughs I and my wicked co-adjutors writhed under, (while I remained undiscovered,) at his simplicity and patience, enduring this infliction day after day, squinting up to discover through what cranny in the blind it was that the sun came in to occasion this annoyance: but at length I was caught in the fact; for, while I thought he was looking in an entirely opposite direction, I found he was looking me and my bit of glass full in the face. I was horsed, and now *really* flogged—barbarously birched; while Pompey Pownall roared out, with a voice of thunder, this facetious moral,—" That, sir, will teach you, I hope, not to cast reflections on the heads of the school!"

Here may be traced my first attempts at mimicry. I remember the flogging fellows to this hour,—their voice, tone, and manner; and my ruling propensity was thus early called into action at their expense.

Another precocious attempt at individual imitation about the same time had nearly proved fatal, and, it might be supposed, would have tended to check that irresistible impulse I had to echo, like the mocking-bird, every sound I heard. I used to amuse my schoolfellows with what I then thought my best specimen in that way. It was of a man who cried eels about the streets, and passed through the Strand by my father's door daily. He was rather short, but remarkably muscular; he had a peculiar, guttural voice, which I remember correctly to this hour, and which I can of course now delineate with more accuracy and truth than my then penny-trumpet voice could enable me to do; still it is quite out of the question that I can give any idea of such an original with my pen, when the whole humour of my delineation depends upon intonation: nor should I relate the anecdote, but to enforce my position of the wonder that I had not given up business in that line in the outset. This fellow's regular cry was, "Live eels! Conger eels! Thames eels!—try my eels—silver eels —Dutch eels—threepence a pound e-e-e-e-e-els!" which, taking a fresh supply of breath from his leathern lungs, he *eel*-longated to such an extent, that the last monosyllable frequently held out in undiminished force and energy while he strided from Craven to Hungerford Street.

An imitation of this odd, perambulating fishmonger, I considered as most desirable. He was a notorious character, and excited various laughs, from the infant snigger to the adult roar; and "What a long eel!" was the constant remark his drollery excited. Even my father's serious friends relaxed so far from their rigidity of muscle as to ha-ha-ha nearly three times at my successful hitting off of his peculiarities. Encouraged by this approbation into boldness, having brought my parody to perfection, I was emulous of the approval of the great original himself; and having due notice of his approach from the long eel on which he was trilling perhaps as far off as Charing Cross, I anxiously awaited his arrival. When he was near enough to observe my action, I placed my hand on the dexter side of my mouth, and commenced my sinister operations, taking him off " to the very life," as my panegyrists had led me to believe I could. Had I been as slippery as one of his own articles of traffic, I might have twisted and wriggled my way behind the counter and escaped; but he was too much for me—indeed I did not apprehend so savage an attack. Deliberately placing his basket at the door, he pursued me into the shop; and as I flinched from the huge and ponderous fist that was poised high in air to annihilate me, I conveniently placed my back to receive his blow. " Next time," said the huge monster, as he felled me to the earth, " as you twists your little wry mouth about and cuts your mugs at a respectable tradesman, I'll skin you like an e-e-" and seizing his whole shop up in his Brobdignagian arms, he finished the monosyllable somewhere about No. 27. For weeks — nay, months—did I suffer from the effects of this punishment.

CHAPTER II.

Methodist Preachers: Brothers Hill, Durrant, Huntington, Berridge.—Fanatics' Tabernacle in Tottenham-Court Road.—"The Oven."—Early Bigotry.—"Wrestling."—First Love.—Musical Mania.—Incipient yearnings after popular applause.—Enfield Races.

LITTLE daunted at my ill success in my first attempt, I commenced, previously to my knowledge of the actors, with the heroes of the pulpit. I was reckoned so expert at my representations of Brother Hill and Brother Durrant, Huntington, &c. that I have been requested, in some moments of hilarity, (alas! they were but few,) to exhibit my imitative powers before some of the stiffest of our visiters, and success crowned my efforts. My father was a joyous-looking person, and his jolly good-humoured face dimpled into delight at the "little dog's impudence:" I need not say I had ample encouragement from my mother in this pursuit.

My most successful delineation was of a huge-wigged old devotee whom we called Daddy Berridge. He had been a preacher in the Whitfield school for many years. He was a very old man at the period I speak of, and had lived long enough to see the progress of the Tabernacle in Tottenham-Court Road until it had become a third larger than in Whitfield's time. I myself remember it before the addition of the gallery to the east end, and when the pulpit was nearly close to the wall; but when the new wing was added, there was an eye to the accommodation of a hundred or two more persons than it would formerly hold. These additional auditors, however, were necessarily only indulged with a back view of the precious wigs of the preachers; and those whose circumstances did not afford them seats in the new gallery were doomed to a dungeon underneath, dark and dreary, and well suited to the dismal predictions and fearful threats held out to all who were not of the elect. This recess was called the Oven:—no misnomer. The inexperienced of these comical clergy, who were not aware of the difficulty which the cakes in the Oven encountered during their baking, as to hearing, (seeing the preacher was, of course, out of the question,) proceeded in the even tenor of their way, apparently unconscious of their presence, and certainly taking no pains to convey consolation to their consciences. But Daddy Berridge was a regular old-stager. He was well aware of the select portion confined in the black hole, and had no idea of hiding his candle under a bushel. He, therefore, when he had any choice bit of consolation for his flock, encored himself in his most eloquent passages. Turning his body entirely round in the pulpit, exhibiting his lank desponding visage to those of the gallery, who were delighted with this indulgence, and then dexterously elongating his neck to the prisoners below, he would roar out the repetition of his last sentence, which frequently reaching their ears without the context, could not, I fear, have tended much to their spiritual comfort. As in this instance—" If, with these examples before you,—if, when these truths are made manifest,—if, with these rules laid down for your conduct, and the consequences of your sins by such awful warnings made clear to you, you do not repent, you will all be damned;" he would elevate his guttural voice to a ludicrous pitch, peep down to the half-stifled wretches underneath, and cry, " You will all be damned,—do ye hear below ?" This being all they heard of the sentence, they might very naturally have asked, " For what ?" He would cite a string of truisms as to the uncertainty of life, the certainty of death, the necessity for preparation, and with pathetic tones chant out, " Since I last sojourned amongst you, my worthy brethren, the fell Destroyer has been busy. I can see before me the outward symbols of grieving spirits within—1—2—4—7—8—10—11 13—18—22 people in mourning—(then wheeling to the right about) 25—(left face) 27—9,"—then, to the Oven, " How many are there there ?" Here again is the lack of manner and tone of voice, but I pledge myself to the truth of my description.

Before I began to have a perception of the ludicrous in these exhibitions, which perhaps would have been much longer in being formed but for my occasional visits to St. Martin's Church with my mother, Berridge's Johnsonian wig awed me, and I was strongly impressed with the belief that these Brimstonians were right, and all others wrong.

Notwithstanding my childish wonderment at these proceedings, I had a strong bias to proceed in what I have since believed the wrong path. I was between the ages of eight and thirteen—as complete a little bigot as ever was begotten by gloom, envy, and spleen, a thorough-going melancholy fanatic in embryo. My charity was that of the fraternity, for I not only believed in fire and torments being prepared for all who were not of "the elect," but most devoutly *hoped* it: and I think it fair to infer, if the doctrines which I heard produced this species of feeling in my mind, that such must always be their effect on the ignorant and uneducated. I shall relate presently an anecdote where these feelings came into full play. But first for a more natural as well as more amiable passion,—incipient love.

About this period there was a little saint of the name of Chater. Brother Chater, her father, was a manufacturer of iron-work for coachmakers. I had "*wrestled*" with her at some of the love-feasts, and I was just old enough to regret we were so far apart during the *wrestling*. I therefore began to think I was in love. Gravity begets gravity, and my sister in the faith and I ogled each other most piously. The first time I ever attempted to *wrestle* with her in her father's house, I received a most mortifying check—not from herself—oh no! I was too young to declare my passion; but I had hoped to recommend myself to her regard and insinuate myself into her affections by the force of melody. The charms of music were summoned to my aid. I popped my flute into my pocket and paid her a visit. Her mother was gone to a " *T and B*" ('Tea and Bible), and her father, as we hoped, with her. I had just prevailed upon my fair one to try a newly-published song on the pianoforte, while I accompanied her on the flute, when the enraged father rushed in, and, with all the meekness and courtesy which such Christians profess, called me by every sort of opprobrious name, boxed my ears, seized my hat, thrust it rudely on my head, gave one of his own sledge-hammer knocks on the top which forced lining and all over my eyes, and caused me to try to escape with the swimming sort of action peculiar to blindman's buff, pushed me from the room, and literally kicked me out of the house,—and all because he caught me in the fact of playing "a song-*toon*" as he called it, and " corrupting his darter's mind" by leading her into the same sinful course. " Keep your devil's *toons* to yourself, you young varmin! don't come 'ere with your Beelzebub's jigs. None o' Satan's 'ymns 'ere! take 'em to 'is hown 'ouses—there's one close by in Common Garden. Shan't play none of your imperance to debauch my gal's mind wi'! Go out, I say! and I'll throw your fife out a vinder arter you."—Brother Cahusac's patent keyed flute to be called *a fife!* " Barbarous blacksmith!" thought I, " never more will I endure the wrestlings of your daughter after the indignity bestowed by your iron fist. Sweetest specimen of a saint-like coach-and-cart-spring maker, adieu!"

Was not this enough to check my musical studies in their early growth, to damp my ardour and destroy my enthusiasm for ever? No.

About this very period I made " my first appearance in public" at my father's chapel at Whetstone, where he preached every Sunday.

" Brother Oodard" (Woodward), the butcher, who was my father's clerk, suggested that a " hopposition to the horgan of the church," though in a minor way, might be attractive. He had a son " as fiddled," and Wilson the Cobbler was reckoned a capital hand at the bassoon; " and if Master Charles would but jine 'em and play the flute," what an effective orchestra might be formed without trouble or expense! The scheme was immediately carried into execution; we had several "practizings," as Woodward called them, which made no little noise in the village, and our first public performance being announced by whisperings into the ears of the pious only (as we hoped), the meeting was crowded to suffocation—literally " overflowed," as the play-bills have it.

Pope's " Vital spark of heavenly flame" was the piece selected for our *début;* and I can as perfectly recollect as I can any event within one week of the time of my penning this, the arrangement I made for " a good part," as the actors would say ; I mean, the care and caution I used to make the flute the " first fiddle ;"—*flauto primo* was not enough for my inordinate ambition. Now, as this was a "*four-part song,*" as our choristers called it, we expressly forbade the rest of the congregation from joining in until the whole had been sung through once ; and then they were to sing chorus *only.* I had been a principal singer in this really beautiful piece of music before we aspired to instrumental accompaniment; but here came the puzzle.—I had been *primo tenore,* and " Brother Wizzun" had a " barrow-tone" voice which he made bass for Sundays, I presume, by the old-established mode of getting his feet well wet on Saturday evening. The interesting elder butcher had a counter-tenor part. Our first notion was to accompany ourselves ; but we forgot, in the enthusiasm of the moment, that those who had to play the wind-instruments could not conveniently play and sing at the same time. The junior slaughterer *Oodard* had here an advantage. Many a blind minstrel had given him a hint that to sing and fiddle together was practicable; but *we* did not produce sweet sounds by force of elbow, but by dint of lungs, and I was emulous to exhibit my twofold accomplishments—I considered myself as the principal performer, and I would be heard. If I was to be merely an accompanyist, who was to sing my old part? At last it was agreed that the fame we had already acquired by our vocal performances was not to be compromised, and an ingenious arrangement was made to satisfy all parties. There were fugue passages, symphonies, &c.; and the cobbler and myself, with an enthusiasm never to be sufficiently commended, so contrived that we made some of the bumpkins believe that we sang and played at one and the same time. I wish it were within the power of my pen to give effect to this scene; it requires the aid of practical and vocal elucidation to convey it with full force.

This was a great musical epoch in Whetstone, the march of music at the first stage on the high North Road. It made a stirring sensation in our community, and I hoped, if not believed, that the Steepleites would be jealous: I felt persuaded that seceders from the Church must be the consequence. I was complimented by my saintly friends, and old Woodward was so pleased with my enthusiasm in the good cause, that he respectfully invited me to see a bullock killed on Monday at eleven precisely, "God willing." I wished that Sister Chater could have been present to witness the effect produced by the very instrument which her father had so contumeliously termed a fife. But his assault on the drum of my ear with his metallic fingers had been resented by my father, and the families never met afterwards. Our separation had cooled the ardour of my regard for her, and I soon discovered that I had not really loved; for I was almost immediately afterwards struck dumb by the beauty of another little saint in petticoats. She was exceedingly pretty and good-tempered.

Sister Hallows was the daughter of a rich ribbon-weaver, who had his country-house near my father's, and was one of his flock. I became as desperately enamoured as a boy of my age could well be, and am compelled now to confess that she was really my first love. I was constant, but "let concealment like a worm in the bud" fester my heart—I had not courage, at sixteen, to declare my passion. She was three or four years older than myself, and never, I dare say, bestowed a thought upon me. I sighed at humble distance until she was torn from me by a ruddy handsome young farmer, and I left to mourn my loss unpitied.

I introduce this story of my seared affections

here, as I so fully recollect that my eyes alternated from the notes to her beaming countenance, watching every expression, and anxious for her approving smile. Little did any of these parties think to what all this might lead! Trifles are the pivots on which turn all the vast wheels of that complicated machine called society. Had I never played the flute in chapel, I might have remained in ignorance of the word fame, or its soul-inspiring power. Had I not received the plaudits of Whetstone bumpkins, I might at this moment have been addressing their descendants from the self-same tub. But I had a soul above tubs. These meeds of approbation so flatteringly bestowed upon my musical exertions were the first dawning indications I had of the value of applause. The seeds of ambition were here sown in my young heart. Emulation fired me; I had an immediate desire to rival the violinist. I occasionally had a ride in his cart as he went his rounds of Frien-Barnett and Totteridge Green. I was envious of his accomplishments. He sometimes took his fiddle with him. I drove while he treated me with a "song-tune." Then, when he stayed long from his vehicle,—sometimes "*a killing time*," while he poked a family pig out of the world,—I would seize up the instrument, and wish that "Heaven had made me such a fiddler!" I was too proud to be taught by him, and dreaded a refusal from my father if I petitioned for a fiddle. Alas! good man, I wronged him! I was not then alive to the liberality of his mind. How could I know, in those tender years, that he did not take his tone from those who were feeding upon him? I was not aware with what nicety of discrimination he separated the ore of pure piety from the dross of blasphemy and hypocrisy. He had no persecution in his heart—he breathed, preached, and practised charity!

The "flouters at our solemnities," the "Steeple-ites," as I contemptuously termed those whom I had not yet learned to respect, were of course an opposite faction in the village; and the customers of the rival butchers and bakers were almost all influenced by their party feelings and religious prejudices. The church-goers did not patronise Woodward, and the chapel-ites would not eat of the bread made by the episcopalian baker. The feuds created by this twofold persecution must be manifest. I seldom passed through the place without some petty insult. "Ah, there goes the Methodist parson's son!" "Ah, fifer!" "There goes a psalm-singer!" &c. Some of the rival faction had determined to kidnap me and carry me off *vi et armis* to Enfield Races. The plot was deeply laid—their plan organised with care. A Mr. Lawson, the son of the most respectable shopkeeper in the parish, with whom my mother dealt, though he did not go to chapel (for, be it understood that though my mother attended the parish church in London, she could not with decency appear to act in opposition to my father on his own ground, where all eyes were on her,)—Mr. Lawson, then, who was a gentleman compared with most of those who joined in the conspiracy against "*Our House*," proposed to treat me to the races, and drive me there and back. He undertook to gain my mother's consent, and, to my astonishment, her "slow leave" was given; though the rest of the party had predetermined that, if not accorded, I should go without.

Behold me, then, at my first race! It would be absurd to attempt to describe now what I felt then. I do not affect to recollect the name of a horse or the colour of a rider; but I do remember that these "terrible, terrible high-bred cattle," being the first racing-blood I had ever seen, had such an inspiring effect, that I was then and there inoculated with a mania that has prevailed until this hour. Yes! lame and worn as I am, I admit no difficulty—I allow of no impediment—I am indifferent as to distance—but to the races I must go, whether Doncaster or Epsom, Leger or Derby. I have left Glasgow with the penalty attached of two nights' travelling, in order to be at Newmarket on Easter Monday, and have witnessed twenty-five contests for Derby and Oaks since 1803. I have frequently ridden on horseback from London to the neighbourhood of Epsom at night after my performance to sup with friends, rather than encounter the dust of the roads on the "great day," as it is called. This will show that my enthusiasm is not abated.

Can it be wondered at that I, who had been debarred from any the most trivial amusement or relaxation from school-fagging, should be dancing mad with joy at such an exhilarating exhibition, the first of any sort I had ever witnessed? — But for my adventure.

The races were over, and my anxiety for return was immediate. I apprehended darkness, robbery, upsettings—my mother's alarm if I should not be at home by the promised hour. I urged all this to my companions, but in vain. They had not studied to amuse me only, but themselves also. The sports were now to commence with them. Then, as now, my pleasure for the day finished with the last race. All my enjoyment had ceased with the shout which proclaimed the winner. I was at the mercy of the party, but I had faith in my protector and guide. It was agreed they must dine there, and go home afterwards. A booth was chosen, and dinner was succeeded by punch. It was no difficult task to intoxicate a boy of my age. I was hardly aware of the probable consequences of the tempting but treacherous beverage. They had resolved upon making me dead-drunk, and I hiccuped out, "No more! no more!" till I was nearly no more myself. All I remember from the time the bacchanalians ordered in a fresh bowl was their noisy chorus of " Drunk, drunk, drunk." My lifeless body was taken out of the gig and carried in triumph on their shoulders through the village, some of them singing, in ridicule of the music in which I had so distinguished myself, "Vital spark," &c. In this way I was chaired round the place like a successful member—like him receiving additional shouts when we passed the houses of obnoxious politicians,—till, wearied with their midnight orgies, and their carrying me like Guy Fawkes about the streets, they shot me out of my triumphal car at my father's cottage-door.

CHAPTER III.

Merchant Tailors' School.—Flogging.—Serjeant Pell.—William Mathews.—Religious experience.—Saintly Epistles.—Religious Fanaticism.—Pious Tracts with odd titles.—Huntington the Coalheaver, and his miracles.—Rowland Hill.—Popular preaching.

I was now transplanted from Dominie the flagellator's garden of knowledge in St. Martin's-in-the-Fields, to Merchant Tailors' School, to gain, what Pope so aptly terms "a dangerous thing," a little learning. This was about the year 1786. Bishop, the head master, wore a huge powdered wig — larger than any other Bishop's wig. It invited invasion; and we shot paper-darts with such singular dexterity into the protruding bush behind, that it looked like "a fretful porcupine." He had chalkstone knuckles too, which he used to rap on my head like a bag of marbles; and, eccentric as it may appear, pinching was his favourite amusement, which he brought to great perfection. There were six forms; I entered the school at the lowest, and got no higher than the fifth, but was of course alternately under the care and tuition of the four masters. Gardner, the lowest in grade, was the only mild person amongst them; the others had a little too much, and perhaps he had much too little, of the severe in him for his station. Two more cruel tyrants than Bishop and Rose never existed. They were great "deck-walkers," as I have always designated those public nuisances who, regardless of the fidgets of poor nervous wretches like myself, mercilessly pace up and down apartments, inflicting pangs unutterable on those who dare not roar out "Sit down, sir!" as old Sam Johnson did. Lord, the fourth master, was rather an invalid, and, I believe, had been prescribed gentle exercise; he therefore put up for, and was the successful candidate for, the flogging department. Rose was so great an adept at the cane, that I once saw a boy strip after a thrashing from him that he might expose his barbarous cruelty, when the back was actually striped with dark streaks like a zebra.

Before I left the school, the pupils had the satisfaction of witnessing the administration of the *lex talionis* in a most summary and somewhat awful manner. The boy I spoke of, like Zanga, remembered "the blow," and on proceeding to college, kept up the recollection of this most gratuitous barbarity; for, shortly afterwards, he came into the cloisters during a play-hour, went to Rose's apartment, lured him to the door of it, and horse-whipped him there before the admiring and approving scholars until he roared for mercy.

This gave occasion to the abolition of flogging in this school; for, the next time Lord made the attempt, at a concerted signal, (the rebellion had been long in preparation,) all the boys, to the number of two hundred, rushed from the school-room into the lobby, where punishment was usually inflicted, hustled the pedagogue, rescued the victim, and scattered the birch into fragments, each one carrying off a twig in token of victory. We then returned into school with perfect coolness, having announced our determination *uná voce* never again to submit to such a degradation. To this arrangement the heads were compelled to submit; for so well was the spirited measure organised, and so completely carried into effect, that no ringleader could be pointed out as an example, and nothing short of the expulsion of the whole number could have been resorted to. The affair, therefore, was hushed up. There were young men from seventeen to nineteen years of age, just ripe for college—amongst them my brother and Serjeant Pell (in our eyes men), and other stout fellows—who swelled the ranks of the rebels.

William, my brother, was my senior by seven years, and, being intended for the church, of course looked to a college education. Thus did my father strike a fatal blow at his own peace. He created a mortifying distinction between the rank in society of his two sons,—the eldest a gentleman, the youngest a tradesman. Having made up his mind to " cramp my genius" behind a counter, he was imprudent in sending me to a public school.

My dear and excellent brother had great natural talents, and was indefatigable in his search after knowledge. He was essentially a gentleman in all his feelings; and his earliest associates were high, if not in rank, certainly in talent. The pursuits that engaged him were not those of other youths,—he was devoted to profound and abstruse studies, mathematics, and had an absolute thirst for languages, six of which he could speak or read before he was twenty years of age. To gain perfection in these, his time was occupied day after day, night after night. The school exercises, of course, were only Latin, Greek, and Hebrew; French was supplied by my father's means; but at the time I was young enough to sleep in the same room with him, he rose at four or five o'clock in the morning to study Italian and Spanish; of which pursuits he was so unostentatious, that he threatened me with the penalty of his displeasure if I revealed to any one the hours he stole from sleep. Thus qualified at a very early age, he entered Pembroke College, Cambridge, already an accomplished gentleman.

If constant trials—if application—if marching and counter-marching could have made a scholar of me, I ought to have been an Admirable Crichton.

At seven I started for the east end; at eleven I came out of school, and went to another in the neighbourhood for writing and accounts, and to a French school in the evening.

On Saturday, during nine months of the year, I went to Whetstone, and stayed till Monday morning. This escape from all descriptions of fagging, and from confinement—this freedom of body and soul from the fetters of scholastic discipline—the contrast between the narrow dirty lane where the school was situated, and the pure air I breathed in my beloved little village, was such a joyous emancipation, that the impression has dwelt in my memory to the present hour; and I feel the same impulse to escape from London with all its attractions, and revel in country pleasures, that I did when I was a schoolboy. Indeed, every feeling, every propensity or peculiarity, I can trace to impressions formed in my school-days. During my first engagement in Drury-lane Theatre I lived at Colney Hatch, and in all weathers returned home after the play about eight miles, and over Finchley Common, in an open carriage: this was from pure love of the country. Four years I lived at Fulham, and paid the same midnight visits, frequently on horseback, to my house; and fourteen years at Kentish Town (commonly called Highgate by my visiters, and not unfrequently Hampstead); and I can truly say, that the same feelings pervade me at this moment. Without enumerating my list of objections to all large cities, and more particularly to London, I can only assert that I always turn my back upon it with pleasure when I have anything like rural enjoyment in prospect.

What an almost universal feeling is the regard for our native place! I have no such sentiment, unfortunately; and yet I could never have been callous on such a subject, or have revisited the scenes of my childhood without emotion, associated as they are with the pleasing dreams of youth—of beloved relatives now no more, or partners in school-tasks now toiling in far-distant climes, or " seeking the bubble reputation." I feel nothing of all this on entering *my* " native village." Its huge masses of unfeeling brick and stone inspire me with frigid indifference as to the street in which I first saw light. 'Tis death to the sentimental. Ah! how different when the associations can be concentrated within the compass of a quiet secluded hamlet! I never whisk through dear Whetstone in his Majesty's mail, that I do not gaze right and left on some object that brings to me pleasing as well as melancholy recollections of the past: I feel that this is in reality my native place.

How many there are who assert that our school-days are the happiest of our lives! The happiest of mine were in flying *from* school; when, feeling the value of my wings, I soared for two days weekly in the picturesque beauty of Totteridge and its neighbourhood, with the penalty, as I at last thought it, of a sermon of one hour and forty minutes from my father on Sunday.

I have already observed on my incipient fanaticism. It was not until my removal to Merchant Tailors' that I began to waver in my faith. The taunts of my schoolfellows, my mother's opposition, my brother's thorough contempt for the whole ignorant crew that he well remembered, first awakened my attention. On his visits at home during the Terms, my mother was always prepared with a budget of "gospel-grievances." "Gospel," that was the grand and leading watchword of the conspirators. "The Church of England clergy are not gospel preachers;" such was their cant. Then, again, the depredations on my poor father's purse—the subscriptions, the "mites for missionaries," the building and rebuilding chapels, the "accommodation paper," &c. were naturally sources of disgust to my mother. These vacation visits brought me in closer contact with my brother than I had ever been before: and the periodical pourings forth of a sad spirit, and the union of sentiment between himself and my mother, made me seriously incline to hear, if not devour up, their discourse.

The following specimen of style will suffice to justify my general assertions of the prevailing ignorance and indecent use of the name of the Deity on all familiar occasions. The date of the letter, which is faithfully copied, will explain that I obtained possession of it many years after the period just spoken of, from my father, to whom it was addressed on the sudden death of one of his servants.

Mr. Mathus

My verey dear Frinds

I simpothis with you under this verey sollom providenc the deth of your survant, may our all wis Covenet God by His blesied Spirrit santefey it to Every one of you and my famley may owr gratious Lord fill our souls with the oyell of his gras that we may allwayes be redey We mest you last Nigt but the Lord wos with us may He Espeselly be with you and der Mrs. Mathus your der Child and famley under this Visettation prayes your ffnat Br. in a der Redemer.

Io Hill.

Doctor Ferean of No 3 Lams Condict plase tould me yesterday he wos goin to part with a good yong womon his housmaid if you thougt proper to inquier after hor you are welcom to maik yous of my Name.

6th Jany. 1804.

I am not disposed now to speak with severity of any sect or sects; there is good in all: but I have evidence of the hollowness of the many I knew, and I am positive that the persecutions of some of the persons I treat of drove me from my home, and my brother from his original profession. Their ignorance, their hatred of those who differed from them, their intolerance and their scandalous mountebank tricks in the pulpit, I have a right to comment upon; and I shall die in the belief that such familiar uses of the name of the Almighty as are exemplified in the pawnbroker's letter are blasphemous; and the eloquence of the first advocate in existence cannot persuade me that these men were not in the constant habit of violating the third commandment.

My mother's visits to St. Martin's and other churches gave me many opportunities of hearing eminent divines, from which my father's pursuits would have debarred me. I was therefore a listener in public and private, between the ages of ten and seventeen, when my mind was somewhat capable of reflection, to the various and complicated tenets and doctrines of more than half a score of disputants; for all the persons I am about to name, with numbers whom I have forgotten, met at my father's house and *wrestled* most vigorously. From day to day they brawled, as if the best use to be made of religion was to quarrel about it; and what they were wrangling for, I never knew, nor do I to this hour. I had, however, the opportunity of hearing, amongst other eminent men and writers on theology, John Wesley, Romaine, De Coetlogon, Dr. Madan, Toplady, Rowland Hill, Cecil, Cadogan, &c. &c.; and they were among the first *gentlemen* I had seen. The clearly-drawn line of demarcation between these and the vulgar herd that embittered my life, and eventually drove me from my family fireside, added to my mother's example and high bearing towards them, and her sincere attachment to the Church of England, may account for my vacillations, and my ultimately settling down as a true and, I hope, sincere member of the established religion.

The bitterness with which I write of the canting hypocrites who infested my father's house will, I trust, be excused in consideration of the cruel persecutions I suffered at their hands. His was, in fact, a sort of house-of-call for sanctified fiddlers, holy hosiers, pious pedlars, and beatified butchers — for preachers of the Huntingtonian, Wesleyan, Whitfieldean, Cantadean sects. Lane at the Minerva Press issued nothing but novels; my father was as well known for religious publications—he was the *serious publisher*. I wish I could recollect the titles of one half of these "pious tracts," as they were called: some of the works which he published are now in existence, and I have seen them lately; others I remember well, such as "Deep Things of God, or Milk and Strong Meat for Babes and Fathers in Christ;" "Nine Points to tie up a Believer's Small-clothes," "Collins' Spouse under the Apple-tree;" "Hooks and Eyes for Believers' Breeches;" "A High-heeled Shoe for a Limping Christian." Some, I, a profane person in their eyes, think too blasphemous to be recorded, and one of Bunyan's too indecent to pollute my pages with.

There was a coalheaver, one Huntington, a

pretty specimen of the mechanics I have spoken of — he who added S. S. to his name, which he intended to mean *Sinner Saved;* but as even my father's waggery extended to another interpretation, I may venture upon it. He one night came home from a "Religious Experience and Christians' Confessing Benefit Club," and found Huntington making love to his cook in the kitchen — "basting her with the hoyle of salivation," as he said. My father, in great indignation, literally pushed him out of the house. I believe he gave him a kick; and as he sleeked his coal-black hair with his dusty paws and their ebony terminations, about to excuse himself, my father exclaimed, "William Huntington, *S. S. Sad Scoundrel.*"

The disgusting *sang-froid* with which the same Huntington used to speak of his actual colloquial intercourse with the Deity would not be believed if related by a mere hearer, had he not put it beyond all doubt by publishing his blasphemies years after I heard him spout forth his fiendish threats.

I find whole passages, with which I used to amuse my schoolfellows in imitation of the Coalheaver, in his printed works. "He, good man! was ashamed of nothing;" and so he has put on record innumerable lies of his dreams, conversations with the Almighty, &c. In order to bear out my assertions of the infamy of this man, I shall copy two or three specimens of what I have repeatedly heard from him, as published by himself subsequently in his " Bank of Faith."

" During the space of three years," says this *Sinner Saved*, " I secretly wished in my soul that God would favour me with a chapel of my own, being sick of the errors that were perpetually broached by some one or other in St. Margaret's Chapel, where I then preached; yet I could not ask God for such a favour, thinking it was not to be brought about by one so very mean, low, and poor as myself. However, God sent a person unknown to me to look at a certain spot, and afterwards took me to look at it. God stirred up a wise man to offer to build a chapel, and to manage the whole work without fee or reward. God drew the pattern in his imagination while he was hearing me preach a sermon. I then took the ground, and the chapel sprung up like a mushroom. I thought, after such large proofs of my prayers being attended to, I would ask a few more favours. My surtout coat was got very thin and bad, and the weather at that time was very cold; and I felt it as I was going to preach, and I prayed secretly for a coat. As soon as I delivered my discourse, I desired a young man to fetch my old great-coat in order to put it on before I went out of the warm meeting-house: when he came back, lo! he brought me a new one. I told him it was not mine; he said it was; so I put it on, and it fitted very well. In one of the pockets there was a letter which informed me my blessed Lord and Master had sent it to me to wrap my worthless carcass in during the very severe winter. I had thought, by my continual coming and begging so many things of my indulgent Master, I should weary him. My mock-modesty had nearly deprived me of this new great-coat.

" At this time," continues the Reverend Coalheaver, " I preached at Richmond, Ditton, Cobham, Farnham, &c. This I found too much for my strength. I found I had great need of a horse; so I went to prayer and asked for more strength, less work, or a horse. I used my prayers as gunners do swivels, turning them every way as the cases required. I then hired a horse to take me to town, and rode into the livery-stables near Margaret-street Chapel; but the ostler refused to take him in, saying he had no room. I asked for his master, and he told me the same story. I was then going out of the yard, when he asked me if I was the person that preached at St. Margaret-street Chapel? I told him I was; he burst into tears. He said he would turn one of his own horses out and take mine in. In a day or two, he said some of my friends had been gathering money to buy me a horse, and that he gave something towards him. Soon after I got the horse, and one person gave me a guinea to buy me a bridle, another gave me two whips, another trusted me for a saddle; and here was a full answer to my prayer."

I wonder how many answers a man might receive in these days, if he prayed that a saddler might be found to trust him under similar circumstances. But he had not half done with the credulous customers that were saddled—ay, and bridled too—by him. The Coalheaver, "set on horseback," still longed for something more; he would not let his dear master have an hour's rest; he bestrode his Bucephalus and rode home.

"I told God," he continues, "as I went along, I had more work for my faith now than heretofore, for the horse would take half as much to keep him as my whole family; but I lived and cleared my way just as I did before, for I could not then get anything either to eat or drink, wear or use, without begging it of God;" *i. e.* he was too lazy to carry out coals, too stupid to make a shoe, found nothing was so easy as to preach to uneducated fanatics, and was not above spunging upon them all.

Often have I heard him repeat the passage that follows, which is nearly verbatim in his book, as far as my memory serves me. "Having now had my horse several weeks, and going a great way regular every Sunday, as might naturally be inferred, my breeches began to wear out. I often made very free with my master in my prayers, but he still kept me so uncommon poor that I could not get them at any rate. At last I was determined to go to one of my flock at Kingston that was in the breeches line, and to get him to trust me until my master sent me money to pay him." Is not this very like swindling?

"I was going to London that day, and called on Mr. Croucher, a shoemaker;" (to diddle him out of a pair of shoes;) "he told me a parcel was left there for me—I opened it, and, behold, there was a pair of leather breeches!"

Now, what can be said or thought of the infatuated wretches who would visit this wretched buffoon to hear "the word," as they called it? Did any one of the "devil's children" ever utter anything in a theatre so calculated to bring the very name of religion into contempt as this? In his book he published the letter which accompanied the present.

"SIR,—I have sent you a pair of breeches, and hope they will fit. I beg your acceptance of them; and if they want any alteration, leave in a note what the alteration is, and I will call in a few days and alter them.   J. S."

Now hear S. S. reply to J. S.

"SIR,—I received your present, and thank you for it. I was going to order a pair of leather breeches, because I did not know till now that my master had ordered them of you. They fit very well; which convinces me that the same God who moved thy heart to give, guided thy hand to cut, because he perfectly knew my size, having clothed me in a miraculous manner for near five years."

Often as I have heard this, I would not have ventured to offer it to my readers if he had not borne me out by his own printed testimony. If this be not the double-distilled essence of blasphemy, I know not what is.

If I were writing only the history of Methodist preachers, I could relate innumerable anecdotes of the absurdities, blunders, and practical jokes, &c. of these people, who have left the same impression upon my mind that a set of strolling actors would have left upon one of them, and about as much respect for their calling as such pretenders to religion would feel for the clowns and pantaloons of a comic pantomime. I have seen even Rowland Hill, (I believe, a sincere and excellent man,) who had the advantage of those I have spoken of in being a gentleman, guilty of such violence in the pulpit, that the impression of those who were not accustomed to his oddities was that he was a maniac. Frequently I have seen him wield and poise in the air, and shake the Bible at his congregation, till he has dropped it amongst his auditory. (It was a common thing to see him stoop to pick it up within the pulpit.) I have seen him, while dealing out brimstone by the bushel and torments by the hundred weight, knock the candles on either side out of their sockets. The pulpit cushion was another plaything: I have often expected he would throw it at me, and I perfectly recollect making the preparatory action of a cricketer as I exchanged looks with some of my companions, youngsters like myself, to catch it when he should hurl it from him in his enthusiasm. He, who had the advantages of birth and association, and a college education, should have proudly maintained his station in contradistinction to the vulgar herd of "the elect," instead of being a kind of leader to them; but he was as remarkable as the most unwashed and uneducated of the set for the preaching-made-easy system—the reducing the sublime to the level of such understandings as theirs to whom they principally addressed themselves—the notion of making Divine truths clear to "the meanest capacity" by vulgar illustration. I shall mention only three or four of his most extraordinary attempts at effect in his way.

"The love of our Lord is like a good large round of beef, my brethren; you may cut and come again."

Again—"You all know how difficult it is to catch a pig by the tail; you will find it equally so to catch the love of our Lord after backslidings."

On an occasion of his preaching a charity sermon he said, "I once got 1000*l.* by a charity sermon. I hope I shall get as much to-day. But observe, if any of you are in debt, don't put any money in the plate. Recollect—take time—deliberate. If any of you owe money, be just before you are generous. Stop though. On second thoughts, those who don't give will be pointed at. 'Oh, he or she's in debt,'" &c.*

I remember Rowland Hill from my infancy. He was an odd, flighty, absent person. So inattentive was he to nicety in dress, that I have seen him enter my father's house with one red slipper and one shoe; the knees of his breeches untied, and the strings dangling down his legs. In this state he had walked from Blackfriars'-road, unconscious of his eccentric appearance.

---

* Since I wrote down these anecdotes, I made the following extract from a newspaper, Dec. 30th, 1831.
"Popular Preaching.
" As the Rev. Rowland Hill was holding forth at the Tabernacle, Tottenham-court Road, a lady remarked the uncommon attention paid to him by a very old person near her. When the discourse ended, the attentive hearer exclaimed, 'God bless his heart, he is as funny as ever!'"

CHAPTER IV.

French School.—Private Theatricals.—Master Elliston.—First Visit to a Theatre, and its effect.—Literary attempt.—Mr. John Litchfield.—Major Topham.—William Mathews.—The Thespian Magazine. — Editorship. — Death of Edwin the Comedian. — Correspondence with Mr. Thomas Harris the proprietor of Covent Garden Theatre.—Apprenticeship to his father.—Macklin.—First Appearance on a public Stage with Mr. John Litchfield.— Richmond *at* Richmond. — The Duke of Clarence and Mrs. Jordan.—Second Appearance in public.—Canterbury.—Last Appearance in the character of a Bookseller.— Introduction to the Agent of the Dublin Theatre. —Engagement, and departure from home.

I NOW approach that period of my boyish days which is more intimately connected with my after-life. I have before hinted that my peregrinations from the Strand to Merchant Tailors' School four times during the day ended in attending a French school in the evening. This was kept by a Madame Cotterel, who had fled from the horrors of the French revolution, and commenced teacher of her own language in England. Her scholars were few and select. She resided in the first-floor of a pastrycook's house near Bedford-street, Strand. The father of the celebrated Flaxman, the sculptor, resided next door, and Miss F. was one of my fellow pupils. In this evening academy the foundation-stone of that fabric was laid which, whether or not raised for the advantage of myself and the public, I must leave to posterity to determine. Here, most unquestionably, ambition for histrionic honours first fired my soul. I had never seen a play, and probably should not have rebelled against my father's authority, and strict commands that I should not visit a theatre, but for this accidental association. I believe all the pupils of this lady had been indulged in this amusement but myself. Some three or four were panting for private theatricals, and amongst them, unluckily for my father's peace, hear it, theatrical readers, with some interest — Master Elliston! He was already a spouter, and I must own much more time was spent in English recitations from dramatic authors than in French exercises. I was fascinated by the specimens I heard, by imitation, of some of the great actors, and, scarcely knowing why, was insensibly led on to emulate these would-be heroes at the French school. This gradually ripened into an overpowering, all-absorbing passion. Elliston, afterwards so justly celebrated, was our prime leader; he was only four years older than myself, yet the distinction between man and boy almost existed between us, I being fourteen and he eighteen.

Having with some difficulty obtained our mistress's permission, the play of " The Distressed Mother" was at length arranged and got up; and

CHAPTER IV.

French School.—Private Theatricals.—Master Elliston.—First Visit to a Theatre, and Its effect.—Literary attempt.—Mr. John Litchfield.—Major Topham.—William Mathews.—The Thespian Magazine. — Editorship. — Death of Edwin the Comedian. — Correspondence with Mr. Thomas Harris the proprietor of Covent Garden Theatre.—Apprenticeship to his father.—Macklin.—First Appearance on a public Stage with Mr. John Litchfield. - Richmond at Richmond. —The Duke of Clarence and Mrs Jordan.—Second Appearance in public.—Canterbury.—La Appearance in the character of a Bookseller. — Introduction to the Agent of the Dublin Theatre. — Engagement, and departure from home.

I now approach that period of my boyish days which is more intimately connected with my after-life. I have before hinted that my peregrinations from the Strand to Merchant Tailors' School four times during the day ended in attending a French school in the evening. was kept by a Madame Cotterel, who had from the horrors of the French revolution, and commenced teacher of her own language in England. Her scholars were few and select. She resided in the first-floor of a pastrycook's house near Bedford-street, Strand. The father of the celebrated Flaxman, the sculptor, resided next door, and Miss F. was one of my fellow pupils. In this evening academy the foundation-stone of that fabric was laid with, whether or not raised for the advantage of myself and the public, I must leave to posterity to determine. Here, most unquestionably, ambition for histrionic honours first fired my soul. I had never seen a play, and probably should not have rebelled against my father's authority, and strict commands that I should not visit a theatre but for this accidental association. I believe all the pupils of this lady had been indulged in this amusement but myself. Some three or four were panting for private theatricals, and amongst them, unluckily for my father's peace, hear it, theatrical readers, with some interest — Master Elliston! He was already a spouter, and I must own much more time was spent in English recitations from dramatic authors than in French exercise. I was fascinated by the specimens I heard, by imitation, of some of the great actors, and, scarce knowing why, was insensibly led on to emulate these would-be heroes at the French school. This gradually ripened into an overpowering, absorbing passion. Elliston, afterwards so justly celebrated, was our prime leader; he was only four years older than myself, yet the distinction between man and boy almost existed between us, I being fourteen and he eighteen.

Having with some difficulty obtained our mistress's permission, the play of "The Distressed Mother" was at length arranged and got up; and

I made my "first appearance on any stage" at the theatre over the pastrycook's shop, first-floor front, in the character of *Phœnix*. Master Elliston enacted *Pyrrhus*, and *Orestes* was really well performed by a very interesting youth of the name of Leftley; a poetical genius who distinguished himself in many of the periodical publications of the day. Miss Osborne and Miss Flaxman were among the performers. But Elliston was our evening star, and distanced us all. It was a fine animated performance, and created as much wonder and elicited as much applause as the acting of Master Betty in later days. He was pronounced at once a theatrical genius of the first order, and his future pursuits in life fixed in the minds of all his auditors, if not in his own.

All I can recollect of my tragic attempt is, that it had an effect — a powerful effect. The audience laughed as much *at* me as, I am proud to say, they have since laughed *with* me. But I had not the advantage of my competitors. They had all seen many plays—I not one. Each had probably selected some favourite actor as a model, while the only specimens of elocution I had to form my notions upon were, with a few exceptions, the drawling, snuffling heroes of the conventicles. From this time I am free to confess that our studies were in some degree neglected, the English drama proving more attractive than French exercises.

At the age of fourteen I commenced author — at least as much so as many of our modern dramatists — for I translated the Princess of Cleves, which was published in monthly contributions in the Ladies' Magazine.

The following year we got up "The Orphan;" (I the chaplain;) Elliston was again our Magnus Apollo. His voice had had twelve months' more mellowing, and he gave a specimen of his vocal powers on this occasion by singing, between the play and farce, "To Anacreon in Heaven" at a table, with punch-bowl and glasses, while the scholars sat round as chorus. A gayer specimen of juvenile jollity I have never witnessed. His joyous exuberance of mirthful enjoyment was worthy Bacchus himself: he looked the rosy god when he chuckled over

"The myrtle of Venus with Bacchus's vine."

His laughter-loving eye and round dimpled face were never displayed to more advantage even in after-days when crowded audiences gave their testimony to his mirth-inspiring comic powers; and to the praise and the good taste of our critics at the pastrycook's, be it spoken, they predicted his future greatness. Having a bad part in the tragedy, I stipulated for a character in the afterpiece. A one-act farce, called "A Quarter of an Hour before Dinner," (written by Mr. Rose, second master of Merchant Tailors' School, and often acted at the Haymarket,) was selected, in which I enacted *Mr.*

Lovel, and, I have every reason to believe, *without the slightest approbation.* I cannot now remember whether by slow degrees I had gained my father's consent to this, or whether it was kept a secret, but certainly neither he nor any of my family were present. Again he was unfortunate; for how could he, good easy man! have anticipated that the reward for his parental anxiety respecting my education should be to find himself thwarted in his best hopes, by my being initiated into the mysteries of Melpomene at a French academy?

I have already stated that a public school was not calculated for a youth destined to stand behind a counter, and deal out " More Last Words of Mr. Baxter," " High-heeled Shoes for Limping Christians," and " Hooks and Eyes for Believers' Breeches ;" for my associations there only gave me a distaste for such occupations, while at the tart and tragedy manufactory I imbibed an actual taste for other pursuits, and, instead of reading "Huntington's Sinner Saved" (S.S.), "Brother Hill's Experience of his sainted Sarah," or " The Last Moments of a Pawnbroker's Laundry Maid," or other such tracts from my father's shelves, I selected the beauties of the living dramatists which nestled unheeded among the great mass of sermons and theological works. They heated my imagination, and, together with the lessons in the French nursery, gave me the most ardent desire to witness a play. On every occasion of my father's absence, instead of standing behind the counter I mounted upon it, and with a round ruler for a truncheon, red ink for blood, the kitchen poker for a sword, and a towering goose-quill fixed on one side of my hat, turned up for the purpose, the skirt of my coat thrown gracefully over my left shoulder for a mantle, and a red tape garter encircling my knee, did I exhibit myself, to the great edification of his apprentices.

At length, on a certain, and oh, fatal night! a dark and gloomy night, suited to the perpetration of such an act of disobedience, with stealthy steps I trod my way. I dared not look right or left, so conscious was I of the " deep damnation of the deed;" but my soul was in arms, my time was my own, my will was free, (my father had departed for Whetstone, his constant custom on a Saturday evening, to indulge his own pursuit,) and I issued forth with my friend Litchfield, of the Council-office, from the bookseller's shop, to make my first *entrée* at a public theatre: this was in the autumn of 1790. Oh the delights of *that* night! that two shillings' worth of disobedience! My companion and I have frequently laughed over the recollection of my frantic behaviour. He could not pacify me. He had long been initiated into the mysteries of the scenic art; but here I was, at fourteen, at "my first play," which Charles Lamb has so beautifully described. The very curtain filled me with anticipations of delight;—the scenery, the dresses, the feathers, the russet boots, the very smell of the theatre, that mixture of orange peel and oil, the applause in which I joined so heartily as to bring all eyes and many remarks upon me, to the great scandal of my cicerone, filled my senses with delight. From that night my mind was in a state of splendid irritation; I could scarcely walk the streets without offering " my kingdom for a horse," to every pedestrian I met. *At night* I could not rest, Macbeth *did* " murder sleep;" and I recited Lear up three pair of stairs to a four-legged bedstead.

My thirst for dramatic fame was now of course increased tenfold. My next appearance was in a private theatre, as we termed it, over a stable in an elegant part of the west-end of the town, called Short's Gardens, Drury-lane. I hope it was rather more respectable as to its inmates then than now. Here I joined a society of spouters, and, having stipulated for the best parts, made my first attempt in comedy. Though Master Elliston monopolised all the attention and applause in tragedy, I thought that in low comedy I could beat him. I accordingly determined to astonish my friends by appearing in *Jacob Gawkey*, in " The Chapter of Accidents," and *Lenitive* in " The Prize." This must have been during the first season of that farce; and thinking that neither the audience nor myself could have too much of a good thing, I favoured them with about a dozen imitations of the favourite actors of the day. Suett and Munden were pronounced to be near perfection. I cannot amuse my readers, as I hope I did my audience, except in relating one most absurd though appalling fact. In the commencement of the second act there are two cases discovered, supposed to contain Chinese bonzes sent as presents to *Mr. Caddy*. The first is opened and discovers the bonze to the delighted eye of the virtuoso. He then proceeds to No. 2, when he starts back with surprise at discovering *Dr. Lenitive* in a new dress, the caricature of the fashion of the day, who darts forward from the cabinet with his lottery-ticket in his hand, by which he has gained, as he supposes, 10,000*l*. During our rehearsals I was much distressed at the difficulties that presented themselves in the way of our obtaining these most important and indispensable adjuncts. The expense of making them was too serious to encounter; and as I was the person most interested, and most likely to suffer from their absence, I gave a sort of vague order to "knock up something" for the occasion. This was not attended to, but I was assured that something would be prepared and ready, when lo! to my horror and amazement, when I came out dressed in all my best, I discovered that the cabinet from whence I was to issue forth was a *shell* from a workhouse!

At this epoch my pursuits took a literary as

well as a dramatic turn, and my delight when "The Ladies' Magazine" first exhibited in print " The Princess of Cleves, by C. M.," was boundless. I thought the eyes of all Europe were upon me, and that the ladies who took in the work would unite in calling on the Editor to insist on the author declaring himself. I erected my crest and craned my neck, as many a modern dramatist has done when taking to himself the compliments upon his new play, properly due to the Messrs. Scribe and Co. My friend Litchfield, afterwards husband of the actress of that name, who first displayed to me the splendours of Melpomene, was shortly after that period connected with the press. My brother also added to the income my father allowed him by contributions. "The Oracle" was a new paper, and Topham, Parson Este, Hewerdine, and a little clique of the elect started a paper called "The World." Litchfield wrote the dramatic articles occasionally for both, under the signature of "Pollio," and I believe these were allowed to be the best criticisms of the day. My brother was for a time parliamentary reporter to these and others: I therefore was insensibly enticed into this knot of literati, and initiated into the mysterious arcana of diurnal despotism. Captain, afterwards Major Topham, was a most prominent character on the canvas. I remember his appearance well,—a scarlet coat, a cocked-hat, a large door-knocker of a tail appended to a carefully powdered head, that seemed to invite you to give a rat-tat on his scarlet and white shoulders, and inquire if the editor of "The World" was within—his knuckles crammed into his pockets, out of one of which peeped a short but very thick stick, enough to show that he was prepared for an attack. Lewis dressed at him in Reynolds' comedy of " Notoriety," and had two lines in his epilogue, which were evidently personal, and were always vociferously applauded :—

"Hey, Tom, how do? Oh! is that you, Dick Docket?
You've stole my stick! Oh, no!—it's in my pocket!"

Boaden, the author of the life of Kemble, Mrs. Siddons, Mrs. Inchbald, &c. was the editor of "The Oracle," and a celebrated dramatic critic. He was enthusiastically devoted to the Kemble family, and on terms of intimacy with "Glorious John." To these men I looked up as arbiters of the fate and fame of many a Thespian hero. In all the freshness of youth, when impulses burst forth without disguise, it was natural that, on associating with these men, I should mistake inclination for ability — endeavour to emulate their example and become one of them.

"The Thespian Magazine" (entirely devoted to the drama—I need give no other reason for its decline and fall) was first edited by several of my friends, and I commenced dabbler, and afterwards editor; but the pay was so contemptibly small, (a guinea per month,) that it soon fell into other hands. During my editorship appeared my first attempt at criticism. I was blockhead enough, after having seen only about a dozen plays, to imagine myself qualified to write upon the subject, and censure those who had devoted their minds and lives to the study of their art. I was willing, though not able to be, as Coleridge forcibly styles such persons, of "the animalculæ that feed upon the bodies of genius."

In the year 1790 the great comedian Edwin died, and had I been a bad boy and stolen to the theatre during that summer when he was acting at the Haymarket, I might have gained many a hint that would have turned to my advantage in after times; but he died in August, and my first play was in September, so that I lost the opportunity of witnessing the extraordinary comic efforts of that great actor, and have ever since lamented that I should have been so tardy in my disobedience. To give an idea, however, of my peculiar modesty at this period, the news of poor Edwin's demise was no sooner made known than I made up my mind, inexperienced and ignorant as I was, to succeed him. I lost no time in writing to Mr. Harris, the proprietor of Covent Garden Theatre, tendering my services for his situation. I luckily preserved a copy of my absurd letter, and have also carefully cherished Mr. Harris's reply in evidence of my own vanity and folly.

"Sir,—The lamented death of Mr. Edwin making an opening in your establishment, inspires me to offer myself as a candidate to supply the vacancy. I have never performed in any public theatrical representation yet, having been much engaged in business, but I trust this will not operate against me. 1 already am perfect in *Lingo* and *Bowkitt,* and know more than half of *Old Doiley.* Salary is no object, as I only wish to bring my powers into a proper sphere of action. I do not wish to blaze out awhile and then evaporate. Being at present bound to my father and under indentures,* of course his consent will be necessary; but this is the only impediment I am aware of. Your immediate answer, if convenient, will be of great consequence to, sir, your obedient servant, C. M."

Mr. Harris's reply was simply as follows:

"Sir,—The line of acting which you propose is at this time so very well sustained in Covent Garden Theatre, that it will not be in my power to give you any eligible situation therein. I am, sir, your obedient servant,

T. Harris."

In justification of this gentleman's rejection of my valuable services, and in confirmation of my vanity, I have only to add, that those excellent actors, Messrs. Munden and Fawcett, were deservedly established favourites in the line to which I aspired.

Had I never turned manager myself, I should

---

* Every frequenter of the "At Homes" will recollect his fine personification of the celebrated John Wilkes—before whom he appeared with his father on the occasion of his apprenticeship.—A. M.

have been under the mortifying impression of being the only silly boy that could be guilty of such folly, but I have since collected stores of such specimens of harmless stupidity, many of them addressed to myself. However, I was not to be stifled in my theatrical cradle; I bought a pot of rouge and kept it in my drawer of best clothes, though I had no chance of using it, and burnt all my father's corks, and put them by against the time I should want eyebrows. Low comedy flamed high within me — *Lingo* danced in my imagination, and *Old Doiley* raged in my soul. The former I used to go through, with all the songs, to my father's apprentices and servants, with the most complete and triumphant success. I procured a wig resembling Edwin's, as I guessed from portraits of him, and sung the songs in imitation of imitations I had heard of him.

Here a blank is left in my husband's narrative, after a pencilled name, which from memory I fill up. I have heard him relate the following account so often that, though I may not be able to give it as humorously as he would have done, I can yet tell it truly.

At this time the aspirant sought an interview with the celebrated Charles Macklin, who had then attained a hundred years and upwards. He had been recommended to recite to him for the purpose of gaining the veteran's opinion and instructions;

and going by appointment to the residence of the aged man in Tavistock-row, he found him ready to receive him. When the door was opened, and the youth announced, there was Macklin in his arm-chair, from which he did not attempt to rise, nor, indeed, take any notice of the entrance of the stranger, but remained with an arm on either elbow of the chair he sat in, looking sour and severe at his expected pupil, who, hesitating on the threshold, paused timidly, nay, fearfully, which occasioned the centenary to call out, in any but inviting tones: " Come *nearer!* What do you stand *there* for? You can't act in the gap of the door!" The young man approached. " Well," added Macklin, in a voice ill calculated to inspire confidence, " don't be *afraid!* Now— let me hear you." This crabbed austerity completely chilled the aspirant's ardour; however, mustering up all the confidence this harsh reception had left him, he began to declaim according to the approved rules of "speech-days." Macklin, sitting like a stern judge waiting to pronounce sentence upon a criminal, rather than to laud a hero, soon interrupted the speech with a mock imitation of the novice's monotonous tones, barking out, " Bow, wow, wow, wow!" This was enough to damp the Thespian flame which had lighted the poor youth into the presence of the terrible old man, and he felt himself unable to make another essay, but stood, with downcast eyes and swelling heart, awaiting the verdict which he expected. At last, Macklin, with increased severity of manner and voice, asked (poking his head forward at the same time, as if to impress his question the more strongly), —" *Young man,* are you at all aware what the qualifications of an actor should *be ?*" The youth sighed out, "I believe *not,* sir."—*Macklin.* " No, I am *sure* you are not. I will tell you, then, sir *;*"—(Poor Charles Mathews had never in his life before been called " sir," and it seemed to him an awfully responsible word at that moment;)— "I will tell you what he *ought* to be : what *I* was ; and what no man was ever eminent without being. In the first place ; an actor ought to possess a fine, an expressive *eye ;* 'an eye like Mars, to threaten and command.'" (His own flatly contradicted his assertion.) " *Sir,* he should have a beautiful countenance." (Charles looked up at his; but so many lines had crossed what of beauty might have once been written there, that nothing of it was legible.) " He should be able to assume a look that might appal the *devil!*" (Here, indeed, he had *one* requisite in full force.) " He should possess a fine, clear, mellifluous voice!"—(alas! his own sounded like a cracked trumpet;)—"a graceful figure, *sir.*" (The lean and slippered pantaloon was an Apollo Belvidere to Macklin) " But above all, young man,"— (and here the speaker's tone deepened into something like solemnity,) "above all,—an—actor—should—possess—that—first—great—natural—requisite—that—test—of—genius—a good—good— *Sir*," (added he, in a loud and angry voice, as if commanding assistance,) — "I want a *word!* — he should, I say, possess a good — retentive —" "Memory!" cried out the young man. "Ay, sir, *Memory!*"

Here the old man seemed to dwell for a while pensively upon the attribute just *lent* to him; then rousing himself from his thoughtful posture, he looked up in his visiter's face, as if inquiring what he did there? "Well, sir?—oh! well, well,"— (as if rising from the abyss of forgetfulness,)—" as I have said—an actor's requisites are many. Amongst the rest, *discrimination.* Sir, in the course of my long life I never knew more than three actors who possessed discrimination. David Garrick was *one*, — *I, Charles Macklin*, another, and the third was—a—a—a—." (Here his voice sank, as if step by step, till it reached a landing-place, where it was stationary and mute for some seconds; he then added, in a sort of mental soliloquy, and with a half sigh, "I *forget* who was the other!" Then, closing his eyes, he sank back into his chair, as if asleep, and was certainly unconscious of the exit of the young Thespian, who, shutting the door quietly after him, flew down stairs like a lapwing, opened the street-door, and ran away rejoicing in his escape, as if he feared the sour old man, who had curdled his blood with his severity, would have shut him up for life in his dreary presence.

Mr. Mathews had not, however, seen him for the last time; for, before he left home for Dublin, he was seated next to Macklin in the pit of one of the theatres, when, totally unmindful that he had ever met the youth before, he addressed him on the occasion of an actress, of a certain age, performing a youthful hoyden, and affecting the lightness and agility of girlhood. Macklin *ought* to have known her—(she was either *Miss* or *Mrs. Pope;* both of the old school) — but that he had confessedly lost an actor's great requisite, memory; and he asked his neighbour the name of the lady, who seemed to amuse him, several times in the course of the performance. At last, on her more than ordinary display of agility, Macklin turned round and observed, in a voice that seemed to issue from a cavern, " Sir, that lady jumps very *high*, but she comes down very *heavy.*"

Autobiography resumed.

From this period I remained at Merchant Tailors' School; and, during vacation time and leisure hours, " served in the shop," as Brother Hill would have said. Dick, in Murphy's " Apprentice," was a mere type of me. He neglected only the shop in pursuit of his spouting propensities, but I forgot counter, cloisters, chapel, father, mother, all; and my master-passion led me at length to an act of open rebellion. I began more than to suspect that the managers of the theatres would not engage a raw inexperienced youth, merely to gratify his silly ambition, when, to my great delight, I heard from Litchfield, who was quite as stage-struck as myself, that the manager of the Richmond Theatre would allow any young gentleman to perform who would pay him ten guineas. What condescending liberality! How could he ask a smaller sum? I negociated with him; and had the great good fortune to bring the potentate to even more moderate terms, namely, that he would allow *two* young gentlemen to perform for fifteen. This I communicated with great glee to my brother enthusiast, who had ambition enough to aim at the highest honours of the art at once. He jumped at the proposal, and declared himself ready studied in " Richard the Third."

Now, it so happened that I had a passion for fencing which nothing could overcome; and this friend of Melpomene and mine learnt the exercise at the same academy with myself. Therefore, for the delight of exhibiting my skill and legitimate love of the art, I kindly consented to take the inferior, insipid part of *Richmond*, who does not appear until the fifth act of the play, I stipulating, however, for a good part in the afterpiece. I cared for nothing except the last scene of *Richmond*, but in that I was determined to have my full swing of carte and tierce. I had no idea of paying seven guineas and a half without indulging my passion. In vain did the tyrant try to die, after a decent time; in vain did he give indications of exhaustion; I would not allow him to give in. I drove him by main force from any position convenient for his last dying speech. The audience laughed: I heeded them not. They shouted: I was deaf. Had they hooted, I should have lunged on in unconsciousness of their interruption. I was resolved to show them all my accomplishments. Litchfield frequently whispered, " Enough!" but I thought with Macbeth —

" Damn'd be he who first cries, Hold! enough!"

I kept him at it; and I believe we fought almost literally " a long hour by Shrewsbury clock." To add to the merriment, a matter-of-fact fellow in the gallery, who in his innocence took everything for reality, and who was completely wrapt up and lost by the very cunning of the scene, at last shouted out, " Damn him! why does not he shoot him?"

His present Majesty William IV. was in a private box, with Mrs. Jordan, on this occasion, having been attracted from Bushy by the announcement of an amateur *Richard;* and I heard afterwards, that they were both in convulsions of laughter at the prolongation of the fight, which that most fascinating and first of all great comic actresses never forgot. Years after, when we met in Drury-lane green-room, I was relating, amongst other theatrical anecdotes, the bumpkin's call from the gallery in commiseration of the trouble I had in killing *Richard,* when she shook me from my feet almost, by starting up, clasping her hands, and in her fervent, soul-stirring, warm-hearted tones, exclaiming, " Was that *you? I was there!*" and she screamed with laughter at the recollection of my acting in *Richmond,* and the length of our combat. She thought it was my friend's love of acting that induced him to spin it out. She was loud in praise of his personation of *Gloster;* and a very sensible, judicious reading of the character it doubtless was. The farce was " The Son-in-law." He enacted *Arionelli,* the opera-singer, a singular effort after so arduous a part as *Gloster;* but he acquitted himself with credit. I attempted, after my fencing mania had been satisfied, to dance myself into favour in the character of *Bowkitt,* in that most whimsical afterpiece. Here I had an opportunity afforded me of exhibiting a third accomplishment. Having convinced *in Richmond* all the people *at* Richmond, that I could fence, and in *Bowkitt,* that I was *maître de danse,* I satisfied them that my musical education had not been neglected. The incipient Paganini delighted the audience by a country-dance tune on the *kit*.*

[In my husband's notices of his early career, he has not put down his second attempt upon a public stage, the particulars of which, as I clearly recollect them, may properly be related in this place.

Early in 1794, he and his fencing friend (Mr. Litchfield) prevailed upon another *liberal* manager to permit them to pay a sum of money to perform at Canterbury, where "Richard the Third" showed them in their former glory, as *Richard* and *Richmond*. The latter, from pure love of fighting (like *Sir Lucius O'Trigger*), was once more performed by the comedian, who afterwards, from equal love of acting, played *Old Doiley*, in the farce of "Who's the Dupe?"

* The following criticism upon his performance I have found in a London paper, dated Monday, Sept. 9th, 1793.—A. M.

"*Richmond Theatre.*

"'Richard the Third' was on Saturday evening represented." After great eulogy upon the performance of Mr. Litchfield in *Richard*, the criticism concludes:—

"Another gentleman also made his first appearance in a theatre the same evening, as *Richmond* and *Bowkitt*. Fear depressed his voice in the former part, and in the latter he frequently spoke too indistinctly to be heard in the distant seats. He manifested some *naïveté*, however, in the *Dancing Master*, and trod the boards with free and easy steps. Had he combatted with a less powerful rival, his attempt had been better justified; as it was, he did not disgrace the company he performed with."

The requisite reserve with their mutual friends (for Mr. Litchfield's family had also a dash of *seriousness* in it), precluded these young men from completely indulging their vanity, by carrying with them any admiring witnesses of their triumphs; so that they were driven to the expedient of inviting " *mine Host*" of the *Fleur de lis*, where they put up, to go and see the performance, who graciously consented to accept a ticket.

In spite of remonstrance from his coadjutor, and consciousness of former ridicule, *Richmond* resolved again to prolong the last struggles of the tyrant; and when *Richard* fell, he poked him up, in the same spirit with the boy in " The Children in the Wood," who says to *Walter*, after he has killed *Oliver*, " Kill him again! such a villain cannot be too dead!" and recommenced the attack. Thus the combat lasted as long as before, and the two fencers gained much applause, without the laughter with which the Richmond folks treated them. On the contrary, the good people of Canterbury enjoyed the stubbornness of the contest, and their interest in it was manifested by repeated cheers at *Richard's* skill in parrying such vigorous and persevering attempts to put him out of the world. They were in fact delighted to see him *die hard;* while it was evident that, had he a thousand lives, *Richmond's* " great revenge had stomach for them all." In fine, the curtain dropped under shouts of approbation from the *discerning few;*

and the two stars lighted each other home, eager to receive the private meed of their exertions, from a quarter whence they were especially due.

After a few minutes, "mine host" placed their supper upon the table with great care and precision: but not one word did he speak. The tired performers sat down, but did not find the food they required. They hungered and thirsted for praise, for which they had a craving, nay, an insatiable appetite. The best carver cut up the chicken more as a form than from a desire to eat of it; and in the course of the operation put several leading questions to the silent landlord. Still nothing satisfactory was elicited. As soon, however, as he and the waiter had carried off the remnants of the supper, which at last the guests had fallen upon in earnest — from the wish to detain their host, they invited him to return for the purpose of *taking some punch* with them. In due time he re-entered the room with a *pipe lighted,* and sat himself down to enjoy the offered glass. Now then was the time. Several *fishing*-lines were thrown, but not one *compliment* did they hook: at last, the friends tacitly agreed to discard all finesse, and fairly drag out with a net the prey they were so determined on securing. *Richard* asked resolutely, "Pray, Mr. ———, how did you like the tragedy?" The landlord paused, with his eyes down-cast, after the approved manner of smokers; and, puff—puff—puff, was the only reply. "How," said the comedian, who was impatient, "how did you like the *farce?*" Puff—puff—puff, again (but not one puff for the actors). The question was then put into a more peremptory and determined form: "Pray tell us really what you thought of *our acting?*" There was no evading so direct an attack. The landlord looked perplexed, his eyes still fixed upon the ground: he took at length the tube slowly from his mouth, raised his glass, and drank off the remnant of his punch; went to the fireplace, and deliberately knocked out the ashes from his pipe; then looking at the expectants for a minute, exclaimed in a deep though hasty tone of voice, "*D—d good fight!*" and left the room. Sir Oracle having thus oped his mouth, not one word more could be extracted; and to this day his opinion upon the rest of the performance remains a sealed mystery.]

Autobiography resumed.

My future fate was now sealed. To buckle to business after tasting of public applause was not within the boundaries of probable expectation. My first act of open rebellion was accompanied by an assault in the eye of the law. From the age of fourteen until the period at which I now arrive, I occasionally served in the shop during the holidays. A purse-proud vulgar customer of my father's, who never would condescend to alight from his carriage, exacted of me, "the shop-boy," the most degrading of all duties, that of carrying articles to a carriage. I had been sent backwards and forwards in the rain too often to agree with my irritability, when, goaded into madness by his haughtiness, I felt at once that I never could suit myself to such purposes. "This is the second edition, I want the first:" again I returned to the shop. "This is bound in russia; calf-gilt will do for me. The boy's a fool!" said he, and then I threw the book in his face. This was about "my last appearance in that character."

Destiny, a word so often repeated by Napoleon, now began to develope her plans. I could not resist my fate. Early in the year 1794, I had made up my mind to make the stage my profession, and began to ponder upon the when, the where, and the how, when chance threw in my way Hitchcock, who wrote the History of the Irish Stage. All authors upon such subjects were welcome to me; and, after an introduction, I heard with great delight that he was a sort of Serjeant Kite to the Dublin corps of Thespians, and was now in London beating up for recruits: in short, I enlisted. He did *not* give me a shilling, and I believe never would if he could with decency have avoided it. I was fairly kidnapped after all; inasmuch as it was quite clear that the

Irish agent, as he was termed, had no power to fulfil the flattering promises he had made to me. It is true I was inexperienced, but this he knew. I did not deceive him, and I never swerved from my original inclination. I stipulated as far as possible for what is termed low comedy; for I had no pretensions to anything above that. Tragedy I never dreamed of. Why he engaged me at all was a puzzle to me when I had leisure for repentance in Dublin. My salary was to depend on my success. Could I doubt that it would be liberal? It was agreed that I should join the corps in Dublin at the latter end of May 1794.

I had now a scene to encounter that required some little courage to support, namely, to break the intelligence to my father that I had determined to quit the parental roof and follow the stage as a profession. He was in some measure prepared for the blow. I requested him to cancel my indentures of apprenticeship. "At all events," said I, "I am resolved to quit this house."

"You will live to repent this act of disobedience," said he.

"I doubt it, dear sir: 'my fate cries out.'"

"Don't shock my ears, sir, with such language," said my father.

"'Tis Shakspeare's, sir; I have heard you quote him."

"I was unconscious then," said he.

"No, sir," said I: "you did him but justice when you defended yourself from the attack of one of your bigoted brothers, by saying the words you used were certainly from the works of an inspired writer."

"Do not be profane, sir."

"Far from it, my dear father, 'I speak it not profanely;' but I cannot be persuaded that the magnificent mind which seems to have unclosed the book of fate, and penned lessons of morality for all ages, could have been so directed by the mighty Mover of all, if in his sight such productions were so wicked as you believe them to be. I can endure no longer the tyranny of those I consider as rebels. They are avowed enemies to the established religion of the country. Besides, if I am to believe them, they are too good for me. I am embarrassed in their presence,—I feel my own nothingness,—I, a sinner, shrink from such purity."

"Your sneering at those good men shows how well you are qualified for the profession you have chosen," replied my father.

"There are some gentlemen, at least," said I, "in that profession; not one, amongst those who have driven me from home. Let me fly from these noxious reptiles,— these persecutors and slanderers,—' I banish them.'"

"That little vagabond, Garrick," said he, "bit you, when he took you in his arms;" and here our colloquy closed.

Our painful interview ended by my kind but rigid parent saying, that, since I was determined on this sinful step, he would furnish me with the means of accomplishing my journey; though even this was an act that warred with his conscience. A day or two after this, and after an afflicting interview with my very truly beloved mother, who slipped a gift into my hand bedewed by her tears, I embarked on board the " Chester heavy," in my way to Parkgate, whence I had been advised to sail for Dublin; a passage, I believe, now nearly abandoned.

I had now the world before me where to choose. There was something of uneasy foreboding in the contemplation of my future prospects. I could not with indifference turn my back on the home of my youth; and yet I bitterly felt what it might have been, and what it ought to have been to me. How different the sensations with which my brother must have left the same home! when every anticipation of his young and ardent mind was joyous;—his college and studies, his youthful and agreeable companions, inhabitants of a world I was forbidden to explore. He could at once renounce the sanctified mechanics, and retain his parents' approbation!

I indulged in one reverie after another during rather a melancholy journey. Before this I had never been from home twenty miles,[*] and was not

[*] Excepting in his visit to Canterbury.—A. M.

fitted by nature or education to encounter the difficulties and hardships of even a stage-coach journey. I was shy of my travelling companions, for I knew nothing of what was called the world; and therefore did not then, as I have done since, to my great profit, extract aught of fun or frolic from my expedition.

It was a dark and dreary morning when I landed at the Pigeon House; and, in spite of myself, a melancholy foreboding stole over me. I had embarked on a dangerous sea of adventure, without rudder, compass, or pilot; and all seemed comfortless. "Where am I? who knows me? In a strange country, without a friend, without a recommendation, and almost without money;" for my pride had struggled with, and mastered my prudence. It was fortunate that I had not been scrupulous with my dear mother, or I might have rued it; for the mite given me by the good man my father was nearly expended before I was well settled in my first Irish lodging.

I landed on the 28th of May 1794; and a thinner and more consumptive specimen of an Englishman never set foot on the Emerald Isle. As soon as Aurora condescended to develope her plans for the day, I was cheered. The goddess shone forth in all her spring splendour; — the exceeding and novel drollery of all the lower orders, with whom I had my first dealings after I left the Custom-house, came upon me with such irresistible force, that I could not negative a proposal, however absurd, for laughing. The powerful contrast that manifests itself on first landing in France is not greater than that experienced by a close observer when he encounters the crowd of whimsical beings who surround and pummel him after his luggage is cleared from the Custom-house in Dublin.

Here the Autobiography, in a connected state, unfortunately terminates; but some detached fragments, intended to have formed a part of it, will be introduced in their proper places.

CHAPTER V.

Early Letters to his friend Mr. John Litchfield.—Departure from Home.—Journey to Ireland.—Dublin.—Introduction to Daly the Manager.—Mrs. Wells (afterwards Mrs. Sumbel).—Owenson.—Miss Campion (afterwards Mrs. Pope).—Miss Farren.—Holman.—Honourable Mrs. Twisleton.—Dishonourable conduct of Daly.—First appearance on the Dublin Stage.—His Salary.—"Fontainville Forest."—Cherry.—John Palmer.—Captain Wathen.—Mathews's Cast of Characters in Dublin, and his quick study.—Mr. Boaden the author.—Mr. and Mrs. Davenport.

At this period of Mr. Mathews's career, I introduce the following letter (the prelude to many others), written on the eve of his departure from his paternal roof. It will show that his affectionate feelings, and love of home, were only interrupted, not destroyed, by the ruling passion; and that his family, however objectionable his bias and pursuits seemed to their preconceived notions, had become resigned, if not reconciled, to the course of life he had determined to pursue.

His last amiable consideration for those whom he nevertheless felt irresistibly impelled to quit, proves the tenderness inherent in his nature, and that in leaving, though voluntarily, for the first time, his excellent parents and the roof under which he was born, he was not therefore divested of that portion of suffering which a good mind and feeling heart ever undergo at a necessity of inflicting pain on those whose love and good intentions are indisputable, even when the manner of evincing them is inimical to the happiness they would promote.

The ensuing letters are the compositions of a youth, *much younger* than his *years,* from the circumstances of his bringing-up, and his too long confinement to.

"Home, where small experience grows."

His health from childhood had been weak; his growth so rapid as to give serious apprehensions that his life would terminate early. He was, besides this, his mother's darling; and he might be said, in familiar phrase, to have been "tied to her apron-string" much longer than male children are expected to be petted. This mode of treatment, while it kept his mind from the contamination of evil, narrowed the sphere of his ideas. He was scarcely emancipated from home-prejudices and fire-side habits, (for his term at a public school was not of long duration,) and the custom, which his fond mother insisted on, of his passing every allowed period of absence from school duties under her own eye, precluded that wholesome and necessary experience which a community of boys inevitably gives, in *little*, of the grown-up world before them.

The modesty of his self-opinion; the generosity with which he judges the conduct and merits of those about him; his manly though meek endurance not only of the trials he had incurred by his resignation of his home prospects, but even of the injustice which he was not prepared to expect; his integrity and good temper; his proud independence and honourable notions — all combine to constitute these letters a most interesting feature in the opening of his eventful history. They assuredly display the native goodness of his disposition, while they must mirthfully amuse every person versed in theatricals and acquainted with the genius which, by dint of the most laborious struggles, and most untiring perseverance, raised its possessor to the height of the profession he so ornamented. What but smiles can attend upon those relations which present him in characters not only of the most insignificant nature, but in style so preposterous, under the present recollections of the performer! *

* I take this opportunity of thanking Mr. Litchfield for the loan of these letters. But for his kindness, the whole of the period of Mr. Mathews's life to which they relate must have been a total blank, excepting a few anecdotes left upon my memory, from my husband's occasional repetition of them.— A. M.

TO MR. JOHN LITCHFIELD, Jun.

Dear Litchfield,   Strand, 28th May 1794.

As I leave town at six o'clock to-morrow morning, I must pass this evening at home. My father and mother have a very particular desire that you should sup with them; and this being the last evening we can spend together for some time, I hope you will favour us with your company.

As for the play, you can see the new piece any other evening; and "Alexander" is not to be endured. We can drink our parting glass as comfortably in our room, nay, I hope more so, than at Williams's.* I must pass this evening with you; therefore do not tear me from home.

Your mother was so good as to ask me to tea before I went; I shall therefore come down this afternoon. Be good enough to look at my books, and send them by George, as I wish to pack them up.

I have sent you Boaden's play; and also "Travellers in Switzerland." This latter is the only new play I have.

Yours sincerely,

Charles Mathews.

TO MR. JOHN LITCHFIELD, Jun.

Dear Litchfield,   Chester, May 31st, 1794.

I arrived in this city last night at nine o'clock, at a very large and commodious inn. Mr. Hitchcock was obliged to leave on Wednesday, but left me a letter of direction to find him in Ireland. I met with an Irish

* A tavern in Bow Street, which was, I am informed, much frequented by the *stage-stricken*.—A. M.

gentleman, of the army, in the coach, who was going to Dublin; and he has recommended me to a captain of a packet, whom we met here. We sail to-morrow morning at eight o'clock, and leave Chester at two this afternoon for Parkgate. I breakfasted yesterday at Litchfield, where I had the pleasure to find that Garrick and Johnson were well remembered. One of the inhabitants showed me where Johnson was born; and there are some of the Garricks now in the town. It is their market-day here; and the situation from the inn is very similar to that in the market at Canterbury, with the same kind of entrance to the cathedral. I have been very fortunate here at breakfast. I unexpectedly met with a couple of muffins; and a fine leg of pork is now being dressed for dinner! I cannot hear from you till I get to Dublin, from whence I will write as soon as I arrive. Remember me most affectionately to all your family, and to all others who think me worth inquiring after; and believe me to be

Yours unalterably,

CHARLES MATHEWS.

(Saturday, one o'clock.)

TO MR. JOHN LITCHFIELD, JUN.

DEAR LITCHFIELD, Dublin, June 4th, 1794.

I left Parkgate on Sunday last at two o'clock, and arrived in Dublin last night at eleven, which is reckoned a remarkably tedious passage, as they frequently cross in fourteen hours. I was extremely well during the voyage, a very uncommon circumstance on board. I slept at a hotel, and found Mr. Hitchcock this morning, who walked about Dublin with me for two hours, to look for a lodging; all of which I found most extravagantly dear. I have got one chamber, with a closet to dress in, for 6s. 6d. a-week, which in English money is only 6s. It is by far the handsomest lodging I met with, and, here, is reckoned *wonderfully cheap!* I met with several inferior, at 8s. and upwards, to 15s.; single rooms, with ragged beds. You recollect, on our last meeting, recommending me to one at 3s.; conceive, then, after walking two hours, to be surprised at meeting with one so *cheap* as 6s.

I was this morning introduced to Daly, who behaved very politely to me. He is as tall and corpulent as Williams in Bow Street. I am to rehearse *Jemmy Jumps* to-morrow morning; and I expect to play next Monday, but am not quite certain what character. The play this evening is "He would be a Soldier," and the farce of "All the World's a Stage," by command of the Lord-Lieutenant. At present they have no professed low comedian. Meadows, a singer, (who performs *Caleb* to-night,) is the only actor of any consequence in this line. I had some conversation with Mrs. Wells this morning in the green-room. I talked of "The World" newspaper to her. She speaks very highly of Fuller and J. Hewerdine, but not so of Swan. When I told her he was in the militia, she laughed most extravagantly. I shall write as soon as possible again to you to tell you something of this very superb city. Direct to me, at Mrs. Moland's, No. 14, Exchequer Street, Dublin; and believe me to be

Yours ever most affectionately,

CHARLES MATHEWS.

TO MR. JOHN LITCHFIELD, JUN.

DEAR LITCHFIELD, Dublin, June 14th, 1794.

I admire Dublin exceedingly. You will no doubt be surprised to hear that I am going to leave it. Daly has behaved extremely ill to me; for he has put me off from day to day with promises of playing, and he has as often disappointed me. I promised Mrs. Wells to play for her benefit. It will be next Thursday. I am to play *Lingo*, and, I believe, *Jacob*. I was recommended by one of the company to apply to Owenson, who is making up a company to go to Kilkenny, one of the most important towns in Ireland. Owenson* has played all the Irish characters in Daly's company for many years past. I was introduced to him, and spoke *Sir A. Absolute*, *Jacob*, and *Lenitive*. He was very well satisfied; and said, if I was going on the stage in that line, I might depend on a first situation in his company. All the players here speak well of him, and would be glad to go with him, and leave Daly. Those who have no articles have not hesitated, some to join Moss, and others, Owenson. Daly is hated by all the performers, scarcely any of whom can get any money from him. Owenson opens his theatre on Monday, 23rd. I expect to leave Dublin on Friday next. Daly met me, and said, he heard I was going with Owenson; and asked me if I would like to play " walking gentlemen." I told him, by no means. It was his intention to keep me in Dublin until I had spent all my money, and then have offered me a small salary, and make me play " walking gentlemen," a proposal which I must have accepted rather than starve. Cherry, the comedian, is coming from York, and Wathen from London; of course there would have been no situation for me in that line. The company here is very small and very bad, Palmer, Clinch, Moss, and several others, having left it. Hargrave is a good actor, and his voice very pleasant. He is the only man in

---

* Owenson was the father of Lady Morgan.

tragedy that is decent now. Mrs. Kennedy is the principal lady in comedy, and a Miss Campion* in tragedy. Mrs. Hitchcock is a tolerably good actress in Mrs. Bland's line. Her husband is much respected in the company; but they all look upon him as a tool of Daly. I have seen Daly play the *Copper Captain* extremely well; that and *Walter* are the only characters I have yet seen him in. There are a vast number of places taken already for Miss Farren's first, second, third, and fourth nights, but very few for Holman and Mrs. Twisleton. As soon as you receive this, look at the Irish paper, and at " The World," and you will perhaps see me advertised for Mrs. Wells's night. I am yours ever most affectionately,

CHARLES MATHEWS.

TO MR. WILLIAM MATHEWS.

DEAR WILLIAM, Dublin, June 14th, 1794.

I have been in this city nearly a fortnight, and of course have had time enough to find out its beauties and deformities, both of which are numberless. I cannot sufficiently admire the buildings. There is a university here — the only one in Ireland. There are several hundred students, who dress in the same manner as those of Cambridge and Oxford. It is a very superb building, and boasts some very fine gardens, which are public. There are scarcely any public amusements; only one playhouse, and a place they call the Rotunda, for concerts. The politicians, I think, are more numerous, and by far more violent, than those in London.

Daly has treated me very meanly, having continually put me off with promises of playing. Mrs. Wells's benefit

* Afterwards the second wife of Pope the actor.

is next Thursday, when I expect to play *Jacob Gawky* and *Lingo*. I mean to leave Daly, and go with a new company to Kilkenny. All give him a most dreadful character; and I shall be glad to escape from him.

Let me know whether you went to the masquerade on the 5th instant. The account of it in " The Courier " mentioned a master of arts as a good mask. Was it you? I am delighted with the walks about Dublin. Adieu.

Yours most affectionately,
CHARLES MATHEWS.

TO MR. JOHN LITCHFIELD, Jun.

DEAR LITCHFIELD, Dublin, June 23rd, 1794.

I received yours last Thursday with a great deal of pleasure.

On Thursday evening I made my first appearance, for Mrs. Wells's benefit, in *Jacob* and *Lingo*. The house was tolerably well filled, and I was received in a manner that exceeded my greatest expectations. The scene in *Jacob*, where he mimics the minuet, was highly applauded; but *Lingo* gained me much more. I had an excellent dress, and my wig did a vast deal for me. The songs were very much approved of, judging from the applause. The two last were encored: " Amo, amas," was one, and " Of all the pretty flowers" the other. Each time I came to the part of " To be sure I did !" I gained bursts of applause. When I had sung it I made my exit; but it was loudly called for again. I was somewhat fatigued, and told the performers to go on for the next scene. *Laura* and *Eugene* went on, and were hissed off. I was, of course, obliged to sing it; and gave very general satisfaction. The musicians declared that the song was never so well sung in the theatre before. I received numerous compliments, and was told that the part had not been so well performed since O'Reilly played it. I was distinctly heard in every part of the house, which is larger than the Haymarket Theatre.* Daly sent for me on Friday, and declared himself very well content with my performance, and offered a guinea per week. I was obliged to accept of it, as Owenson has been disappointed of his theatre in Kilkenny, and cannot open it before August. Cherry is coming here from York, and Wathen from Richmond. Though I was so well received, I cannot expect to get all the capital low comedy parts at first. Hitchcock behaves very well to me, and will ensure me every farthing of my money. I am to play second and third parts in tragedy and genteel comedy, and occasionally parts in low comedy. I am promised *Rundy*, in "The Farmer," when Wathen plays *Jemmy Jumps*. They never give more than 1*l*. 1*l*. to a young actor. Most of the salaries here are what they

* The criticism in the Dublin paper upon this performance fully corroborates the foregoing account.

"Theatre Royal, Dublin, June the 19th, 1794.

" Mrs. Wells's benefit was on Monday the 19th of June, when 'The Chapter of Accidents' and the 'Agreeable Surprise' were performed to a very elegant audience.† Independently of her unrivalled imitations, there was the attraction of a new performer, of the name of Mathews, in the characters of *Jacob* and *Lingo*. The introduction of a young actor in two such different characters on the same night was rather singular, and the task to the performer indisputably very arduous. He went through them both, however, in a very creditable style, and received the most flattering marks of approbation. He assumed the Somersetshire dialect very happily, and dis-

† Mrs. Wells, afterwards Mrs. Sumbel, was the original performer of *Cowslip*.

call " play-house pay ;" that is, payment only each night they play; so that a man engaged at three pounds a-week, if he performs three times a-week only, has only half of his salary. I am to be paid if I play only once; and am not obliged to take " a benefit." Daly deducts money for a benefit from all those who are engaged at the play-house pay. I am therefore equally well situated with those who have three pounds. Daly bears the worst of characters; but I have dependence on Hitchcock, who is much beloved, and has great influence in the theatre. As manager, he disposes of all the characters. Of course, he will sometimes serve me. He treats me very well, and invites me frequently to his house. I see my name now in the bills for the first time: — " To-morrow evening, ' Lear ;' *Albany*, Mr. Mathews!" It is a pretty part for its length; and each one I perform will make me more used to the stage. Hitchcock has promised to let me play *Lenitive*, if he can get up the piece. It has not been played

covered in the course of the performance very extraordinary talents in low comedy. The scene where *Gawky* mimics the minuet was highly relished by the audience. Flattering as was his reception in *Jacob*, his performance of *Lingo* was certainly superior, and met, if possible, with still louder applause. The songs of ' Amo, amas,' and ' Of all the pretty flowers,' were sung with infinite humour, and were universally encored. The turn of ' To be sure I did!' was neatly managed, and gained him repeated applause. The two above-mentioned songs were never so well given in this theatre, and the part, on the whole, has not been so successfully played since O'Reilly.* Moss was very inferior. Mr. Mathews's manner of playing is quite original, and he has tolerable freedom in action. The turn of his features is irresistibly comic; and, on the whole, we may reckon him a very desirable acquisition to the Irish stage."

* A great comic genius, who died young.

since Moss left them. They have lost their *Label, Juba,* and *Caroline;* so that its revival will be attended with some difficulty. Holman, it is said, has arrived, but I have not yet seen him. He is advertised to play in " Romeo and Juliet" on Wednesday: Mrs. Twisleton* the *Juliet.* Among their plays are, " Don Sebastian" (Holman, *Dorax,* Mrs. T., *Almeyda*), " Fontainville Forest," " Venice Preserved," and " Alexander." Miss Farren† is expected every day. She will draw very crowded houses, as the boxes for her nights are extremely well taken. Holman and Mrs. T. are not expected to draw much. We have played since I have been here, " He would be a Soldier;" " Recruiting Officer;" " Rule a Wife and have a Wife;" (Hargrave, *Leon*—very good acting; Daly, *Copper Captain; Estifania,* Mrs. Kennedy — both well;) " Jane Shore" (*Shore,* Mrs. Wells; *Alicia,* Miss Campion,—this actress, who has been the heroine at the private theatre in Fishamble Street, played here two years back, and is a great favourite); " Grecian Daughter;" " Gamester;" " Chapter of Accidents" (*Jacob,* moi-même,—of *course!* very well! hem! *Bridget,* Mrs. Wells); " Wild Oats." " The Children in the Wood" is played extremely well. The *Children* are superior to those in London. Hargrave is a very improving actor; Daly, good in genteel comedy; Mrs. Kennedy, in genteel comedy, a very good actress. Hurst, in Hull's line, admirable. Cunningham in "fops" is a very good actor; I think he would succeed very well in London in R. Palmer's place. He is a very genteel young man, and a pleasant companion, and the only one in the company with whom I associate. Miss Brett, a very good singer, and very pretty actress in Mrs. Bland's line. Miss Farren's plays are, " Know your own Mind;"

* The Hon. Mrs. Twisleton.
† Afterwards Countess of Derby.

"Hypocrite;" "School for Scandal;" "Belle's Stratagem;" &c.; and the farce of "The Citizen." Hargrave is the only man, except Hurst, who is decent in tragedy. They give him five pounds a-week certain; and he is very regularly paid. They are terribly at a loss for tragedians; and every man is obliged to play in them, whether suited or not. "Fontainville Forest" is printed in Dublin —a very paltry edition. When it is performed, Hargrave is to be the *Marquess;* Hurst, *Peter;* Cunningham, *Louis,* and myself the *Phantom.* I expected to have been *Louis,* but Cunningham was cast for it before I came out. Boaden said he wished me to be the *Ghost.* Remember me to him, and tell him of my success, and the cast of his tragedy. I have dined with W. Palmer, to whom Cunningham introduced me. He is very much like his brother Bob, and was a great favourite here. He is married, and lives elegantly. He had six pounds per week; Moss, ten. I will thank you not to tell any one what salary I have got, as you know people unacquainted with the stage will expect to hear I receive much more, and if they hear this, they will perhaps judge unfavourably of my reception. My salary is to be raised in the winter. I mean to board with a family, as I cannot otherwise live on the money I receive. The wardrobe and conduct of the theatre are much better than I expected to find them. They dress their plays in general very well. The *Grecian Daughter* was dressed entirely in "shapes," all belonging to the theatre; and the dress of *Gloster* in "Jane Shore" was equally elegant with that worn by Harley[*] at Covent Garden. I expected to be some distance hence before I could receive another letter from you. It is, however, much better to be in Dublin than in the country parts of Ireland, where very little reputation is to be gained. I thank you

[*] The tragedian.

for your concern about my "wiggery," which escaped the officer's "rude gripe," without discovery. They only opened the tops of my trunk and portmanteau, but proceeded no farther. Adieu! and be convinced of the unalterable affection of yours,

CHARLES MATHEWS,

of the Theatre Royal, Crow Street, Dublin.—Hem!

In the foregoing letter, it is impossible to read his comment upon the merit of *Albany,* in "Lear," without a smile. " I see my name in the bills for the first time.—*Albany,* Mr. Mathews! It is a pretty part, for its length." (!) Let those who have known Mr. Mathews in his high-day remember this character, and amuse themselves at the idea of his representing it.

It is noticeable, that his comments upon the performers named are very judicious. Their merits, well known afterwards, proved his judgment to be correct at that time. Mr. Hargrave performed as a tragedian at Covent Garden Theatre in 1804 or 1805, previously to his retirement from the stage.

TO MR. JOHN LITCHFIELD, JUN.

DEAR LITCHFIELD, Dublin, July 20th, 1794.

" Fontainville Forest" has been played three times with very great success. I played the *Phantom,* and got great applause. I had a very fine dress, and very like that which Follet wears. The dresses in general were new, and the scenery also. Holman's dress was plain, but very handsome. Hargrave's, for the *Marquess,* extremely splendid. Holman played some parts of *La Motte* very finely; and Hargrave did great justice to the *Marquess*. The same points told each night, as in London, but particularly that where *La Motte* tells the *Marquess* he buried Adeline " in a chest." Each night it gained five or six peals of applause. Holman and Mrs. Twisleton perform only three nights more. They have had but very poor houses, in comparison with Miss Farren, who is entirely the fashion. Cherry came out in *Sir Peter Teazle* and *Lazarillo* on Wednesday last. He is a very good actor, but extremely short, much more so than Quick. Miss Farren has played eight nights, and has ten more to come. Each night has been an overflow. There is some talk of Kemble coming here. I want to hear how they go on at the Haymarket, and of the alterations at Covent Garden. I see very few English papers here, and know nothing of the London theatricals. Is the anecdote of Palmer and the Prize case true?*

I am very pleasantly situated in a house, where I board and lodge. I have a room to myself, and live extremely well for a half a guinea per week. There are two other

* This inquiry alludes to Mr. John Palmer, whose embarrassed circumstances caused him at this time to live in his dressing-room at Drury-lane Theatre; and when the Haymarket re-opened for the summer season, at which he was engaged, the fear of arrest suggested the expedient of conveying him with a cart full of scenery, in one of the cabinets used in "The Prize;" and in this manner he actually was removed from one theatre to the other. Formerly a patent theatre was considered as a sort of theatrical *Alsatia* for money-owing criminals—a sanctuary from "John Doe and Richard Roe." Indeed, I remember several cases of a more recent date where such shelter was deemed inviolable, but I believe the march of knowledge has since that period stepped over this fallacy.—A. M.

performers, both English people, who board with me. The landlady of the house is a widow, and a very pleasant woman. I can make my cash hold out very well, but am in want of many stage properties, particularly for tragedy; buskins, russet boots, Spanish hat, cocked hat, sword, ruff, &c. Yours ever most affectionately,

CHARLES MATHEWS.

Direct to Mrs. Byrn's, No. 24, Temple Bar, Dublin.

TO MR. JOHN LITCHFIELD, JUN.

DEAR LITCHFIELD, Dublin, August 3rd, 1794.

On opening your packet I found a letter from my father, a few lines from my brother, and an introduction from Boaden to Holman.

I am very much obliged to you for the satisfaction you express at my success. My sentiments were exactly similar to your own. I was very doubtful of the event, eager as I was to embrace so hazardous a profession; I was however much encouraged from my attempt in that "hole"* which you mention, and thought myself extremely fortunate in having the opportunity of performing *Jacob*, of which my friends in London on that occasion were good enough to approve. The attempt fully answered my wishes. Everything was superior here. I had room on the stage, and every advantage of regularity, with the aid of performers who understood what they were about, and were able to assist me. I had also the advantage of being the only person who had played the character for two seasons. But if these were my advan-

* The private theatre, in a dirty street called "Short's Gardens."

tages in *Jacob*, it was not so with *Lingo*, the recollection of Cornellies, who was a great favourite, and the original in *Lingo*, being fresh in the minds of the audience, and coming after Moss, who had played it within a fortnight. These were powerful reasons to make me fear success in that character. Thank heaven, however, I combated these; and, on my entrance the second time to perform it, I was saluted very flatteringly. It is the custom here, in the galleries, previously to applauding a performer on his entrance, to call for it. For instance, when *Cherry* enters, the cry is instantly, " A clap for Cherry !" and if any performer displeases them, a groan is called for. This has several times happened when I have been on the stage in an inferior character in tragedy. On such occasions they have called out " A clap for Lingo !" which is very flattering, and frequently gives me that confidence which I very much stand in need of.

I do not think myself at all ill-used by having only a guinea a-week. A young performer cannot expect a large salary; and the salaries here are by no means great. However, I thank you for concealing the sum from people whom you have told of my success. It is a general idea with those who are unacquainted with the theatre, that the salaries are much larger than they really are. I have not entered into any articles with Daly, nor do I mean to do so. I should always wish to have it in my power to leave him if a superior situation offered.

I was much entertained by your account of the masquerade; and am much obliged to you for sending me the sham bill. On opening one of the packets, this bill fell out in the green-room, where I opened it. At first I was deceived and thought fortune had been uncommonly favourable, but was very soon undeceived. However, I did not tell the people to the contrary, who all supposed

I had received a bank bill. It is a good thing to be imagined rich.* Daly was in the green-room at the time, which I was glad of. I really think that he does not deserve so bad a character as he in general bears. He has behaved very well to me, and takes great notice of me; I have been paid very regularly, and have not been fined a farthing. You desire to learn the " exact progress of my stage business." I will give you my regular number of characters. Wathen and Cherry have the low comedy; so I could not expect to get that kind of business, particularly at first. What I have done, to be sure, is only poor, but it will make me used to the stage, and that at any rate is a service. Daly has said to several of the performers that I have great merit in comedy, and he will give me good business in the winter. I do not doubt that I shall get better if I stay with him. But when I have had some bad characters offered me, I have been very crusty; and if he does not keep his word, I certainly will go into the country.

> *Jacob*, " Chapter of Accidents." *Lingo*, " Agreeable Surprise."
> *Lamp*, in " Wild Oats." (Because I played the violin — bad second appearance part!)
> *Albany*, in " King Lear."
> *Paris*, " Romeo and Juliet."
> *Melidor*, " Zara." *Lingo*, " Agreeable Surprise."
> *Thesalus*, " Alexander." *Beaufort*, " Citizen."
> *Elliott*, " Venice Preserved."
> *Charles*, " Know your own Mind."
> *Rossaud*, " Fair Penitent." *Benin* (the black), " Highland Reel."
> *Count Louis*, " Peeping Tom."
> *Hounslow*, " Beaux' Stratagem." *Apathy*, " Children in the Wood."

---

* He had reason in later years to change this opinion.—A. M.

James, " Provoked Husband." 1st *Scholar*, " Padlock."
Phantom, "Fontainville Forest." *Sambo* (the black), "Divorce."
Coachman, " Devil to Pay."
Sexton, " Much Ado about Nothing." *Beaufort*, " Citizen."
(Mrs. Twisleton's Benefit), *Captain of Guards*, in " Tancred." *Hortensio*, " Catherine and Petruchio."
David, " Natural Son." *Priest* (Chorus), " Arthur and Emmeline."
Muley, Zedan, " Don Sebastian." (Part Middleton played at Covent Garden.)
Brush, " All in the Wrong." *Beaufort*, " Citizen."
Paris, "Jealous Wife." *Sailor*, " Glorious First of June." (Holman's Benefit), *Guildenstern*, " Hamlet."

These are all the characters which I have yet performed. Of these, *Count Louis, Apathy, Phantom, Sexton, Paris*, (" Jealous Wife,") have done me some service; and I gained applause in each of them. *Apathy*, in " Children in the Wood," was a very lucky circumstance for me. It was originally played by Moss; since he has gone, by a man of the name of Callan (very excellent in Rock's line). About four o'clock on the 8th of July Mr. Daly sent for me, and asked me if I would undertake to study *Apathy* by the evening, as Callan was then very ill. I told him I would; and was perfect to a letter. I got the music, practised it, and sung the duet with great applause. An apology was made in the usual form; and I was received with great good-nature.

I delivered my introduction to Holman yesterday. We had a hearty laugh together at its arrival the day after that on which he had intended to leave Dublin. He has been extremely polite to me; and Mrs. Twisleton also, who is the most amiable creature in existence. When

Holman first arrived I made myself known to him, as being acquainted with Boaden; on which he took a great deal of notice of me, and made me pay him several visits. He plays *Romeo,* and Mrs. Twisleton *Juliet,* for Wathen's benefit, on Tuesday next, the 5th instant. The houses have been very bad on Holman's and Mrs. T.'s nights. Miss Farren has been all the fashion; and nothing else would draw money. Holman made a very good benefit; that of Mrs. Twisleton was very poor, for which reason her friends have desired her to take another. It is to be " Fontainville Forest."

The company leave Dublin for Cork on Friday the 15th. Miss Farren is to play twelve nights there.

I left England without calling on Wayte, to whom I am indebted for a few articles; among which are the dresses for the private play. I shall be very much obliged to you if you will call on him to make an apology for my neglect, and tell him I will remit the money as soon as it is in my power.

My brother tells me that Boaden mentioned me in " The Oracle." Will you copy it for me, and send it with what he said of " Fontainville Forest," in your next packet? This will save me 1*s*. 1*d*. Everything helps on these occasions, and I must be frugal.

I very much feel the loss of my box of plays, which would be very useful to me here; but the expense of having them over would be too great, and I cannot afford it. They are already packed up at home, but I believe there are upwards of 200 cwt.

There are two people from this theatre engaged at Covent Garden — Mr. and Mrs. Davenport. He is a very respectable performer in a general line, but mostly " old men," and she is a very good actress in Mrs. Webb's line.* She is also very serviceable to a theatre in second-rate " genteel comedy" and tragedy. She played *Madame La Motte* very well.

Believe me to be yours ever most affectionately,
CHARLES MATHEWS.
24, Temple Row.

When mentioning his performance in " The Citizen," he omitted, for obvious reasons, the particulars attending the representation. He was naturally unwilling to enter into a detail of every mortifying result of his wilful pursuit to his friend, hope ever pointing forward to the moment when, surmounting all such disadvantages, he should be able to relate his " moving accidents" without vexation to himself; and, as he hoped, a time did arrive when he felt the amusement he afforded others, by narrating his history of past degradations. Although I furnish the following account from memory, I can assert its correctness.

During the engagement of Miss Farren (afterwards Countess of Derby) Mr. Mathews was obliged to play — as the foregoing list shows — the part of *Beaufort* in " The Citizen." Now, of all " walking gentlemen," as such are technically called, *Beaufort* is the most dreaded by young men; — being an insipid, sighing dangler, the

* Mrs. Davenport, since, the inimitable " Old Woman" of Covent Garden Theatre, having succeeded Mrs. Webb in that line soon after this period.—A. M.

character is generally given to the most insignificant actor in the company, if he be young enough to be "sent on" for a lover. Imagine, then, a novice in this part, one whose intention to be a "low comedian" was thwarted by the wily manager, whose agent had in fact kidnapped him over, as cunningly as gipsies delude children from their homes, with sweet and fair promises, only to break them as soon as they have their dupes in their power. Daly was so well known by experienced people in the profession, that he was fain to entice the young and unsuspicious, and therefore sent one of his agents to England occasionally in order to entrap those whom he might meet there, for a cast of characters he found it difficult to get filled. Mr. Hitchcock discovered a young man who wished to play *Lingo*,— this, then, was the bait with which he covered the hook; and with such *taking* promises he flattered and led him on with hopes never intended to be realized, tickling him like a trout, till he fell a willing victim into the hands of his tempter. It is true, as he has related, that he *did* play his stipulated part of *Lingo*, but it was immediately followed up by *Lamp*, *Albany*, the *Noble County Paris*, and such like dawdling worthies, and *Beaufort*, the dreaded *Beaufort*.

Imagine, then, a tall, thin, awkward youth, with a deportment utterly unfit for a stage-gentleman of that starched day, with a craving appetite for *Old Philpot,* which he in after-years performed so admirably, compelled to submit to be the *butt,* not only of *Maria,* but of all the audience, in *Beaufort.* Miss Farren, accustomed as she must have been to the worst sort of acting in the part, probably never before saw a total novice represent it; and it was with dismay that she observed him appear in the green-room dressed in a scarlet coat (the only one provided by the theatre for the occasion) which had obviously been made for a man a head shorter than himself, and whose arms were in proportion with his stature, for the sleeves reached only within an inch of the wrists of the present unfortunate wearer;— a yellow embroidered waistcoat, a pair of black satins scarcely covering the knee, and showing more of a leg guiltless of calf than grace or fashion demanded; his hair liberally powdered and tied in a *queue,* according to the mode; a *chapeau bras* which he scarcely knew how to dispose of, and which now and then in his embarrassment he was tempted to put upon his head. Fancy Mr. Mathews in such a dress, and at the age of seventeen playing a puling, sentimental drawl of a lover to a woman of elegant, easy figure and accomplished manners! When he came before the audience there was a general shout, as if a clown in a pantomime had made his appearance, succeeded by an almost simultaneous shriek from the gallery, and then the following delicate *innu-*

endoes !—" Oh ! see the mop-stick !"—" Ah ! Pat, hould yer breath hard, or y'll puff him off the stage."—" Oh ! and it's the only puff I'll give him, any how."—" Oh ! the crethur ! what a slice of a man ! Arrah ! where's your other half ? Why didn't ye bring it with ye, jewel?" These and such like pleasantries greeted his first appearance. When *Maria* came on the stage to him, he being directed by the author to look thoughtful and embarrassed, Miss Farren *felt obliged* (by the same authority) to imitate the performer's peculiar action, and then laugh in derision of it. Hereupon followed, from *on high*, a dreadful noise, that might be supposed to resemble the war-whoop of American Indians, in token of their approval of the imitation.

At length, when the love-sick *Beaufort* made his exit, he was followed by a universal whoo !!! After this had subsided, one of his tormentors got up and proposed "*a groan for the long lobster,*" which was loudly and heartily accorded with due honours, as far as the gallery was concerned, to the infinite amusement of the rest of the audience.

When the piece was over, Miss Farren went up to the young actor behind the scenes, and apologized to him for having been an unwilling accessory to the ridicule his unpractised manner and appearance created, owing to the necessity she was under of obeying the author's intention, and following up her own character in the farce. She kindly expressed her concern at seeing a young gentleman thrust into a part so obviously out of his line, and which in itself was so contemptible as always more or less to draw ridicule upon the actor. She added, that his inexperience, and the disgraceful dress the theatre had provided for him, had of course rendered the result still more distressing.

These delicate alleviations soothed, but did not heal his feelings; he begged, almost in tears, that Mr. Daly would on a future occasion give the character to a fitter representative. But managers, as well as fathers, have "flinty hearts;" and, moreover, Daly could find no one else to take such a part, unless he paid a long arrear of salary. *Beaufort* was not worth so high a price, and therefore the part was assigned to a good-for-*nothing* actor, as *he* was deemed who had last been ridiculed in the character, and whom it was not the manager's intention to pay much longer. The best apology that could in the first instance be adduced for such an unprincipled determination was, that Mr. Daly, in kidnapping a young man of respectable family and friends, stage-struck as he was, believed that he possessed resources independent of the paltry salary agreed upon, and therefore might afford to go on without pay after his first probation, and, from his own confessed dramatic ardour, not feel the injustice, or at least not be inclined to question it. This, at first, he might believe; but he was afterwards quite aware of the privations and difficulties his dishonourable treatment occasioned the poor novice.

I have heard Mr. Mathews say, that he has gone to the theatre at night without having tasted anything since a meagre breakfast, determined to refuse to go on the stage, unless some portion of his arrears was first paid. When, however, he entered the green-room, his spirits were so cheered by the attention of his brethren, and the *éclat* he met with among them whenever he put forth his powers of amusement, added to the gaiety of the scene altogether, that his fainting resolution was restored, all his discontent utterly banished for the time, and he was again reconciled to starvation; nay, he even felt afraid of offending the unfeeling manager, and returned home silent upon the subject of his claims. Then came in succession the London performers, Miss Farren, Kemble, Incledon, &c. some of whom he beheld for the first time. Fancy a young enthusiast witnessing and becoming familiar with such talent in the profession he doted upon. He devoured their every look; he drank up every tone; he was enrapt with their excellence, and gloried in the choice he had made. In short, he was content to live on in the hope, remote as it seemed, of being one day received by an audience with the same enthusiasm with which they were received. Such a hope was worth all present suffering, and suffer he did manfully.

Throughout his correspondence it will be found that he made no positive admission, after the first disappointment, of ill-usage from Daly; not even to his most confidential friend did he complain of any subsequent injustice. Not a hint of actual pecuniary distress was given to Mr. Litchfield or any of his own family, nor of his consequent privations. When he alludes to stoppages of salary from occasional closing of the theatre, he touches so lightly upon the consequences to himself, that his friend would hardly have been justified in proffering assistance, which, after all, his pride, and a determined constancy in suffering, would have rejected as uncalled-for and unnecessary.

TO MR. JOHN LITCHFIELD, Jun.

Dear Litchfield, Cork, Aug. 24, 1794.

I arrived here on Wednesday last, in the mail, and am much pleased with this beautiful city.

The expenses of the journey I knew would be so great that it would be impossible for me to afford it; I therefore told Daly, in Dublin, that I could not undertake it unless he would pay my expenses. I knew this was not the custom, and by no means expected he would consent; this, however, he did. He took a place for me in the mail and paid for it, giving me money to pay my luggage and expenses on the road, and promising not to deduct it from my salary. He has kept his word, for this day I received the money. Mr. Daly has always paid me, which has made the situation very pleasant, and he always gave redress in any complaint I made to him. He has spoken very much in my favour to several of the performers, praising my attention to my business in the theatre, and regularity out of it. I am sure I am a great favourite with him, because the travelling expenses of no other person are paid.

I have given imitations very frequently to the performers here of those in London; and of some of those here, particularly Wathen. Some one told Daly of this circumstance, and he asked me yesterday morning to give him my imitations, which I consented to do, and gave several before him and Miss Farren, and a number of the performers, in the green-room. Daly and Miss Farren both paid me a number of compliments. My imitation of Wathen gave very general satisfaction. When I had done, and went out of the green-room to rehearse my part on the stage, some of the performers followed, and cried out, " By Jasus! Mathews, your fortune is made; Daly swears he'll put you forward in the winter."

Miss Farren is to play six nights; she opened with *Bizarre*, in " The Inconstant," and has played *Lady Bell* and *Beatrice*. She plays *Violante* to-morrow. The house has been crowded each night that she has played; she was never here before, and is very well received. The theatre holds about 200*l.*; the boxes, 4*s.*; pit, 3*s.*; gal. 2*s.* It is a very handsome house, and very neatly built, like the Canterbury Theatre. There are several dressing-rooms, and the stage is immensely large; it was built by Woodward and Barry. I dress in a room with only one other performer. Wathen had a benefit here, and one in Limerick; his engagement ends on the 20th of September.

"The Jew" was performed in Dublin, and he played *Jabal;* being a very *starved* figure. Daly has promised it to me when he goes. Cherry's *Jew* is one of the finest pieces of acting I ever saw; I think it very superior to Bannister's, who certainly played it well, but neither spoke the dialect nor looked the character so well as Cherry. He is an extremely little man, I think less than Quick, with a droll face; he is one of the most humorous men in the world off the stage, and a very good actor on it.

The Company go to Limerick on September 7th, and play there during the assizes. They then return to Cork, play three weeks, and open in Dublin in November. Miss Farren plays in Limerick six nights, and goes thence to England. I shall be very sorry when we lose her, for she is one of the most agreeable women I ever saw, and behaves as politely to an underling as to a first-rate actor. She made a most excellent benefit in Dublin.

Mrs. Twiselton took "Tancred and Sigismunda" for her benefit, and had a most dreadfully poor house; she afterwards solicited Miss Farren to play for a second night, which she consented to do. The play was "Much Ado," and Mrs. T. played *Hero*; Holman, *Benedict*. It was as full as the house could hold; at least 350*l*. I am very glad of it, as she and Holman were very much neglected on their nights of playing. Holman also made a very good benefit Wathen had but 90*l*. in his house. The houses were full on Miss Farren's nights, even to the last, which proves how well they can support a house when there is any object of fashion. I believe Cooke is engaged for the winter, from Manchester.

I have got very good board and lodging, on the same terms as in Dublin. The provisions here of every kind are wonderfully cheap. The dialect, besides a very strong brogue, has a mixture of the Somersetshire in it. They say "steage," "feace," "neame," and so on. It is a rule with the shopkeepers to ask three times as much as they mean to take. If 7s. 6d. is asked, it is not thought indelicate to bid 2s. 6d. They will not allow that anything in England can be equal to Ireland. I must say, however, that there is a great degree of hospitality among them. The gratitude of the lower people is amazing: I have seen two or three instances where they would lay down their lives for a man from whom they had received a favour. An instance happened since I have been in Cork, of a labouring man fetching twenty or thirty men to the assistance of one who was ill-used, merely because he was of the same name and country as himself. The Irish language is very much talked here: it is a very singular kind of language, and very discordant to an English or a musical ear.

I shall be glad if you will write to me directly on the receipt of this. I wish to hear how Fawcett succeeded in *Lingo,* and the success of the new comedy, if it has appeared; in what part of the world my brother is, and any other news you can muster. Are Mrs. Leicester and Mrs. Henley discharged from Covent Garden? If so, there will be a fine opening for Mrs. Davenport, who I most sincerely hope will succeed her. They both are very worthy people, and have been very great friends to me. Tell me, is there a character in that line in Boaden's new play? She would do great justice to it, I am sure. Remember me to all at home, and be assured of the lasting affection of yours ever most sincerely,

CHARLES MATHEWS.

Mrs. Malony's, Bear-street, Cork.

TO MR. JOHN LITCHFIELD, Jun.

Dear Litchfield, Limerick, 15th Sept. 1794.

We opened here on Monday the 9th, with " Know your own Mind," " The Village Lawyer." *Lady Bell* in the play, Miss Farren. She was most rapturously received by a very elegant audience; for, besides numerous people of fashion residing near Limerick, the assizes brought together an immense number of people. She played every night last week to crowded houses. The theatre here holds about 130*l.* at the Dublin prices. The stage is very small, and there is no green-room, which is very unpleasant. There was a dressing-room built on purpose for Miss Farren, which I am told is to be the green-room for the future. We close on Saturday, and open in Cork next week. Daly has engaged the Chevalier D'Eon to fence on the stage; and I believe Mrs. Bateman is engaged for a few nights. " My Grandmother" has not been played yet. I believe it will be played in the winter; but *Dicky Gossip* would, of course, be given to Cherry, as he is very fond of it, and has played it often in Yorkshire.

Wayte's account, I believe, is correct, to my *sorrow*. I now repent running into some foolish and unnecessary expenses, which have involved me in debts that I shall find it difficult to pay out of my small salary. I cannot pay him at present. He will not, I hope, take the bill to my father. If you should hear such an intention hinted, and can prevent it, you will confer an additional obligation upon me. My father mentioned it to me while I was in Dublin: his reproof was very gentle to that which I could have expected on such an occasion; but I have always found him make allowances for these kind of follies.

Miss Farren was much pleased with my imitations, and frequently requested me to give them. Of the London performers, Suett and King struck most forcibly; but Wathen pleased them best. I gave Kemble in *Octavian,* which Miss Farren expressed great satisfaction in hearing. Daly asked me two or three times to give imitations at his benefit in Cork, which I was rather fearful of at first; but at last consented to do, not a little pleased, you may imagine, but somewhat fearful of success. "The Manager in Distress" was the piece fixed upon; and instead of giving the imitations in the balcony, I came down upon the stage, where I had plenty of room, and gave several with very great applause. The house was crowded; and those of Munden, Kemble, and Wathen, were received with roars. Kemble was strong in their recollection. Munden had been there last season; and I gave Wathen in *Sheepface,* which he had played very often in Cork. It did me a vast deal of service.—Adieu.

Yours most affectionately,
CHARLES MATHEWS.

CHAPTER VI.

Study in the fields.—In danger of being drowned.—An Irish *humane society.*—Virtues of Whiskey.—Mrs. Bateman and the Chevalier D'Eon; their fencing.—Mathews's prospects.—Buck, the Artist.—Daly's engagements.—Mathews's first appearance on the stage as a dancer.—Mathews's characters.—Cooke's performances in Dublin.—Supper with Cooke, and *a scene*, principal characters by Cooke and Mathews, and Mrs. Byrn.—Whiskey Punch and the Passions.

AMONG some detached and undated memoranda for his Life, I have found the following account, in my husband's hand-writing, of an accident that befel him about this period, which I well remember his relating at various times.

" During Miss Farren's performance in Ireland 'The Wonder' was one of the plays announced. From one of those irregularities which were common, the performer of *Lissardo* was not forthcoming, and I received commands from my superior officer to get ready in the part; having only the few hours from rehearsal time until evening to study it in. I therefore sallied forth to walk and learn, preferring the open air and exercise, to in-door fagging. I crossed Limerick Bridge, and was strolling by the banks of the Shannon, intent upon my book, when I met a brother actor—as it turned out for me, most fortunately met him— occupied like myself, in conning over his lesson. I asked him to read some of the dialogue to me, that I might ascertain how much I had got by heart. We then separated, mutually agreeing to assist each other in this way in another half-hour or so. In the mean time, the weather being sultry, I thought I would bathe. I accordingly stripped for the purpose, and having frequently paddled about near the same spot with impunity, I believed there was no part of the river where I could get out of my depth; for, be it known, that I had nothing but an 'alacrity in sinking' to qualify me, as I never had a notion of swimming. With some confidence in the solidity of the bottom, I walked, and splashed, until I imagined I had reached the deepest part, when I was instantaneously overwhelmed with the horrors of drowning! I felt the sensation of slipping down a precipice! Cataracts, thunder, lightning, seemed suddenly to environ me! The agonizing sensation of finding myself irrecoverably shut out in an instant from all human aid! a thousand racking thoughts of my distant home! my parents' distress! succeeded each other with the most frightful rapidity during the brief space of time that I was impotently struggling for recovery. But oh! the ruling passion, strong in death — dare I confess it? — my mind was occupied, for a brief second, by conjecture who could act *Lissardo* that night if I were drowned. ! Then, the worse than agony of renewed hope, when for a brief second I beheld the fair face of day, the sunny, cloudless sky, after my immersion below; for I rose twice, sufficiently above the surface to see distinctly my friend Seymour seated in the meadow, intent upon his book. I made an impotent attempt at a shout to him. I hoped I had articulated, but it must have been a faint scream. Alas! he saw me not. Again I sank! — and can comprehend the ' catching at a straw,' for my sensations, which are now vividly before me, were those of perishing in an unfinished building, where the beams of the floor were above my head. I struggled to grasp them, with a wild and frantic action, with my hands above my head! — Drowning has been variously described, and is generally supposed to be a very easy death. I have not experienced any other manner of dying certainly, but I cannot conceive any mode more painful. The tremendous noise of the rushing waters in the ears; the frightful flashing of light, as if surrounded by sparks from fire-works; the sense of suffocation! and oh! who can describe the sensations I briefly felt upon my second bound from the bed of the river to the surface! Again I attempted a feeble cry! Again I saw my studious companion; and again I had the conviction that I was unseen! Every hope now fled; and I gradually lost all sensation except that of struggling to reach the beams that floated in my imagination. To the last, I was under the impression, that by desperate efforts I might grasp this apparent substance, and so save myself. This is all I am capable of relating from my own knowledge; for I was near death, most decidedly, before I was providentially rescued.

" It appeared from the evidence of my friend, that the 'beam in my eye' was my latest vision, for he had jumped into the river with his clothes on, to save me. He was an expert swimmer; and made for the spot where he had last seen me rise, when, in almost despair of rescuing, or even finding me, he felt his legs suddenly seized with violence, and he was dragged by my dying struggles, feeble as they were, to the bottom. He was a most accomplished swimmer and diver, or I should never have related the tale. He contrived to get me on shore! I have no recollection of anything that occurred from my third sinking until I saw a heterogeneous collection of human figures and humorous countenances about me; and was almost suffocated afresh with the aroma of 'mountain dew.' I was carried, much in the state in which I am to believe I came into the world, by two soldiers, under the command of my preserver Seymour, to the first public-house that presented itself; and there they rubbed me down, and rubbed me in all directions; and I was recovered by the means prescribed by the humane society—of whiskey dealers. Curiosity brought numbers to see what was on table; and the jokes that were passed upon the occasion were something like the following:—

"'Let's luk at the face of him. Rub away, ye devils! I've seen the eyes of him opening. Don't trust the potteen near the mouth of the cratur, or he'll leave you none for the rubbin'. Pour a drop down to rouse the heart of him. Niver fear!—keep the sowl inside the body of him, and he's safe! How did he get in the sea itself?'—'Sea! sure, it's the Shannon. There's no sea there, you tief o' the world. Did he jump in?'—'Sure, he went a swimming, and had never learnt?'—'He had one lesson only, I heard, and that was to teach him how to sink.'—'By my sowl, then, he was an apt scholar. What name's upon him? Has he a woman itself that owns him? Sure, I heard the Englisher red-coat say, he was one of Daly's *divarters*.'

"The most zealous attendants of the Humane Society, however, might have here taken a lesson in adroitness in restoring animation. Suffice it to say, their *means* were effectual, and I acted *Lissardo* with the accomplished Farren that night."

TO MR. JOHN LITCHFIELD, Jun.

Dear Litchfield, Cork, October 16th, 1794.

I returned to Cork on Monday, September 21st, and we opened on the Friday following. We have played every night since, which, with the new pieces got up for benefits, has made our rehearsals very tiresome. They are frequently called at ten; never later than eleven; and they generally last till four. Then comes dinner, and preparation for the play; therefore, you may judge there is but little time for study; and I declare upon my honour, that since I received yours, except to-day, I have not had time to write a short letter.

Mrs. Bateman, and the Chevalier D'Eon, are here; and both have had benefits, which were tolerably good. Mrs. B. has played *Little Pickle, Caroline* (Prize), *Bridget, Widow Brady,* &c. She is thought very little of here, as an actress; and off the stage, she endeavours to sport the woman of fashion. She is the most talkative woman I ever met with, and has afforded great entertainment to the green-room. She wishes to convince us that this is merely a fashionable trip, and, in great measure, on the " dear Chevalier's account," whom she makes great merit of having supported for some time past. Her husband, she says, is in India, and at present allows her 1000*l.* per year, and that she soon means to follow him, where, as an actress, she says, she shall be " the sun."

The Chevalier has fenced several times with a gentleman whom she brought from England. Her figure, when dressed for the business, was the most ludicrous I ever saw. A helmet, with a plume of feathers, on her head; a piece of armour on her body, and a white satin petticoat; and so on to the feet like a woman. She wore a wig to resemble the hair dressed, which unfortunately fell off the first night, on taking off the helmet, and discovered her bald head, to the no small entertainment of the audience. Her figure generally produced great merriment among the gods; but on her own and Mrs. B.'s benefit she assumed the uniform which she wore formerly in the army, when captain of dragoons, and looked amazingly well.* The following singular announcement appears in the course of the bill :—" As several ladies and gentlemen have solicited Mrs. Bateman to fence, she will (for this night only) *push*, *quarte* and *tierce*, with any gentleman who will accept the challenge."

We close here on Saturday next, and play in Dublin for the government play on the Thursday afterwards; but I believe we shall not open till several days after that.

Adieu. Yours ever sincerely,
CHARLES MATHEWS.

DEAR LITCHFIELD,   Dublin, Nov. 9th, 1794.

I returned here about ten days ago, and am again situated in my old lodgings; two of the performers, a gentleman from Manchester, the widow and her son, form our family, where I pass my time very pleasantly. I shall now be able to form some idea as to what degree of happiness I may expect to pass my time in this company. It is five months since I left "my father's home," my friends, all that was dear to me, and became a voluntary exile; left all the dear delights of a native city and country; crossed the seas to a strange land, where I had no one

---

* It may be unnecessary to remind the reader that the *Chevalier* D'Eon was *not* a female, as was supposed at this period. —A. M.

hand to welcome me; entered with a dreadful uncertainty of success into the most precarious profession that could be found,—under the government of a man who was represented to me as the worst of men, the greatest of villains. With this prospect I came: thank Heaven, I have found him misrepresented, have had the good fortune to prove a favourite, and have had very particular attention paid me. I have passed through what the performers reckon the most disagreeable part of their work, that of travelling to play in the country; and it has turned out very pleasantly. I there improved myself by playing a very decent line of business, much more so than as a young performer I could expect, and had the pleasure of travelling through a very beautiful country. I have now returned safe and sound to winter quarters; and have a very good prospect of advancement in the profession I have adopted. If my salary were somewhat larger it would render me more comfortable, as my two blue coats begin now to look rather rusty, and my clothes in general exbibit very fatal symptoms of decay. I purchased a piece of nankeen in the summer for 6s. which made me two pair of breeches. This was a very cheap purchase, and they were very serviceable to me in the genteel parts I played.* A pair of shoes that I got made, and a hat that I have been obliged to buy since I returned, are the principal articles I have yet been able to spare money for. A coat will very soon be absolutely necessary, and I shall find that a great pull out of a guinea a-week. My debts in London make me very uneasy, as I thought it would be in my power to save sufficient money in the winter to discharge them, which would be the greatest pleasure to

* A "*genteel*" waiter, in the present day, would disdain to appear in such a material.—A. M.

me in life; but I find it can scarcely be possible. We have now been three weeks without salary.*

I was introduced to a very agreeable elderly lady in Cork, by Mr. and Mrs. Davenport, who behaved very politely to me. She is a person of tolerably good fortune; on which she lives in genteel style. I breakfasted with her, while in Cork, generally twice, and sometimes three times a-week, and found her a very pleasant acquaintance. Her house overlooked a convent garden, where I had the pleasure of seeing the nuns walk as I breakfasted. She introduced me to a very genteel family, of the name of Buck. There were three sons, all of whom are miniature painters. Two of them live in Cork, and are very agreeable men; and they gave me a letter of introduction to the third in Dublin. He received me very politely, and gave me an invitation to see him as often as possible, of which I have availed myself, and find him an extremely pleasant man. He lives in very elegant lodgings, and is a charming painter. †

Daly returned in the beginning of the week from England, where, I believe, he has made very few engagements. Richer, Mrs. Parker, King, and Smith, all from Sadler's Wells, are engaged for dances and pantomimes. A capital clown of the name of Davies is engaged; and great preparations are making for a pantomime to be got up under his direction. Daly gives him five guineas per week; Richer, ten. Kelly's brother, whom you have often seen in London, and who is a great favourite there as a singer, is come home with Daly, and is engaged at

---

* And yet in this same letter, when so affectingly summing up the particulars of his situation, he thanks Heaven that he has found Mr. Daly misrepresented in respect to the bad report of him.—A. M.

† The artist well known in London some years ago.—A. M.

a very capital salary. Palmer is re-engaged. He is a very pleasant man, and we often visit each other. Cooke is expected every day; some say that he is arrived, which I rather suppose is the case, as "Hamlet" and "Othello" are put up to be played next week. Daly misses Mr. and Mrs. Davenport very much; and so do I, for they are two of the worthiest people living, and behaved with the greatest kindness to me.

We open to-morrow (Monday 10th) with the comedy of "The Young Quaker," and the farce of "The Highland Reel." Richer dances on the rope. Mrs. Parker and King dance in " The Caledonian Lovers," in which I am obliged to dance as figure-dancer. This is rather a bore, but at any rate it will give me an opportunity of practising. Tuesday, "Chapter of Accidents," " Spoiled Child," *Bridget* and *Little Pickle*, Mrs. Bateman. The Chevalier D'Eon fences.

Pray write soon, and send me some theatricals. Daly has brought "The Rage," in manuscript. Send me an act of it. Remember me unto all my old friends, and be assured of the sincerity of

Yours ever most affectionately,

CHARLES MATHEWS.

The good temper with which the foregoing account is delivered, the liberal construction of the ill-usage he had endured, and the philosophy with which he reconciled himself to it, after the defeat of the hopes and expectations which seduced him to Ireland, are truly admirable. How few (having a just confidence, as he must have had, in his own merit,) could so mildly have spoken of their insulted feelings!

Dear Litchfield,   Dublin, Dec. 28th, 1794.

I am extremely obliged to you for the papers you sent me; they afforded me a fund of entertainment.

I shall expect your prologue in the next letter, which you spoke at the Wells.* I don't exactly recollect where I left off my list of the characters I performed, but will continue them as nearly from the time as I can remember.

Kingstone, "High Life below Stairs."
Beaufort, "Citizen."
Town Clerk, "Much ado about Nothing." *Petruchio*, "Chances."
Villiard, "Foundling." Last night of performing.
Bravo, "Inconstant." *Beau Trippet*, "Lying Valet."
Count Louis, "Peeping Tom."
Vasquez, "Wonder." *Sambo*, "Divorce."
Rodolpho, "Tancred and Sigismunda."
Edmund, "Purse." *Orasmin*, "Zara." *Label*, "Prize."
James, "Provoked Husband."
Captain Sightly, "Romp." *Harry Stukely*, "All the World's a Stage."
Gent. in Balcony, "Manager in Distress." *Robert*, "High Life."
Roger, "Stoops to Conquer." *Thomas*, "Agreeable Surprise."
Sir Harry Lovewit, "Know your own Mind." *Charles*, "Village Lawyer."
Sanchio, "Rule a Wife." *Sambo*, "Divorce."
Conrade, "Much ado about Nothing." *Thomas*, "Agreeable Surprise."
Prompt, "Heiress." *Beau Trippet*, "Lying Valet."
Captain of Guards, "Maid of Normandy." *Gabriel*, "Children in the Wood."

* After the Richmond and Canterbury affairs, these youthful friends performed one night at Sadler's Wells, (on what is called a bye-night,) when Mr. Mathews played *Sir David Dunder*, in "Ways and Means."—A. M.

Sandy, " Highland Reel."
Waiter, " Jew."
Worthy, " Recruiting Officer."
Crotchet, " New Brooms." *Stukely,* " West Indian." *Captain Seymour,* in " The Irishman in London."
Lounge, " Young Quaker."
Goatherd's Son, " Mountaineers." *First Scholar,* " Padlock."
La Warrene, " Battle of Hexham." *Endless,* " No Song," &c.
Edmund, " Purse."
Captain Harcourt, "Chapter of Accidents." *Nephew,* "Irish Widow."
Servant, "Every One has his Fault." *Coachman,* "Devil to pay."
Crookfinger'd Jack, " Beggar's Opera." *Younger Brother,* " Comus."
Player, " Heigho for a Husband." Duet from " Prize."
Stukely, " West Indian." *Bagatelle,* " Poor Soldier."
Bates, " Gamester."
Placid, " Every One has his Fault."
Government play—*Footman,* " Love in a Village."
Twig, " Young Quaker."
Dance. *Label,* " Prize."
Robber, " Castle of Andalusia." Dance.
Second Muleteer, " Mountaineers."
Messenger, " Othello."
Will Scarlet, " Robin Hood." *Waiter,* " Hotel."
Messenger, " Othello."
Ranger's Servant, " Suspicious Husband." Dance.
Seyton, " Macbeth." Dance.
Janizary, " Two Misses." *Priest,* New Pantomime, " Harlequin in Persia."
Sailor, " Inkle and Yarico." Dance. *Archer,* " William Tell."
Cuto, " Columbus." *Priest,* Pantomime.
Norfolk, " Richard the Third." Dance.
Twig, " Young Quaker."
Starved Citizen, " Surrender of Calais."
Cudden, " Agreeable Surprise."

Archer, "William Tell."
Priest, "King Arthur."
Priest, Pantomime.
Grizzle, "Dead Alive."

I have now brought down my list to the last character I performed. My business has been by no means what I wished, as I have got more genteel parts than low comedy; but Daly has so few young men, in comparison with the low comedians, that he has not enough to do the business in that line. Nothing can be more disagreeable to me than doing any dress part. It was very painful to me to be obliged to perform *Norfolk, Paris,* and more particularly *Beaufort;* though, if anything could make it agreeable, it was playing it to the *Maria* of the divine Farren. The low comedy business which I did get was of considerable service to me—*Bagatelle, Endless, Gabriel,* and particularly *Label.* Wathen acted *Lenitive,* and in the duet I mimicked his voice, was always encored, and very frequently called for. Such a favourite was it, that it was inserted in two or three benefit bills—" An Interlude from the favourite farce of ' The Prize,' with the duet by Messrs. Wathen and Mathews. Since Wathen's departure, Cherry plays *Lenitive,* and I think is very superior in it. I am convinced that what merit I may have is in that line,* particularly now I have played before the most difficult audiences to please in the three kingdoms (Cork

* This genuine estimate of his own powers may serve to confute *one* of the many erroneous assertions published since his death, wherein Mr. Mathews was charged with the implied weakness of a belief in his possessing the attributes of tragedy. Perhaps, had this been true, such an impression might have found excuse with those who had felt and witnessed the effect of his *Monsieur Mallet* and the *Ruined Gamester,* which at

and Dublin). The only part in gentleman's clothes in which I gained applause or credit was *Placid*, which I played in Cork, and a very few nights after Wathen had played it, who had then gone to England. Daly has told me several times that he would give me characters in my own line, but that from my youthful figure he was under the necessity of putting me in some young parts. At any rate, everything I do is so far useful that it will make me used to the stage, and able to face an audience with more boldness. Upon the whole, I think, for a young man who has been on the stage no more than six months, I have done extremely well, and particularly in the theatre of a metropolis.

Cooke, of whom you have heard so much, has been here these three weeks, and his merit has not at all been exaggerated; for I think him a most excellent actor, and one of the finest declaimers I ever heard. He came out in *Othello*, and was received with a vast deal of applause, though *Othello* was not his choice for a first appearance. He played it most delightfully, but I do not think it by any means one of his best characters. Mr. Daly's *Iago* is a most excellent piece of acting. *Othello* was dressed in a modern suit of scarlet and gold, which I do not think has half so handsome an appearance with a black face as a Moorish dress. His address to the senate was spoken in a different manner from what I have heard it

least established his power for the pathetic. While alluding to these notices of my husband, I may add, for my own pride and satisfaction, that out of the numerous periodical publications, one *only* has been the medium through which a word has met the public eye, tending to disparage his genius, or impugn his good sense. His good *character* was above the reach of the writer's hands to throw a blot upon.—A. M.

before, being more familiar, and indeed more natural, than the customary mode of delivering it. The more impassioned parts were wonderfully fine; nor do I think the second scene with *Iago* was ever better played. His second character was *Macbeth*, which is certainly superior to his *Othello*, and he has played it three or four times to very great houses. He has played *Columbus; Ghost*, in " Hamlet ;" *Friar*, in " Romeo ;" *Eustace de St. Pierre*, and *Richard*, which is certainly his masterpiece (that is, of the characters he has played here). His figure and manner are much more adapted to the villain than the lover. His countenance, particularly when dressed for *Richard*, is somewhat like Kemble's, the nose and chin being very prominent features, but the face is not so long. He has a finely marked eye, and upon the whole, I think, a very fine face. His voice is extremely powerful, and he has one of the clearest rants I ever heard. The lower tones are somewhat like Holman's, but much harsher, and considerably stronger. The most striking fault in his figure are his arms, which are remarkably short and ill-proportioned to the rest of his body, and in his walk this gives him a very ungraceful appearance. I forgot to mention that he played *Harmony*,* which I think was as fine a piece of acting as I ever saw, and I like it much better than Munden's. He played it as a plain gentleman, not at all *outré* in his dress or manner. He delivered the sentiments in a natural and easy style, and his whole delineation of it is so chaste, that it becomes a much more interesting character than it appeared to be before. After playing *Harmony* the first night, he came forward to make the usual announcement, and had six successive rounds of applause. Next week he plays *Cato, Zanga*, and *Cardinal*

* In " Every One has his Fault."

Wolsey. Mr. Daly is very much pleased with him, and he draws money every time he plays. I have the pleasure of living in the same house with him. He is one of the most intelligent men and agreeable companions I ever met with, and I think myself extremely fortunate in getting into the same house with him.

Hitchcock is now in London. He went last week to engage Madame Mara, if possible. Write as soon as possible, and give me another theatrical treat.—Adieu. And be assured of the lasting sincerity of

Yours most affectionately,
CHARLES MATHEWS.

It is remarkable how true Mr. Mathews's early perceptions of acting were, young and inexperienced as he was in the art. What clearness and truth appear in his critical view of Cooke's talents in the foregoing letter! The reader need only turn his recollections back to the peculiarities and acting of that highly-gifted performer, and he will feel how judicious and faithful is this description and opinion of his manner and powers, given at least ten years before a London public had decided on his merits, and the best judges had determined what were his best efforts. The youth's remarks were not an echo therefore of higher judgments, but emanated from his own untaught, genuine impressions. During Mr. Cooke's residence in the same house with Mr. Mathews, (kept by a widow of the name of Byrn, who was a retailer of the "mountain dew,") it appeared that a mutual liking had taken place between the great and the little actor. Walking home together one evening from the theatre, the former invited the novice into his room to supper. This was irresistible; and the invitation was promptly accepted.

The giant foible of this celebrated actor is so well known, that no indelicacy, I presume, can be placed to the account of the describer of a scene which has for many years past been well known from Mr. Mathews's description of it in private. Mr. Mathews described Mr. Cooke's excesses as not habitual; yet, when once he exceeded the bounds of strict sobriety, the fit would be of long continuance, and was succeeded by as long an abstinence, for he would then drink only water for weeks together, shrinking with disgust from anything more potent, and speaking with unaffected loathing and contempt of a drunkard. In his natural mood he was most refined, bland in his manners, simple and gentlemanlike in his habits, full of kindness to everybody, and ready to do service to all who required his aid; charitable to imprudence, if it is possible so to be. The following anecdote has been related before in print, but always imperfectly; and as Mr. Mathews was the only witness to the scene, his version of it, from my memory, may be relied on.

On the night in question, Mr. Cooke had performed *Sir Archy M'Sarcasm* in " Love à la

Mode;" and the young actor had been intrusted with *Mordecai*. During the early part of the night the host was a most charming companion. He feelingly entered into the young man's embarrassing situation with Daly, and offered to frank him home, if he would consent to return to his respectable family, and give up the uncertain result of the trial he was making as an actor,— but without any effect upon the aspiring candidate for dramatic fame.

After supper, whiskey punch, which was a novelty to Mr. Cooke, who had never before been in Ireland, (though by some erroneously supposed to be an Irishman,) was introduced, and he evidently was quite fascinated with the pleasing beverage. He grew gradually more animated in its praise; declared, as he sipped and sipped, that there was nothing like it! it was the nectar of the gods! His spirits increased in animation; and jug after jug was brought in. The young man had very early cried, " Hold! enough!" Cooke, however, knew not satiety when once the brimming cup had been emptied. " Another! and another!" would then " succeed, and the last be welcome as the former." Mrs. Byrn, up to a certain time, felt bound, both by duty and interest, to supply her distinguished lodger with what he called for; but at last, the night growing old, and her eyes not growing young, she felt disposed to give them rest; and, entering with the sixth jug, inquired respectfully, "whether Mister Cooke would want anything more?" At this moment her lodger was warmed up into the most contented of beings. He glanced at the capacious vessel just replaced upon his table, and, believing its contents sufficient, exclaimed, "Nothing more, my *good* Mrs. Byrn; nothing more." Mrs. Byrn wished her two lodgers a good night, and retired. Mr. Cooke refilled his glass, and, being somewhat sentimental, advised — admonished his young friend; above all, cautioned him to be industrious in his profession, sober in private, and not to allow company, "villanous company," to be the ruin of his youth. And thus he lectured on sobriety, till glass after glass vanished, and with it the reality of the virtue he so eloquently recommended. At last the jug was again empty. Mr. Mathews rose to go. "You shan't stir; we'll have another *croosken lawn*,* my dear fellow, and then you shall go to bed. I have much more to say to you, my good boy. Sit down. You don't know me. The world don't know me. Many an hour that they suppose I have wasted in drinking, I have devoted to the study of my profession; — the Passions, and all their variations; their nice and imperceptible gradations. You shall see me delineate the Passions of the human mind."

The power of the whiskey punch, however,

* White pitcher.

acted in diametric opposition to the intent on his strong and flexible features, and only produced contortions and distortions, of which he was unconscious. He, nevertheless, endeavoured to illustrate the passions, while his visiter was to guess them. " What's the meaning of that, eh?" said the tragedian, with a most inexplicable twist of his face. " Sir!" said the timid spectator, puzzled what to call it. Cooke reiterated " What's the meaning of *that*? What passion does it express? Does it not strike you at once? There! What is it, I say?" While he to whom he appealed could only reply, " *Very fine*, sir!"— " But," persisted Cooke, " what *is* it?" He was then answered, " Oh! I see, sir; *Anger!* to be sure!"—" To be sure you're a blockhead!" said Cooke, showing him the genuine expression of what he imputed to him before. " Fear, sir! it was *Fear!* Now, then — what is *that?*"—" Oh, sir, *that*, I think, is meant for *Jealousy*." Again the *passionate* man declared that the *guesser* was wrong. " *Jealousy!* Pooh, man! *Sympathy!* You're very dull, sir.—Now I will express a passion that you *can't* mistake. There! what's that?"

Fearing to increase Cooke's anger by another misconception, the young man apologized, blamed the portion he had swallowed of the punch; declared that it had stolen away his brains, and left him unfit to judge of Mr. Cooke's representations. But Cooke was not in a humour to be so put off.

K 2

"Look again, sir!" he exclaimed, in a terrific voice; and he then made up a hideous face, compounded of malignity and the leering of a drunken satyr, which he *insisted* upon being guessed; and his visiter, trembling for the consequences of another mistake, hesitatingly pronounced it to be " *Revenge!*"—" Despite o'erwhelm thee!" cried Cooke, in his most tragic rage. " Revenge! Curse your stupidity! That was *Love!* Love, you insensible idiot! Can't you see it is Love?" Here he attempted the same expression, in order to strike conviction of its truth; when a mixture of comicality with the first effect so surprised the risible muscles of the young man, that he laughed outright. This infuriated the delineator of the Passions almost to madness. " What, sir! does it make you laugh? Am I not George Frederick Cooke? ' born to command ten thousand slaves like thee!' while you'll never get salt to your porridge, as an actor. *Who am I, sir?*—curving his arms just as if preparing to make a minuet bow (his well-known attitude when *dignified*). " Doubtless, a very great actor, sir," allowed Mr. Mathews.

" Very well, then. Do you mean to insinuate that I cannot express the passion of love?"

" I beg your pardon, sir; the whiskey punch has stupified me." Cooke accepted the excuse. ' True, true, *'tis out*"— (his guest wished he was out too). " Mistress Byrn, my love, another jug!"

At this his companion made an attempt to go away, when he was forcibly dragged back with "'Stir not, on your life! The man that stirs makes me his foe.' Another jug, sweet Mrs. Byrn!" Mrs. Byrn, it appeared, slept in the room under which this scene occurred; so that whenever Mr. Cooke addressed her he looked down upon the floor, as if more certain of his wishes reaching her, at the same time tapping with his foot.

" Mistress Byrn, my darling, another jug, *sweet* Mrs. Byrn!" which she answered in tones quite audible through the slightly-built ceiling.

" Indeed, Mr. Cooke, and I'm gone to bed, sure, and you can't have any more to-night."

" Good night, sir," said Mathews, once more moving to go.

" Sit you down, man; you're a d—d black sheep. Charles, my dear boy, one jug more."

Mat.—No more, sir. Besides, Mrs. Byrn won't let us have it. (Here the following dialogue took place.)

Cooke.—Won't she! I'll show her that presently (stamping and looking down). Do you hear *that*, Mrs. Byrn?

Mrs. B.—Indeed and I do, Mr. Cooke.

Cooke.—Will you let us have another jug, then?

Mrs. B.—Indeed, and I will *not*, Mr. Cooke.

Cooke (laughing and looking at his guest).—
" Was ever woman in this humour wooed — was

ever woman in this humour won?" I'll have her up—" I'll have her, but I will not keep her long." Mrs. Byrn! hear me: if I'm not indulged with some more whiskey, I give notice, I'll destroy all your furniture. Do you hear *that*, Mistress Byrn?

Mrs. B.—Indeed and I do, Mr. Cooke; and the devil a drop more do ye get to-night.

Cooke (breaking the jug over her head).—Do you hear *that*, Mistress Byrn?

Mrs. B.—Indeed and I do, Mr. Cooke, sure enough!

Cooke (throwing in turn chairs, poker, tongs, and shovel down with a clash).— Do you hear *that*, Mistress Byrn?

Mrs. B.—God knows and I do, Mr. Cooke.

Mr. Cooke then began to throw the fragments he had made out of the window. The young man, apprehensive lest he might force him to make his exit after the damaged furniture, made another bold attempt to decamp. "Stay where you are," roared the now frenzied tragedian, grasping him violently. "I will go," said the now determined youth. "Will you?" said Cooke. He then dragged his victim to the window, and roared out, "Watch! Watch!" A watchman, who had been already attracted by the clatter amongst the moveables, asked the cause of the disturbance; when, to the horror of his struggling prisoner, Cooke exclaimed, "I give this man in charge; he has committed a capital offence — he has committed a murder!"—" I!" said his amazed companion. " Yes," said Cooke to the watchman; "to my certain knowledge he has been this night guilty of a cruel, atrocious murder, in cold blood. He has most barbarously murdered an inoffensive Jew-gentleman, of the name of *Mordecai*, and I charge him with it in the name of Macklin, author of ' Love-à-la-Mode.'" At this moment the supposed criminal slipped out of his grasp, and made for the door. Cooke followed him, and taking up the candles, ran on the staircase with them, crying out, as he threw them and the candlesticks after him, " Well, if you will go, you shan't say I sent you to bed without light!" But the young man reached his room, and, securely fastened in, he heard a long colloquy between the watchman and the tragedian, who had some trouble in explaining away the account he had given to him of the *murdered* " Jew-gentleman."

CHAPTER VII.

Leaf out of Cooke's Common-place book.—His talents as an actor.—Death of Parsons, the comedian.—Captain Wathen's kindness.—Cherry. — Miss Wallis.—Holman.—Imitations.—Theatrical perplexity.—Quarrel between Cooke and Daly.—Cooke withdraws from the Theatre.—Miss Campion.—Mathews's distress in Dublin.—Kemble's appearance in Hamlet.—His recognition of Mathews.—Incledon and Miss Poole.—Cooke enlists as a common soldier.—Anecdote.—Incledon.—Mathews's characters.—His performance of Clown in a pantomime.—Resolves to quit the profession of an actor, and return to London.—Mr. Montague (Talbot) and Henry Ireland.—The Shakspeare Forgeries.—Voyage from Ireland.—Arrival in Swansea.—The theatre of that town.—Talbot's dismay at sea.—His finikin manners.—Anecdote.

AFTER we came to London, when Mr. Cooke was at the height of his celebrity, he often visited us, and a more cautiously abstemious person could not be found. Indeed, it was difficult to imagine that he could be ever otherwise than the grave, dignified gentleman he then appeared. Amongst Mr. Mathews's collection of autographs is found a leaf taken out of Cooke's common-place book, (the only leaf my husband ever took from his book,) in the owner's writing, and which contains the following extract:—

"When a sober, moderate, and silent man drinks wine in a quantity more liberal than ordinary, it has the effect of cherishing and rousing his spirits and genius, and rendering him more communicative. If taken still more freely, he becomes talkative, eloquent, and confident of his abilities. If taken in still larger quantities, it renders him bold and daring, and desirous to exert himself in action. If he persist in a more plentiful dose, it makes him petulant and contumelious. The next step renders him mad and outrageous. Should he proceed still farther, he becomes stupid and senseless."—Aristot. Prob. Soct. 30.

DEAR LITCHFIELD, Dublin, Feb. 9, 1795.

You ask me if Cooke is as good an actor as Kemble; but I do not think it necessary to be a good actor that he should be so good as he is. My opinion of Kemble is so fixed and on such solid principles, that it is nearly impossible for me to think any actor so good. Cooke is, nevertheless, a most admirable performer. His figure and walk are, however, so much inferior to Kemble's, that, whatever merit he may display in the conception of a character, his execution cannot possibly be equal to his. In many characters he is the best actor we have, I think, next to Kemble. Those characters suited to Harley* are the best adapted to Cooke's manner. I do not recollect, since my last account, his having played anything particular, except *Shylock* and *Stukely*, both of which were remarkably fine, but parti-

* The tragedian.

cularly *Stukely*. I think him very superior to Palmer, or any one I have seen. He is increasing rapidly in the favour of the Irish audience, and very deservedly.

I was never more concerned than to hear of the death of our old favourite and most excellent comedian, Parsons. This is, indeed, a most severe loss to the theatre, and to every lover of true comic humour. Can you send me any account of his death, funeral, and will?

Hitchcock, it is said, has made engagements with Madame Mara, Kemble, and Mrs. Siddons, who are to come over in the after-season. The laugh is very much against Kemble here and everywhere. I am told there was a great roar in the house when he was addressed by *Lady Randolph* in "Douglas," "Thou flower of modesty." Be assured, my dear fellow, of the sincerity of

CHARLES MATHEWS.

DEAR LITCHFIELD, Dublin, March 31st, 1795.

Wathen's conduct to me, while he was in Ireland, was uncommonly polite and kind; he offered several times to pay my passage to England, and particularly urged it when he left Cork for Bristol, when he said he would endeavour to get me an engagement with Dimond. However tempting an object this appeared to me, I did not exactly like to be under so great an obligation, particularly when I was not in immediate want of an engagement. Wathen endeavoured to make me believe my situation was very disagreeable, which I cannot say I altogether felt. Notwithstanding this, if I could have conveniently paid my *own* passage, I think I should have attempted an engagement in Bath. At any rate, I shall always feel his kindness.

Parsons' loss, I should think, will not soon be forgotten; neither will his situation be easily filled again. Where shall we find an *Old Doiley?* and a *Sir Fretful Plagiary?* The latter, scarcely any one will be vain enough to attempt, for a considerable time.*

I do not think that any comedian out of London would be so well worthy an engagement, after Parsons, as my very worthy friend Cherry. Cherry's merit is by no means confined; his old men are uncommonly rich, and his country boys are the most simple and humorous of any I have seen, after Blanchard;† indeed, in any line of comedy, he is a charming actor. He is a very excellent judge of dressing, and has capital clothes, and the best wigs I ever saw. To give you one great instance of his *judgment*, he adores *Kemble*, and " will allow no competition between him and any other;" nor is Kemble insensible to *his* merit. He has been in a Dublin theatre with him, and played with him in Hull last summer. He was extremely pleased with his *Sadi*, and promised him an engagement at Drury-lane, should anything happen either to Dodd or Parsons. Miss Farren also, to my knowledge, promised all *her* interest; so that I should not be surprised if he is engaged there next winter.

Miss Wallis is engaged after Mr. Kemble, as she will

---

* It is curious that the writer of this question was the *first*, after Parsons, that ever made any *sensation* in this character! Mr. Mathews's first appearance in *Sir Fretful Plagiary*, in London, was in 1807, and future pages will show with what effect. —A. M.

† The celebrated performer of vocal countrymen, a line of character which died with him. He was the original singer of " The Flaxen-headed Cow-boy," a popular air in that day in the farce of " The Farmer."—A. M.

not play with any other "star." I do not doubt she will draw money; and it is necessary, for she is to have a most extravagant salary; it is reported that it is larger than Miss Farren's, and she had 50*l.* every night.

If you could procure me an introduction to Kemble without making it appear vanity in me, I should be extremely indebted to you. My principal motive is this: I have boasted of having been introduced to Kemble; talking to him in his study; now and then, in my way, mimicked some of his conversation, " too tall for low comedy," &c. After this, (and this I have not been a *little* vain of,) I say, after this, if he should not take any notice of me the first day he comes into the green-room, I should feel ridiculous; and, being afraid to presume on my introduction, *I* should fear to speak. *He* would not know me; and my good friends would think my acquaintance with him, " by Jasus, was all *bodder*, do you see?" My vanity, without untruth, has led me into a scrape. I should wish to tell him (for perhaps it will be necessary for me to tell him before he can know it,) that my "*forte* is *comedy*," by way of apology for the grinning figure I shall cut beside him in *Richard;* when, with my lisp and confounded crooked face, I shall describe the " host of tattered scarecrows," he will perhaps laugh in his sleeve, and say—" Like yourself;" but when he knows my *forte*, I may tell him they are used to *laugh* at me. You understand me, eh? " Be quiet; I know it." Do the best you can for me. I know you will. I depend upon you.

I thank you for the trouble you have taken about Bellamy's book. Does he print subscribers' names in his second volume? If so, let mine be—" Theatre Royal, Dublin." You understand.

Your theatrical intelligence was very acceptable and entertaining. I was rather disappointed in not seeing a sketch of "The Wheel of Fortune." No matter. Daly, who has it in manuscript, promises me a sight of it. Kemble's increasing popularity gives me the greatest pleasure. Oh! how I shall feast on the applause he will get on this side of the Channel!

How your dislike to Holman breaks out, with a dash here, and a dash there! I must own, it is tolerably just; but I liked him much better here than I did in London: I mean as a man. Do not be alarmed. By the by, his speaking "Alexander's Feast" was one of the finest things I ever heard. It was beyond himself.

Palmer's idea was a very good one. By the by, I am a little jealous of your praise of Caulfield.* Not that I doubt his deserving it. I never heard of his talent that way.—But, to say a little more of myself. I am increasing in reputation "that way." My imitations of some of the people here are by far my best. That of Wathen, of which I told you, was very close. But the most exact I ever attempted is that of Hurst, both in private conversation and public performance. Though a good actor, he is extremely peculiar, and the tones of his voice are very numerous. His manner and his walk, from his great age, are very feeble, and in some degree comical. His expressions and manner of speaking in private, have caused many inattentive imitations of him; but from great study of his manners, uncommonly queer phrases, and oaths, I have made up an imitation which has given great satisfaction to the performers, and to Daly in particular, who glories in imitations. He has heard that my observa-

---

* Still remembered in London, as a superior imitator.—A. M.

tions are extended to *himself*, which, *sub rosâ*, is fact; and he is continually asking me for his own likeness. I have always evaded it, not knowing how he might relish one of *himself*, though he is so much pleased with that of others; and I by no means wish that a talent which was the original cause of his polite attention to me, should be the cause of putting a period to it.

A few nights ago I played *Lord Grizzle* in " Tom Thumb," entirely through in the manner of Hurst, which caused roars both before and behind the curtain. I had one of my wigs dressed in Hurst's manner, and took every pains to resemble him; and, without communicating my intention to any one, I went on in the soliloquy, and copied his walk and voice in such a manner, that the audience took it immediately, and gave me the greatest applause. Daly and Hitchcock were standing at the stage-door, and enjoyed it heartily, as indeed did all the performers. Cherry and Miss Brett came on to me; and the sudden and unexpected imitation made them laugh so much that they were scarcely able to speak. This was joined in by the audience, (the house was very full,) which was not a little flattering to me, you may easily imagine, and has done me a vast deal of service. This was absolutely necessary; for I must tell you in what a very ridiculous situation I was placed during the play. It was the benefit-night of Mrs. Mahon, a person of very fashionable connexions. Some of the most distinguished people were present. The Lord Chancellor, his lady, Chief Justice, &c. Mr. Montague (Talbot) was advertised for *Doricourt* in the " Belle's Stratagem," and while he was dressing, was taken suddenly ill, and sent Hitchcock notice that he was unable to play. The little man was almost mad. The greater part of the company were in the play, and those who were not, were not in the theatre. What was to be done? It was nearly time to begin,—nobody to play *Doricourt!* Change the play? Impossible! But to be brief: the little man came to me in my dressing-room. I was dressing for a little bit of comedy (*Dick*). He asked me whether I had ever played *Doricourt?* I laughed at him. "*No.*"—" Will you *read* it?" —" No; don't like to be *grinned* at."—Went down to the green-room.—Would you believe it, he went on his knees and entreated me. I was impenetrable, till Mrs. Mahon herself offered to appear in the same humiliating posture. I consented. I had Mr. Montague's dress; nothing could be more elegant; and fitted me well. And now, see your unfortunate object of pity, dressing all in haste; surrounded by hair-dressers, tailors, manager, prompter, &c. Hitchcock's distress very entertaining. At last, being equipped, I sallied down; court suit, bag, sword, chapeau bras, &c. *tout ensemble.* I never looked so well! General opinion. Apology made.—Taken ill! short notice! read part! usual indulgence!!! I took the book and went on very boldly. The audience very politely applauded me on my entrance: and I absolutely read the part with tolerable *éclat.* I was confoundedly frightened at first, but their good-nature soon reconciled me to so very difficult a task. My situation was rendered worse from the circumstance of the house being filled with so many fashionable people. I had, however, the united *opinions* of the Chancellor and the Chief Justice.

I am extremely sorry to inform you that Cooke has withdrawn himself from the theatre. Daly was advertised for *Don Felix,* Mrs. Parker's benefit: being unable to play, Cooke was applied to the day before, and said he would play it. Daly's name was taken out, his own inserted. The night came — there was no dress for Cooke. He had sworn in the day-time, without a *new* dress, he would not play. No dress: he kept his word. The part was read; he was very much enraged, and swore he would play no more. I am sorry to say that in that particular he has also kept his word. Mr. Daly, thinking himself the injured person, has never attempted to make it up. Cooke expected entreaties. Daly is too proud to make them. And both are too proud to make up the breach; though, I believe, both wish it. Daly was by no means in fault. He was shut up, and would see nobody. The tailor would make no dress without his orders. It is a misunderstanding which ten words would make up. But obstinacy and pride prevent it. So the town is deprived of an excellent actor. Daly could arrest him for 200*l.* breach of articles, but would not distress him for the world. Daly likes him much. Cooke likes Daly; does not say one word against him; says he has treated him like a gentleman: lays the blame on poor Hitchy. Cooke is a great loss. The benefits suffer much for want of him. He knows his own consequence in the theatre, and when he is at all slighted is the most resolute man, and most to be dreaded in his resentments.

Mrs. Daly has been dangerously ill nearly two months. Given over. Daly was one night dressed for *Sir R. Ramble*, and just going on when he received a note. She was supposed to be dying. The circumstance affected him so much that he only spoke three or four lines of *Sir Robert*, and ran off the stage, bursting into tears. Apology, and some one else did the part. He is a very feeling man, extravagantly fond of his wife, and has nine children. Even his worst enemies pitied him on this occasion. He has not played since. Mrs. Daly is still ill. You may judge to what a situation this has reduced the company. From Daly's playing the principal business, of course we miss him, and Cooke much more so: but our greatest loss has happened since; Miss Campion has now left us. This is indeed a serious loss. There are very few such actresses to be met with. She possesses a very beautiful face, extremely elegant figure, and delightful voice; added to every advantage of nature in mental qualifications, and every accomplishment of education. No lady was ever a greater favourite in Dublin. The term of her articles, I believe, expired March 10th. Daly could not prevail upon her to renew it; as I believe she has an engagement in Belfast. She would succeed, I am sure, in Bath.* Daly has now no actress good enough to play with Kemble. I forgot to tell you that I have played *Tagg*, with great success. I introduced several imitations, with applause. (Excuse me again.)

I was very much affected a few days back (the 25th), at the departure of Lord Fitzwilliam. All the shops were shut, and thousands of people followed, to see him embark. His horses were taken from the carriage, and the coach was drawn by the populace. The place of embarkation is nearly four miles and a half from the Castle. The number of people collected was astonishing, and greater than ever was known on such an occasion. Both himself and lady were very much affected. They left the country with the blessing of everybody for their safety, and sorrow for their departure. Lord Camden arrived in

* This lady's *Juliet* (when Mrs. Pope) was much admired in London; and a beautiful portrait of her in that character, by Sir Martin Shee, is in my husband's gallery at the Garrick Club; engravings from which are still to be met with in every part of London.—A. M.

the usual state, on Tuesday last (31st). He came under very unfavourable circumstances; but, although the congratulations were not very warm, his reception was polite.

The theatre is always closed in Passion Week, but we have been shut up a fortnight. Rather a bore. No SALARY. The houses were very poor: thank Heaven, we have lost no more time. Be assured, my dear fellow, of the lasting sincerity of

CHARLES MATHEWS.

Mr. Mathews's distress at this period I have heard him describe as extreme, notwithstanding his determined endurance of it. He has declared to me, that he sometimes fasted two days, wandering about the streets for amusement, when weary of practising his flute and violin at home, and studying characters which he never expected to be allowed to act. Although he believed that he concealed the wretchedness of his situation from general observation, it is pretty evident from his letters that it was but too apparent; and hence the friendly offers from Messrs. Cooke, Wathen, and others, to assist him with the means of returning to his father's house. I have heard him relate, that he had no hesitation in owning his distress and starvation to Mr. Hitchcock. As to Mr. Daly, he never allowed himself personally to appear on unpopular occasions. His manners were refined and fascinating, and he preferred being cruel by deputy. Mr. Mathews considered Hitchcock to have been the cause of his leaving

London, and therefore naturally responsible for the result. But, though hunger would at such times " speak with most miraculous organ," little effect was produced on a mind rendered callous by custom; and a smooth-tongued pity was all he obtained to fill the " aching void" occasioned by a failure of salary for weeks together. Mr. Hitchcock was, to use my husband's expressive words, " one of those provoking people who are never in a passion, the scourge of the ardent and the irritable, who pour oil upon the fire of impetuosity by way of extinguishing it;" and such a person's reception of a complaint was more likely to exasperate than to soothe the feelings of the sufferer.

DEAR LITCHFIELD,   Dublin, July 5th, 1795.

Nothing material happened in the theatre here from the date of my last letter, which, I believe, was April 5th. The theatre has been closed for three weeks, during which time of course I received no money, which was rather a bore; however, I managed extremely well, as I had a great many invitations during the time, which gave me assistance. The theatre opened for the after-season on Monday, May 25th, with " Hamlet" and " The Village Lawyer." *Hamlet*, Mr. Kemble, his first appearance these six years. If twenty guineas had been offered for a ticket or a place in the boxes, it could not have been purchased. In all my life I never saw people more anxious to get into a theatre. Every avenue was crowded at an early hour; and after the theatre was filled, I may safely assert many hundreds went away. To see this, you may judge, gave me no small pleasure. Kemble's reception was quite rapturous. Every one seemed delighted,—those who had seen him, at the return of their former favourite; and those who had not seen him, at his figure and appearance. The applause was continued to six or seven peals. Being out of the play, (for I had the pleasure, after long holding *Guildenstern* as a " stock part," to get rid of it,) I went in front, and never had so great a treat. His *Hamlet* certainly must be ranked as one of his best parts. In the scene with *Rosencrantz* and *Guildenstern* after the play, it is customary with other actors when performing that character to address themselves entirely to *Guildenstern*—"Can you play upon this pipe?" But Kemble, after speaking to him, and "entreating," turns to "*Rosencrantz*, "Can *you?*" when standing between them and alternately surveying them with scorn, he addresses them, " How poor a thing," &c. This, however trifling the alteration may appear, has a much better effect than addressing only one, as it disposes the three figures better, and by the other mode, I think, it appears as if *Hamlet* spoke partially to *Guildenstern*. Kemble dressed the character in modern clothes, which I do not like so well as a shape; neither do I think it so well becomes him.

You may remember that I was anxious Kemble should remember me, and I took care to try if he did; but on his first coming into the green-room, his salutation to me was in common to the rest of the people, which rather mortified me. I did not, however, expect at such a distance of time that he would recollect me. In a few days, as usual, Mr. Daly introduced my imitations, which he always does to strangers, and he was much pleased with them. In consequence of this he inquired who I was, and Cherry mentioned my having been introduced to him; and he immediately afterwards spoke to me about Mr. Boaden, and recollected the circumstance very well. He afterwards paid me very particular attention, and often talked to me, and several times mentioned you, of whom he spoke in handsome terms.

Nothing could be more agreeable than Kemble's conduct in the theatre, and no one more agreeable or easier to be pleased at rehearsals. Ever willing to give instructions without the smallest ostentation; every one was sorry when he went away. He took leave of us all after *Richard;* and taking me by the hand he said, " God bless you, Mathews: can I do anything for you in London? But, for God's sake, get out of this place as soon as you can; it is no place for you to get up in." He left Dublin for Glasgow the next morning at five o'clock. Incledon and Miss Poole * played on the Monday following his last night " Love in a Village." Several songs were introduced— " Streamlet," and " Old Towler," which is become a general favourite. Incledon sings it every night he plays, and it has made a great noise in Dublin. It was a very fine house, which, after Kemble's drawing so much, was unexpected. Miss Poole was received extremely well. Miss Wallis played on the 6th of July " Child of Nature" and *Roxalana* in "The Sultan;" but, notwithstanding the great expectations which were formed of her attraction from her connexions, we have been disappointed, for her audiences have not been numerous; as the people seem to prefer two singers to one actress in comedy or tragedy. Mr. Daly offered her 30*l.* per night, which she refused, and would share the house; by which she is the loser, as on some nights she has not shared 10*l.*

People all say she is a charming actress, but not fit to come as a star after Miss Farren or Mrs. Siddons.

* Afterwards Mrs. Dickons.

" I am extremely sorry to inform you that Cooke has enlisted. The regiment went to the Isle of Man about a week past. Daly would have been glad to re-engage him; but such was his pride, that he would rather turn soldier from real want than come to terms. If he does not get out of that situation, he certainly will be a great loss to the stage, for he is really an excellent actor. Many of the performers saw him in his military garb when he was going off; but he seemed to wish rather to avoid speaking to them, appearing quite melancholy. He was drunk when he enlisted.

Adieu! God bless you, and depend on the everlasting sincerity of yours,

CHARLES MATHEWS.

The above circumstance in the history of this extraordinary man is not generally known. Such was his madness at all times while under the influence of drink, that no extravagance was too great for him to commit. Mr. Mathews once witnessed a quarrel he fell into during one of his excesses with a low man in some public place; whom he at last invited to fight. The man declined, under the pretence that Cooke insulted him because he (Cooke) possessed more money than himself. Upon which Cooke indignantly emptied his pockets, and threw all the money he probably had in the world into the fire, exclaiming, as he resumed his boxing attitude, " Now, you vulgar scoundrel, we are upon equal terms!"

DEAR LITCHFIELD, Cork, August 1st, 1795.

I suppose we shall close here about the 12th. Incledon has cleared a vast deal of money; he has fifteen guineas each night, and a benefit in each place, two of which have been very great; and I do not doubt that will be the case with the third here. I heartily wish it, for I am convinced he is a very good-hearted fellow. Whatever ill-natured people may say of his ignorance or vanity, I think he has sense enough to conduct himself like a gentleman, and infinitely less vanity than could be expected from a man who had not the advantage of a good education, or polite introduction to the world. I have been very intimate with him since he has been here, and, from his conduct in general, I should say he was as generous as a prince; and never ashamed to mention his former situation when at sea, or when in a strolling company at *half-a-guinea per week*. This is but very seldom the case when men are raised from low situations.

For myself, I assure you I am improving very fast, and expect in a little time to get a regular situation in " low comedy;" at any rate I have the manager on my side. I played *Jemmy Jumps* in Dublin the last week we were in the theatre, and Cherry there at the same time; but he is so very small, that they could not cast it to him, and I expect to keep the part. I have played since I have been here *Mum, Squire Richard, Harmony, Peregrine, Forrester, Lissardo, Bagatelle, Endless, &c.* This is certainly all very well. I however still retain some trash, which if I can once get rid of, I do not doubt I shall in time become a favourite comedian. Unfortunately, my figure is suited to some of your " walking gentlemen." I yet retain *Paris* in " Romeo and Juliet." My greatest pest, by the by, a pantomime, is being got up for a benefit, and some grimaces of mine have made them cast me the clown. It is all very well for once; but I suspect, if Daly approves of me in it, I shall play it next winter in Dublin, as there is not anybody engaged, and nobody in the company fit for it. I hope this will not be the case. I could not endure the fatigue of playing through the run of a pantomime. I am getting some lessons of the person who plays *Harlequin* (a musician in our band) of the mechanical part of the business. God bless you! Yours eternally,

Charles Mathews.

Dear Litchfield,   Cork, Sept. 3rd, 1795.

It is with great pleasure I take up my pen to inform you, that if the winds do not conspire against me, and other accidents should not happen to prevent it, I shall most probably have the happiness of seeing you in about a week. You will no doubt be surprised at the news, as it is so sudden. Montague has for some time past resolved to visit London during our great vacation, and two or three times expressed a wish that I would accompany him. The inexpressible pleasure of paying a visit to my friends, and the horrid prospect of five weeks' idleness, made me happy to embrace the offer, and accordingly we both made the resolution of setting off for England when the season should close here. We have been kept two or three days by a foul wind; but there is every prospect of a happy change. We think of sailing to-morrow (Thursday) on board a trader, bound to Bristol.

This is the first time I have known what it was to be absent so long from home; and, therefore, the idea of seeing "long parted friends" is rapture to me. All the delights of a meeting which I have so long pictured to myself will, I hope, in a few days be realised. Montague has a great desire to know you; I think an introduction will not be unpleasant to you, and we may spend some pleasant evenings. God bless you!

Yours ever most sincerely,
CHARLES MATHEWS.

The cause of this journey to London was a determination in fact to settle there, if the path still remained open to him. He had suffered much, and would willingly have suffered more, had hope remained; but, with the *Noble County Paris* and *Beaufort*, unsustained by any higher prospect, hope so deferred grew sick. The poor young man, in fact, at last wearied and disgusted with the treatment he had received, and despairing of any elevation above the degrading cast of parts allotted him in Daly's company, together with his distresses for want of regular pecuniary supplies, with a feeble constitution, weakened by starvation, and spirits eventually depressed to the lowest ebb by the heartless cruelty of the manager's system — in a moment of despair listened to a well-timed offer from Mr. Montague Talbot, then going to England, to frank him home, where he might repay the charge of his journey; and it was decided by the almost broken-hearted youth to conquer his long-suffering pride and accept this accommodation until his father should repay the debt, resolving to return to *the shop*, and never more *run counter* to his parents' wishes, but remain the tradesman he had been designed for. He consequently packed up the *sad remains* of the wardrobe with which he had left home, and joyfully quitted Cork with his friend, fully resigned to the dull but decent future.

The motive which led Mr. Talbot to England was nothing less than a desire to see *Ireland*. This may appear a paradox, but is a mere matter of fact. Henry Ireland had been an early associate and friend of Montague Talbot. They resided *vis-à-vis* in chambers on the ground-floor in a narrow court in the Temple, when youths. They had but one heart—one mind; all between them was candour and confidence. It happened, however, that all at once Talbot found his friend reserved in his manner and secluded in his habits. The suddenness of the change was remarkable. It was evident that Ireland had some secret and absorbing occupation; and whenever Talbot attempted to enter his friend's chamber, he found the door locked, and always had to wait a few minutes before he obtained admittance. He then observed that Ireland's desk was closed and all papers hidden—a new custom. At first Talbot rallied Ireland upon his unwonted reserve, then reproached him for it; all was alike in vain; Ireland seemed resolved that he should not penetrate the " heart of his mystery;" and Talbot's curiosity was upon the rack. He was therefore determined to be continually on the watch, in order to surprise his friend; but the care and caution maintained by Ireland baffled every attempt of the kind. One morning, the day being warm, Ireland had opened the window of his *den*, and placing himself before it at his desk with his door locked, he was so situated as to be able to discern an interloper, and defeat any possible view of his employment, by closing his dusky window on the first intimation of approach towards it. Thus it seemed impossible that a surprise could happen; but what will not the demon curiosity effect rather than remain to prey upon itself? Talbot withdrew from his own desk — also at the window — for some time, in order to lull suspicion in Ireland's mind; and afterwards crept out of his door upon his hands and knees, till he arrived under the window where his unconscious friend sat in fancied security. Talbot then raised himself slowly and quietly, and, when he had attained the window-sill, dexterously darted up, and pounced upon Ireland's papers, refusing to take his hands from them until he was made a sharer of their contents. This, at the first blush of the thing, appears to have been a most unjustifiable device to enforce a reluctant confidence; but, in palliation of this ungenerous expedient, it is necessary to say, that Talbot never imagined the nature of his friend's secret was of a more serious character than the perpetration of a poem, or the construction of a novel, of which he fain would wait the acceptance and success, before he committed his labours to his friend's inspection. Thus caught, poor Ireland made a merit of communicating what he could no longer withhold; and ingenuously owned his Shakspeare forgeries to his friend, before public detection, in a no less determined manner, compelled him to make his confessions to the world. From this moment Talbot saw the progress of his clever imposition, although he did not assist in it; and it was his interest in the success of " Vortigern and Rowena" which caused his present visit to London.

Dear Litchfield, Swansea, Oct. 9th, 1795.

I expected long before this to have had the pleasure of seeing you; but we cannot command the winds, which in this instance have counteracted all my intentions. I left Cork on Friday, September 25th, in the brig *Defiance*, bound for Kidwelly in Wales, as we were disappointed of the vessel in which we originally intended to have sailed, and which was bound for Bristol. We got to sea on Saturday morning with a fair wind and a very fine breeze, and expected to have made our destined port by the next evening. After sailing about nine leagues, the wind veered about and blew directly in our teeth. We were then blown about a considerable time in a very rough sea, and not being able to make any hand of it, the Captain resolved to put back; and we had the mortification, after having lost sight of the coast of Ireland, to come to anchor in the harbour of the Cove of Cork. It is about nine miles from the city, and is a very beautiful bay. We put in on Saturday night, and were unfortunate enough to be wind-bound for a whole week. It was a great disappointment to us, and very inconvenient, as we agreed with the Captain to find our own provisions, which were now all eaten; and we were obliged, two or three times, to recruit before we sailed a second time. We amused ourselves as well as we could by studying, (for Montague brought some plays with him,) by going on shore with the boat, fishing, &c., every day hoping for a fair wind, but which never proved the least favourable until Friday night, October 1st; and on Saturday morning we set sail a second time. We arrived in Kidwelly on Monday, and immediately set off for this town, which is twenty miles from it. The passage was extremely pleasant until Sunday night, or rather Monday morning, about two o'clock, when the mate discovered land unexpectedly, as we sailed faster than they thought, and, being dismally dark, they were uncertain where they were. The Captain, who was in his hammock, was called, and was most dreadfully alarmed, fearing that we were near some rocks, which were very numerous on that part of the Welsh coast. We were all in great consternation, a circumstance not to be wondered at when the Captain was almost frantic. He tacked about as fast as possible; and we were relieved from our fright by day-light. We came close to the coast four hours before we expected, and must in consequence have sailed nine knots an hour, when they thought they were only sailing four. During the whole passage I was extremely hearty, but Montague was very sick. I slept every night for nearly a fortnight in my clothes, so that I enjoyed my bed amazingly on shore.

We arrived in this town yesterday at noon. It is a very pretty place, and one of the largest and best trading towns in Wales. The first object which attracted our notice was a play-bill—" Theatre, Swansea—This Evening 'Wild Oats,' and 'Ways and Means.' This was a pleasing sight. Montague dressed himself and waited on the manager, Mr. Masterman; talked about acting, and he asked him if he would try a night, to which Montague consented, and is actually to play *Othello* this evening. We saw the play, which was very respectably performed. The hero is Fotteral, a very good actor, who was in Dublin many years. The theatre holds 30*l.*, at 3*s.*, 2*s.*, and 1*s.* The manager seems a very respectable man. His circuit is confined to Wales; and he gets in general very good business. He has a very respectable wardrobe, and the business is very regular.

We are here in an inn, the Red Lion, the master and mistress of which put me in mind of the host and hostess of Canterbury. They are extremely curious; and, having heard that one of us is to play, are pumping to hear which, " his honour in white, or his worship in brown."

I never was among the Taffies before; they bear a strange contrast in their manners to the Paddies whom I have just left. The country is beautifully romantic. We mean to sail from hence to Bristol as soon as possible. Adieu. With every hope of seeing you soon,

I remain yours most sincerely,
CHARLES MATHEWS.

During this voyage an instance of ignorance and superstition occurred worthy of relation. Talbot was a very precise person, and somewhat finikin in his manners, and what in his day was called a *beau* (in the present, a *dandy*). These characteristics were not likely to recommend him to the rough sailors on board the ship in which they sailed.

Indeed, it was plain that they leered at him from time to time with ill-disguised contempt, if not aversion. One morning, while pursuing his elaborate toilette, a noise on deck attracted his attention, and running up with his tooth-brush in his hand, he inquired with alarm the cause of such unusual sounds; which being simply explained as arising from some necessary process in the ship, he remained looking on at what had drawn him upon deck, resuming the action of brushing, which had been interrupted. One of the men, an old gruff sailor, looking askance at Talbot with an expression of ineffable astonishment in his face, inquired of Mr. Mathews, who stood at some distance from his friend, "What his companion there was about?" "About!" asked Mr. M., not quite comprehending the question. "Ay," pursued the inquirer, "what is he *at*, with that *thing* in his mouth?" "Oh!" replied Mr. M., "he is cleaning his teeth?" "What! cleaning his teeth!" thundered out the man: "Well, it's the first time I ever heard of such a d—d trick as *that*. Cleaning his teeth!!! the milk-sop!" and away he rolled, putting a pinch of tobacco into his mouth by way, as it seemed, of compensation for the disgust he had felt, and which, if possible, appeared even to exceed his wonder. When the alarm was afterwards given of the ship's danger, and the Captain with clasped hands in the agony of his despair declared that he knew no more where they were than "Tom the devil," the old sailor, who had remarked so pointedly upon Talbot and "that thing in his mouth," exclaimed aloud with an oath, "I *knew* we should have no *luck,* when I saw that lubber *cleaning his teeth!*" *

* This instance of *superstition,* I heard exceeded in a very profane degree, on board the "Canada," on our passage to America, in 1834. Service had been performed each Sunday morning on deck by a clergyman. Most of the steerage passengers attended, and were very intent and well conducted. One, however, a very ruffianly man, always absented himself, and one afternoon, when this religious duty had taken place, a violent storm ensued, which gave occasion for the absentee to remark with bitterness, and even rage, to the officiating clergyman, " Ah! this is what comes of your preaching and stuff — I never knew it answer."—A. M.

CHAPTER VIII.

Mr. Mathews at the Swansea Theatre.—Memoranda of his performances there.—His success.—Engaged for the season.—Mr. Mathews appears as Clown.—The Shakspeare Forgeries.—"Vortigern and Rowena" condemned.—Dr. Parr deceived.—Ireland ruined.—Mr. Mathews performs at Carmarthen with Mr. Nash, afterwards the architect, and Mr. Pugin, the architectural draughtsman.—Lee Sugg, the ventriloquist.—His dislike of Mr. Mathews, and murderous attack upon him.—An entertainment by Lee Sugg described.—His scheme to outwit the Welsh, and its failure.—His tricks and annoyances to obtain money from Mr. Mathews.—His death.

IN a volume of playbills collected by the young actor at this period, there appears on the back of each, in my husband's hand-writing, memoranda of every circumstance of interest which occurred in relation to the night's performance. Some of these I shall intersperse, according to their date, with the correspondence. Together, they will carry the reader through the dramatic portion of Mr. Mathews's Welsh history.

Mem. "October 1795. — 'The Wheel of Fortune' and 'The Agreeable Surprise.' Montague played for the second time; and I made my first appearance in the farce of 'All the World's a Stage,' and was received in a manner very far beyond my expectations. We were again solicited to perform the next night for the benefit of Mrs. Giles."

Dear Litchfield,   Swansea, Oct. 17th, 1795.

I am detained as usual by contrary winds. I told you in a former letter from hence, that Montague was to play *Othello* here on Friday last, which he did, and was very well received. Masterman, the manager, as soon as the play was over, finding his performance had been attended with so much success, asked him to play *Penruddock* on the Monday. He at the same time asked me if I would perform *Lingo*, which I consented to do. Montague pleased very much in *Penruddock*. I played *Lingo*, being in great spirits, with a vast deal of applause. As the theatre is very small, I felt great confidence, and went through the whole with much credit. It has given me a greater idea of myself than ever, and shows how much a performer may do when he has advantages. You may be sure I felt very grand at playing as a star, — " *Lingo*, for this night only, Mr. Mathews, from the Theatre Royal, Dublin;" and this had great weight in so small a company. As much attention was shown to us as Kemble received from us in Dublin. I had paid particular notice to the getting up of "The Wheel of Fortune," in Dublin, and gave directions at the rehearsal here, which made them look upon me with more respect. The house being extremely full, and entirely attributed to our attraction, Masterman insisted on our accepting a guinea a-piece, which was no unpleasing offer at this time, as, from being detained, our stock was terribly reduced. Finding the wind still foul, we were again pressed to perform, which we did on Wednesday, for a benefit. Montagúe, *Charles Surface;* myself, *Crabtree* and *Diggory* in " All the World's a Stage." Their comedy wardrobe here is really capital; and I wore one or two of the best dresses I ever saw.

You may expect me in London immediately.

Yours ever most sincerely,
Charles Mathews.

Mem.—" October 21st, 1795.—I was well received, and encored in 'The Rushlight.' Very much elated at my success. Fresh fuel."

"October 28th, 1795.—' The Wheel of Fortune.'—'The Prize.' Montague's business now growing urgent, he was under the necessity of coming to a determination of quitting the town, in opposition to all the arguments that friendship could invent to induce him to stay: in consequence of which, after the performance of *Penruddock*, he took leave of the audience amidst the loudest acclamations.

" When the play was over, we spent a pleasant farewell evening with our friends. In the morning breakfasted with Mr. Masterman, and had appointed nine o'clock, once more to take leave of the town. We walked with him on the Burrows, where he was giving us directions as to our intended journey, when we were met by Messrs. Cooke and Bower, who came with the intention of offering proposals to us to stay. They stated that it was the wish of many persons in the town that we should remain through the season, and take benefits; adding, that they would ensure Montague twenty-five guineas, and myself twenty; and should the receipts of the house be less, they would make up the deficiency.

The proposal was accepted, and Montague agreed to go by the mail to London that night, transact his business, and return at all events, in a week. And I agreed to stay during the season."

It may be well here to explain that Mr. Talbot having received a letter from his friend in town, which served to "whet his almost blunted purpose" of visiting London, left Wales in the middle of his great popularity there; but, as may be seen, he did not find himself accompanied by the young comedian, whose dramatic fires were rekindled, and blazing in all their first ardour. Instead, therefore, of joining his family, as he had intended when he sailed from Cork, he despatched a letter by his friend, with a strong injunction to him, to call and satisfy his parents of his present prosperity, without a hint of past misery, or his recent intention of quitting the profession. In the mean time he pursued the "even tenor of his way;" for his success continued, though from his own records he was not then the object with the Welsh manager that he afterwards became; for, in the first place, Mr. Masterman had engaged him merely to ensure the more brilliant star Montague; and in the next he found that he could not, even though he was becoming a favourite, take possession of all the characters his ambition pointed to, as a popular man had long held undisputed sway over most of those in his line. But it will be seen from his next *Mem.*

that his broadest humour was called into play at this time.

" Nov. 2nd, 1795.—' The Belle's Stratagem,' and ' The Whim, or Harlequin's Frolics.' *Hardy*, in the play, and *Clown*, in the pantomime."

DEAR LITCHFIELD, Swansea, November 5th, 1795.

Immediately after Montague's playing the first night, he was asked to take a benefit, by some gentlemen of the town, who said they would ensure him a great one. He declined it, knowing that his business in London was pressing. I believe I never told you that he was principally concerned in the discovery of the much-talked-of new play of Shakspeare, being a particular friend of Mr. Ireland, and present when the first writings were found.*

But to return. Though much disappointed at not having the pleasure of seeing you in London, I think my stay here so much to my interest, and find that in two or three weeks I am making such rapid strides in my profession, that I cannot but feel very happy. I have greater confidence in playing to an audience who have paid me such flattering attention. In short, I must confess, that, from the bad business I have done in Ireland, and other disadvantages, I had very melancholy doubts of my success; but I am now convinced of what I can do, and that I have been cruelly depressed in Ireland. No comedian ever gained more applause in public, or encomiums in private, than I have done. I have played *Lingo*, *Crabtree*, *Diggory*, *Polonius*, *Doctor*, ("Animal Magnetism,")

* Mr. Mathews, of course, was not at this time acquainted with the real state of the case, as related in the foregoing pages; and merely repeats the account given to him by Talbot, in relation to the Shakspeare papers.—A. M.

Weazel, *Rutterkin*, *Kecksey*, *Hardy*, and *Clown*. Sung songs each night with the greatest applause. "The Rushlight" constantly every night twice; and I am sure never better received. In short, I am so highly flattered, that I have become too much of an egotist. The bearer of this is a Welsh gentleman of a good nature, who is in London about law. Show him civility, will you?

Yours ever most affectionately,

Greyhound Inn.   CHARLES MATHEWS.

Talbot returned to Swansea, chap-fallen at his friend's woful defeat. The play of "Vortigern and Rowena" was condemned, and pronounced an imposition. The distended bubble burst when it had attained its height, and fell an "airy nothing" to the ground. The *Shakspeare Forgeries* stood confessed. The ingenious young man, who had so misdirected his great talents, was disgraced and ruined. That his error was to be severely reprobated, who will doubt? but perhaps his youth might have pleaded at the bar of literary judgment in mitigation of extreme punishment. His ingenuity, perhaps, was his worst plea; yet, who but must regret such talent driven into obscurity, under the ban of mortified vanity? Those whose judgment he had so artfully compromised by his skill, could never forgive the wounds inflicted on their *amour propre*. Could the boy-deceiver expect pardon from the *men* whose fallibility he had proved?*

---

* Doctor Parr was seen to fall upon his knees in reverence of Shakspeare's (*i. e.* Ireland's) *Profession of Faith!*" the sublimity of which he declared to be beyond anything of the kind he ever before read.—A. M.

In the year 1814 Mr. Mathews often invited Mr. Ireland to visit us. On these occasions, he used to interest us much by the facility with which he imitated various autographs, and his account of the manner in which he obtained his means, and the whole progress of his fatal deceit. He was a very intelligent, pleasing man, and deserved a better fate. Mr. Mathews some years after bought one volume of the original forgeries, which was in the sale of his theatrical library of 1835.

DEAR LITCHFIELD, Swansea, November 12th, 1795.

I come on apace. I played the *Deaf Lover* last night with great applause, though I never saw anybody but Benson act it. I want comic songs terribly. To-day I dine here with some twelve or fourteen principal men of the town. Very flattering. I have not a moment to spare.

Yours with the utmost sincerity,
CHARLES MATHEWS.

Greyhound Inn, full of jolly fellows.

Mem. " Nov. 18th, 1795.—My own benefit. ' Fair Penitent,' Songs, Imitations of London Performers, and ' The Prize.' Mr. Moor played *Horatio* for me, and acquitted himself very respectably.* In addition to the imitations proposed in the bill, I introduced *Hayes* and *Gloucester*, who being generally known, my efforts were well received. Though I had previously made known my intentions to both parties, the latter was offended. Mi-

* He was announced in the bill as follows: — " *Horatio* by *a gentleman*, for *his amusement*, who *never appeared* on any public stage."—A. M.

micry, dangerous ground — too often creates enemies. The receipts of the house 18*l*."

" Swansea, November 30th, 1795.—' Othello,' and ' The Prize.' On Thursday, we positively, absolutely, and indefinitely, took leave of the town, and our friends; and set off on horseback, in company with Mr. Masterman and family in a post-chaise. We slept at Lannon."

" Friday, set off for Carmarthen; arrived in the afternoon: slept at Ivy Bush. Saturday, went into lodgings."

My dear Litchfield,   Carmarthen, December 3rd, 1795.

I have just time to tell you that I have engaged in this company, and shall probably make an advantageous scheme of it, as I am likely to be a great favourite. My benefit produced twenty guineas, which is a very good one.

We opened here on Tuesday. "Othello" was advertised for Monday; but *Iago* was taken ill, and we commenced with " The Wheel of Fortune." I was remarkably well received in *Lenitive*, which I think is one of the best parts I ever attempted. I shall play nothing but principal parts. It is a beautiful theatre, and holds 30*l*. The scenery is really capital. A swelling in my hand has forced me to keep it in a sling nearly three weeks, which is very awkward. Adieu. Yours ever most sincerely,

Charles Mathews.

P. S. Show the play-bills to my father. Direct to Mr. Doel's, Market Place, Carmarthen, South Wales.

Mem. " Carmarthen, January 8th, 1796. ' The School for Scandal,' and ' The Farm-House.'— Nr. Nash,[*] Mr. Hughes, and Captain Vaughan, performed *Sir Peter*

[*] The late celebrated architect, John Nash, Esq.

Mr. MATHEWS as LENITIVE in the PRIZE,
Swansea 1795.

Teazle, *Charles*, and *Trip*. The house very full. I performed *Shaklefigure* in the farce, instead of Mr. Saddington."

"February 17th, 1796.—' As You like it,' and ' Rosina.' This evening the receipts of the house were 11*l*. 17*s*. Mr. Taylor being too ill to perform, I undertook *Jaques* at a short notice." *

" March 4th, 1796. — ' The Chapter of Accidents,' and ' The Sprigs of Laurel.' This evening the receipts of the house were 6*l*. 8*s*. Mr. Hayes being ill, I performed *Jacob* in the play, and *Sinclair* in the farce."

During this engagement in Wales, Mr. Pugin, since well known as an architectural draughtsman and by his many published works, was scene-painter to the theatre. Here he became acquainted with Mr. Nash, who afterwards employed and brought him forward in London.†

Unhappily, these were not the only people in Wales who were destined to mingle in my husband's future history. There was a person in the company of the name of Lee Sugg, who took a deadly dislike to the young actor; first, because he had shrunk from his advances towards intimacy; and next, because his own striking peculiarities had been imprudently, though not ill-naturedly, touched upon for the amusement of their brother

---

* The '*melancholy* Jaques' ! ! ! The character must have exchanged its attribute for *this* night, at least.—A. M.

† It was to this gentleman that Charles was placed to learn architectural drawing in 1819.—A. M.

actors, with great success. But Lee Sugg, who probably was aware that his prominent points were open to much dislike as well as laughter, could not forgive the man who placed them so ludicrously in view. He was a tall, powerful person, and resolved, in lieu of retaliating in the same manner in which the offence was given, to take private vengeance, and punish with his hand what his head was unable to resent. Not, however, trusting too implicitly to his own personal strength, he called in to his aid an auxiliary in the shape of an iron bar; and, thus doubly armed, he lay in wait one night in a dark corner for the young offender's approach, who, in passing, received a blow across his back, which, had it alighted on his head, would have cured him of all further attempts to take *others off*. Mr. Mathews felt the effects of this ruffianly attack a long while.

Lee Sugg now became watchful and jealous, and fancying that he also possessed talent for something of which he had caught the first intimation from Mr. Mathews, under the name of *Ventriloquy*, he from that time put himself forward as one who, to use his own printed account of himself in after-years, possessed "A power which God had given him, and which the devil himself couldn't take away!" In short, after this man had got up a very coarse imitation from his study of what he had heard and seen done, he set up for himself; and few there are who have not heard or read, in large type, of "*Lee Sugg, the great Ventriloquist.*" Sometimes, by his bills it would be seen (not, however, till my husband's fame was sufficiently established to make it a worthy boast) that he was " The Original Instructor of *Mathews At Home,*" &c. However, as may be supposed, these attempts did not improve the originally low state of his finances. He had one recommendation to the sort of audience with which he contented himself—a good loud voice; and he bawled out some of the hunting songs of the day with as much effect as a thick impediment and lisp would permit. His first attempt to amuse an audience without any auxiliaries, was in Wales; and was a fair specimen, it may be supposed, of what he in after-time presented, and highly entertained at least *one* of his auditors.

It appeared that he was too prudent an exhibitor to trust the receipts to any hand but his own: he therefore added to his versatile undertakings that of door-keeper; and consequently took his station near enough to the entrance of the room he had hired for the occasion, to be able to reach the lock of the door, without any other movement than what was requisite for the purpose of opening it. He then received the price of admission, which he sounded upon a little wooden table on his right hand, placed there it appeared for the sole benefit of this experiment, but so low as to compel him to stoop his tall figure whenever he tested the validity of the proffered coin; this, if satisfactory, he placed immediately in his waistcoat-pocket, thanking his patrons, and directing them forward to seats. Each arrival was announced by a loud tapping at the door of the room, and this he immediately attended to. Finding at length a sufficient number assembled, and the hour exceeded which he had given out as the precise time of commencement, Lee Sugg began to satisfy the impatience of his audience, and struck up his first song—" Old Towler," without the aid of an accompaniment. The *tapping* and jingling of the silver must be remembered as accessories; and the following account will in faint colours paint the scene.

"' Bright Chanticleer proclaims the dawn— And—' (One shilling, if you please, sir. Much obliged.)

"' Spangles—' (Sixpence for your little girl, ma'am.)

"' Deck the thorn—' (Front seat, if you please, ma'am.)

"'The lowing herds—' (I can't help your hissing, ladies and gentlemen, I *must* admit my visiters.)

"' Now seek the lawn, the lark springs from—' (The third seat, if you please, gentlemen.)

"'The corn—' (That's a *very* bad half-crown, sir!)

"' With a heigho! chevy !'—(If you observe, there's no sound in it.)

"'Hark forward! hark forward! Tantivy.'— (Go on, ladies and gentlemen.)

"'With a heigho, chevy.'—(I'm sorry, ladies and gentlemen, for your displeasure; but I *can't* let people in for *nothing*.)

"'Hark, forward!'—(One-and-sixpence for you and your baby, ma'am.)

"'Tantivy! Arise the burthen of my song.'— (One shilling. Pass on, sir.)

"'This day a stag must die! this day—' (There's no half-price, ma'am.)

"'A stag must die,'" &c.

Lee Sugg ruined himself with the honest Welsh folks, by one of those tricks which he was always practising to entice people to the places in which he performed. An instance of this description, and of their simplicity, occurred about this time. In imitation of Foote's evasive title, he advertised for his benefit that "Lee Sugg would present '*Tea*' to those who honoured him with their presence on his benefit night." This proved, as he suspected, an interesting and attractive line in his bill; and many were the speculations concerning the meaning of this announcement amongst the simple folks. Lee Sugg, however, did not intend to leave a doubt about the matter, and contrived an ingenious plan for misleading the lower class of the town's people, trusting to the same ingenuity to get him out of the scrape, after he had induced them to purchase tickets and attend. He called upon a woman who retailed butter, and asked her on the market-day, (which happened to be the day fixed on for his benefit,) whether, when she went to purchase her weekly stock of that commodity, she would allow him to accompany her. To this she innocently consented; and when she had made up her amount, which was to a rather large extent, he insisted upon helping to carry it home for her. He then made a circuit with it, calling out, as he went along, "Here, boys and girls—here is the butter for your *tea.*" The trick had its effect. The people, however, were so exasperated at being lured in under false pretences, that they insisted upon their money being returned. Very few remained; and the evening's entertainment proved little more than "*Tea and turn out.*"

Lee Sugg, from improvident habits, and a very slender stock of professional merit, became sadly necessitous; and, after my husband came to London, he proved a great plague to him. I had often heard Mr. Mathews speak of him, and relate most amusing accounts of his knowledge of him in Wales. One morning, when in London, I was told that "a strange gentleman wanted to see master." But master, not being yet dressed, and always disliking "strange gentlemen," requested me to ascertain the nature of so early a call. When I entered the breakfast-room, I found a very "strange gentleman." He was tall and bony, with a flaxen wig upon his head, not capacious enough to cover the remaining part of the carroty *natural* hair which it was intended to match. His coat was a faded pea-green; he wore a *white* waistcoat— not *very* white — a pair of dark-coloured pantaloons, made tight, and very pale-coloured silk stockings, and thick, uncleaned shoes. I started when I beheld this apparition upon the sofa, with my child. The visiter was evidently disconcerted at my appearing, instead of the person he came to see; and, rising in embarrassment, (rather a novel sensation, I was afterwards told, for *him* to feel,) addressed me hesitatingly—"I expected, madam, to see an *old* friend,—that is, Mr. Charles Mathews. My friend *Charles* and I have not met for many years." I asked, "Your name, sir?"—"Oh! madam," he replied, "I have not the *pleasure* of knowing you, nor have you the *honour* of knowing me." With this unnatural and inappropriate application of the word *honour*, the strange gentleman, being assured that his "old friend" would not appear, bowed and shuffled out of the room, promising, at my suggestion, to write to him; and he kept his word, for, from that day to the latest of his existence, he kept up a regular succession of importunities, occasionally varying them from money to clothes—from clothes to money—orders and benefit tickets, with personal applications whenever he could find the way open to this kind of attack. In short, he was a pest to Mr. Mathews for years. Lee Sugg had no claim whatever upon my husband's purse or sympathies; they had not even been intimate when they met in Masterman's company. Hence Lee Sugg's long enmity towards Mr. Mathews, whose conduct to this person furnishes one of the many minor evidences of that kind, forgiving spirit which actuated him throughout life, and urged him to do good to those who used him despitefully. Lee Sugg, as I have shown, once tried to kill him, and pleaded drunkenness as an excuse for the attempt; perhaps his inebriety prevented the attack being so well directed as to make the consequences fatal. He afterwards endeavoured to affix the stigma of mean ingratitude upon his intended victim, who, he asserted, "had suffered his first instructor to pine in poverty and neglect." Various were his modes of persecution. Sometimes, a large placard would proclaim, "*Mathews At Home, for one night only, at the Harp Public-house,*" by which the careless reader would be deceived — though the more curious observer might detect, by a nice scrutiny, in an artfully diminutive type preceding the announcement in large letters, the words, "Charles Lee Sugg, the original instructor of MATHEWS AT HOME;" in the same manner that adventurous haberdashers would formerly draw in the unwary with the name of *Flint*, the invisible *from* being ingeniously wrapt up in the flourish of the first letter.

At another time my husband would discover announcements upon the walls and posts of our rural vicinity, purporting that he would positively perform that night at the Swan Tavern. Of course, our neighbours disregarded this; no one went; and the next day the perpetrator of this falsehood would throw himself upon the mercy of him he so attempted to disgrace, and beg for relief on the plea that he was detained at the tavern for printing the bills and other expenses incurred by him in anticipation of receipts. This was impudent enough; but the fact of his real destitution covered the remembrance of his offence, and drew forth the amount which would extricate him from his difficulty, and a trifle over and above, from my good-natured husband, who was, however, often exasperated beyond measure at this kind of annoyance. One day Lee Sugg came to a little cottage we had taken for a short period at Clapham, and, breaking through the opposition of the servants to his unannounced entrance, rushed into the breakfast-room, (whence he had from an open window descried his "friend and pupil" at breakfast,) exclaiming, as he presented himself, with the most frantic gestures and tones, "I am a desperate man! I am famishing with hunger, while you are seated here in luxury." He would then drop this exaggeration of his wants as the servant disappeared, and calmly and even jestingly urge his petition for a few shillings. My husband was for some time too angry to yield, but ultimately dismissed him with the required aid. Upon one occasion, Lee Sugg got a crowd round Mr. Mathews in the streets of London, by pointing him out to the passers-by in the following manner:—" There! there goes Charles Mathews, whom I have known for years. I taught him all he knows, and he won't give me a pound, to save me from starvation!" This occurred just after he had been assisted by my husband to double that sum. I perfectly remember his poor harassed victim coming home one day, really ill with mortification and rage, vowing that he would never give " the villain" another shilling. In a few hours after this would follow an abject apology, in the shape of a letter, representing the offender's state of destitution to be such as to affect his brain. It was true that this improvident being was often in the distress he represented; and in the conviction of his necessities my husband's resentment was appeased, and his humanity again exercised.

Somehow, at length, Lee Sugg became less persecuting, though still importunate, and he showed symptoms of a softened feeling towards the man who had returned so much good for evil. Whether Lee Sugg's nature became tamer from time, or whether the untiring bounty and good-nature of his benefactor had at last touched the heart of his ancient foe, is uncertain; but the effect was an acknowledged sense of his obligations to the goodness of my husband, with every appearance of sincerity. It followed that Lee Sugg took occasion ever after to make a ready allowance of his great professional deserts, to which he at last bore *public testimony*, in the astounding assertion in the bills of his own performance, that he would attempt something for the amusement of the public, " after the manner of *Charles Mathews, Esq.* THE GREATEST COMEDIAN that EVER REIGNED!" If this was not compensation for former disparagement, I know not what more could be asked. It then became the habit of Lee Sugg to witness the entertainments of Mr. Mathews, and interrupting the audience frequently with his raptures, he was sometimes turned out. On the first night of any performance the door-keepers had instructions not to admit him on any terms; for, strange to say, he would *pay* when orders were refused him. Notwithstanding all these precautions, he contrived to establish himself somewhere, and as certainly to interrupt the actor and annoy the audience with his expressions of admiration, and his vehement applause at everything. In short, he beset my husband in every possible way that could annoy and distress him. Mr. Mathews really had a horror of encountering him, and used to describe him as Frankenstein's monster, whom he would run to the world's end to avoid.

Lee Sugg has for some years paid the debt of nature; and, from the moment my husband heard of the event, all anger towards his tormentor ceased. He felt none of the satisfaction at the death of this man that he often in his moments of exasperation said he should; on the contrary, I could almost have fancied he was in some degree affected at the intelligence; and after all it might be so, for this person was a link (though a troublesome one) in the chain of his early recollections, and such are, in spite of ourselves, of some value to us ever after.

CHAPTER IX.

Wynne, the leader of the Swansea band.—His romantic and melancholy history.—His irritable temperament.—His peculiarities.—Wynne at a musical rehearsal, and the tricks played on him by the wags of the theatre.—His antipathy to dogs and unintentional cruelty.—Ludicrous mistakes by Wynne.—Mr. Mathews's successful imitation of his peculiarities.

AMONGST the eccentric people in the Swansea Theatre, the most amusing, and I may say interesting, was the leader of the band, whose name was *Wynne*. The mention of this person will at once recall to many of my readers the exquisite imitations of man and manner with which Mr. Mathews was so fond of pleasing his friends, and which always had the effect of creating not merely amusement, but even a regard for the original. The history of Wynne was romantic. It began with a hackneyed incident in stories of fiction, but was nevertheless in his case true.

He was the son of a gentleman of large fortune in Wales, who, becoming a widower while his child was a mere infant, placed it under the care of a nurse in whom he felt great confidence, while he sought alleviation to his sorrow for the death of his wife, in travel. This woman, after a short time, conceived the idea of exchanging her own baby (the foster-brother) for the nursling intrusted to her care; and, in order to destroy the identity of the rich man's child, she determined to put out the little innocent's eyes; for which barbarous design she employed a red-hot knitting-needle, and thus succeeded in destroying one eye, and severely injuring the sight of the other. When the father, after a considerable absence, returned, he saw his supposed child without surprise; and, unsuspicious of any change, save what might naturally be produced by time in the no-features of an infant, and its general appearance, he unconsciously received the nurse's child, which was destined to take his name, and be the successor to his wealth, the real heir remaining with the cruel woman who had deprived him of his rightful place and his future comfort.

After a few years, illness and consequent compunction for this two-fold crime, seized upon the body and mind of this miserable woman, for the acts she had committed; and, when too late to be of any solid advantage to her victim, she confessed on her dying-bed the fraud she had practised from a vague notion of serving herself, through the future elevation of her child. The father of poor little Wynne, for the child was called by his nurse's name, had followed his wife to the tomb; and the woman's story was naturally rejected by the friends of the acknowledged heir. Indeed, independently of their reluctance to displace the child to whom they had attached themselves, for a poor infirm creature, that as a stranger they could not be supposed to love, the story was at best but a suspicious one. The poor wronged boy, therefore, remained unbenefited by the disclosures of the dying penitent, further than by a little assistance given towards his education; but his history, as it spread, carried with it the great and universal commiseration of the hearers, and a deep interest in his fate was evinced by his humane countrymen. It was with them a matter of care in what manner the poor afflicted orphan was to be provided for, after his brief schooling had terminated. All at once it was observed that young Wynne evinced a decided taste and love for music — that sweet and merciful compensation so frequently substituted by an Almighty Providence, for the " one sense quite shut out"—for, though this poor child was not actually in darkness, yet his power of discerning objects was so feeble from the total loss of one eye and the imperfection of the other—that it could scarcely be called sight: in fact, at the best, all was to him but "a palpable obscure." His kind friends resolved to contribute to the means of Wynne's acquirement of the science for which he showed such a predilection, since he was so obviously unfitted for any trade, or other mode of obtaining a livelihood. Thus in time he became a tolerable proficient as a violin-player, and ultimately a teacher of music in various towns in Wales, filling up his time by leading the little band in Mr. Masterman's orchestra.

Wynne was at the time Mr. Mathews met him a man of middle age, and was generally respected and beloved, although of the most irritable temperament imaginable; yet he was at the same time so amiable, so benevolent in his nature, that no one ever felt disposed to be angry with his little foibles. This fretfulness generally exhibited itself either in soliloquy or side-speeches, never direct to the object of his annoyance, if of an intelligent nature. His early misfortune and general ill-usage from his reputed mother had tended to render him a timid nervous creature ever after; and the inconvenience he necessarily experienced from his imperfect vision, served often to excite his natural impatience and restlessness of manner, which was always apparent, even in his happiest moments. He had a remarkably fine ear; and his *not*, in fact, first-rate violin always requiring the greatest trouble and patience to screw into anything like tone, would exasperate him to the most violent pitch of harmless rage. The young and thoughtless wags of the theatre loved to divert themselves with this excellent but whimsical person,—my husband in particular, to whom it was meat and drink to see a *character.*

On the mornings of a musical rehearsal, they would cautiously keep out of the reach of Wynne's dim view, in order to excite his complainings, and then listen to the oral evidences of his impatience at their supposed want of punctuality. There would he sit in the middle of the little orchestra, perched upon a high seat, "raised by his merit to that bad eminence,' alone, and waiting for the appearance of those who were witnessing his solitary distress. The height of his seat enabled him from time to time to crane his neck over the stage, and peer about for the expected comers: then, taking out a warming-pan sort of watch, he would hold it so close to his half-eye as almost to defeat his own intent; and, as he ascertained the wasting time, his rising anxiety and anger broke out half-audibly, until it reached the concert-pitch of his feelings, which were in harmony with the occasion, and discoursed most eloquent music to his hearers. While he proceeded to draw up the refractory strings of his wooden torment, the mischievous group, unseen, but close to him, would enjoy the effects of their supposed absence. Even the prompter, who ought to be the regulator of stage propriety, Saddington, (or, as he was endearingly and familiarly called, " Saddy,") humoured these tricks, by his concurrence in poor Wynne's annoyance, who would rise up and call upon " Saddy!—Saddy!" in hopes of a response : " Saddy ! anybody *come?*" then, receiving no answer, he would resume his tuning, and with now and then an unformed but implied oath, (which, from the non-existence of what he swore by, might be said to be rendered a nullity,) would bewail his uncomfortable feelings. " Saddy ! anybody come?—Demmy *eyes!* it's very hard! just ten o'clock! I've a lesson to give at Mr. Sheldon's at eleven. Demmy eyes ! it's very hard, I'm *sure!*" He would then attempt again to draw up the bad strings of his intractable instrument, while his face was full of the contortion which a very nice ear caused him to wrinkle into an expression of agony, that at last would break into an exaggerated mimicry of the false sounds it uttered. " Demmy eyes ! what, *you*'ll plague me too, will ye? Saddy,—Saddy! anybody *come?* Where are they all?" (And echo answered, "*Where?*" Then looking again on the moon-faced features of his watch, he would replace it in his fob, with an adjusting shake of his head, a drawing out of an immense frill from his bosom, rubbing the dust off one sleeve with the cuff of the other,—

a common usage, and almost as fallacious a notion of nicety as when a cat transfers the soil from her skin to her tongue. Repeated execrations at his violin, and the inutility of his labour and pains, followed. At last raising it to his eye, and rubbing his nose down the strings, in order to examine the cause of failure, accompanying the scrutiny with a sort of low whispering whistle, which he always practised under occasions of strong provocation or excitement, he would resume his self-inflicting torture, in its course relieving his feelings towards the obstinate and ungrateful object of his care, by the utterance of every imaginable term of disgust, until all expression was exhausted. He would then lift aloft the execrable fiddle, as if wringing its neck, and then apostrophize it again as if it had ears as well as voice, and possessed as much feeling as himself, summing up the amount of his detestation in, "Demmy *eyes*! if I'd *another*, I'd break you all to *pieces!*" *

Wynne, as I have said, had a very correct ear, which of course his *band* (that is to say, his *second* fiddle and *bass*,) never satisfied; nor were the singers much more successful. Their vocal enormities

* The difficulty of written attempts to explain *manners* so amusing, which in nine cases out of ten describe the greater part of a character, will perhaps render the present effort unsuccessful in conveying an adequate idea of the man, Mr. Mathews's imitation of whom would convulse with laughter all who witnessed it.

he was wont to check by quickly rising from his seat, and casting up his moiety of an eye in the face of the offenders and drawing his bow forcibly, in order to impress them with a sense of the time or tone violated, at the same time muttering audibly in a stage-like *aside*, " Demmy *eyes,* can't you *hear?* "

After the wags had amused themselves sufficiently with poor Wynne's murmurings and impotent rage, his final threat of " I'll *go,* if they don't come *soon,*' (not that he meant what he said,) was the cue for them to advance in affected haste and concern, and apologize for having kept him waiting. This, as they knew, immediately caused a revulsion of feeling in the good-natured musician, and disarmed him at once; his anger softening into an embarrassed re-arrangement of his frill, and brushing off, as I have before described, the supposed dust from his *other* sleeve; his face unsmoothed, however, from the recent wrinkles of vexation, he would reply, " Oh dear sir, don't mention it; it's of no consequence." In answer to their "belief that it was not *much* after the time," poor Wynne, with his features and his body convulsed by nervous agitation, would assure them that they were right, and that "he had not been there *long,*" and then proceed in his duty in the required music with his customary contortions and correctness.

Amongst the effects of his constitutional or acquired timidity of character, which often struggled with his kind-heartedness, his terror of all animals was excessive, and he would not stay in a room with a dog if he could avoid doing so, nor could he rest with one near him. Mr. Mathews was dining with him at the house of Wynne's great patron, Mr. Sheldon, when a favourite spaniel found its way into the dinner-room, and, as it always happens, took a fancy to importune the only person present to whom its notice could be unwelcome. At first, Wynne withdrew his hand with a start, from the offered devotion of *Phillis*, and, by an effort which the necessity of the case prompted, uttered from time to time sentences of a *soothing* kind, in the manner and feeling of the Brentford tailor, when he deprecates the kicking of his restive steed by patting, and "So ho! my poor fellow, and that's all!" In similar ways, Wynne endeavoured to hide his inward fear of Phillis by outward flattery; shrinking, however, from the animal's touch, and starting from time to time with a convulsive motion which made him appear as if under the influence of galvanism, whenever the dog rested her paws against him: jerking out sentences of affected fondness for his friend's favourite, "Pretty dear, pretty creature!" &c. with an excruciating look across the table at my husband, and with drops of terror upon his brow, as if appealing to his humanity to relieve him.

"You're *fond* of dogs, Mr. Wynne?" asked Mr. Sheldon, not suspecting the truth. "Oh yes, sir, *certainly,*" at the same moment again starting from Phillis's caresses, which had now become constant, in consequence of the unintentional encouragement he had given by the little bits of meat dropped for the purpose of directing the creature's notice from himself. At length a favourable movement of Wynne gave Phillis an opportunity to jump upon his knees. This was too much! He lost all sense but that of his imagined danger. It was a moment of indescribable horror to him; he had no reason left to direct him; " madness ruled the hour," and, unconscious what he did, in the impulse of his terror he plunged the two-pronged iron fork which he had in his hand, into the body of the poor harmless favourite, whose yells told the perpetrator the cruelty of which he had been guilty. Forgetting in an instant all his dread of the victim of his unpremeditated attack, Wynne caught up the animal, from the touch of which he had previously shrunk, and full of horror and compunction for the act he had been betrayed into, ran wildly round the room with the sufferer closely pressed to his bosom, entreating, while tears poured down his cheeks, that somebody would take out the fork from the "poor dear creature's back." The instrument was extracted, and no great mischief ensued; but poor Wynne was deeper wounded, and long after and often was he heard deploring his unintended cruelty with the truest sorrow and remorse; nay, had he injured a human creature in the same way, from *malice prepense*, his conscience could not have harboured a deeper sense of criminality, and from the time of the accident he visited and *almost* caressed poor Phillis, in atonement for the injury he had done her.

He was morbidly tenacious of anything looking like personal neglect or disrespect. He knew himself to be by birth a gentleman, and every feeling confirmed the belief; but conscious that his history gave him but a dubious claim to the world's consideration beyond his acquired and humble place in society, he was scrupulous in all that seemed to arise from the knowledge of his misfortune. Mr. Mathews was amused with this good man's peculiarities, and studied them, besides having a real regard for him, and often made a point of walking home from the theatre of a morning with him, seeking occasion for amusement. Poor Wynne's dimmed vision caused him to make numerous mistakes, from the necessity he was under of taking objects upon guess. Going up the main street of Swansea one day, he passed a shop kept by a tall, bulky woman, at whose door were piled a number of large baskets—the commodity she dealt in. To this temporary structure Mr. Wynne bowed with great respect, taking off his hat; and the next moment, while my husband was trying to subdue a laugh at this blunder, Wynne, drawing out his frill, and rubbing his coat-sleeve down, with his natural quickness of feeling exclaimed, as to himself, " Demmy eyes! she might have *spoken,* I think !" While he walked, he was assisted by my husband in crossing the market-place, where a great many carts were congregated, to the inconvenience of foot passengers. Mr. Mathews led him by the arm behind a pack-horse that was near the crossing, and which backed with its tail a little against Wynne, who, finding himself pushed rudely, as he thought, by a stranger, turned furiously round, exclaiming, "Demmy *eyes*, sir, can't you *see?* You are no gentleman, whoever you are."

Mr. Wynne, in fact, was a never-ending still-beginning subject of entertainment to those about him, and to Mr. Mathews in particular, whose imitation of him was as diverting as faithful, and was so agreeable to all who heard and saw it, that the person and character of the Welsh musician became as familiar to every one of Mr. Mathews's friends, as if they had been personally acquainted with him;* and, whenever this imita-

* In evidence of this, Mr. Denman, of the York and afterwards of the Haymarket Theatre, was engaged some years after he had witnessed my husband's imitation of this character, in one of the English provincial theatres, and going on the first morning to a rehearsal of "The Quaker," in which he was to play *Steady,* he was so struck that when the symphony of the first song had begun he looked into the orchestra, and burst into a fit of loud laughter and turned away. As soon as he could speak, he said to the manager, who was wondering what had caused his mirth, "I'll bet you five guineas, *that* man's name is

tion occurred, there was sure to be seen *three* or *four* attempting to copy the portrait so faithfully drawn by my husband.

Wynne;" and so it was, for he had quitted his native place. Poor Wynne, equally amazed at the conduct of the new performer, stood up peering at him, and adjusting his frill, &c., with fiddle under his arm, *making the faces* Mr. Denman was so familiar with, and which he ever after cautiously avoided looking at during a performance.

CHAPTER X.

Mr. Mathews and Miss Strong.—His engagement to her, and his Father's letter to him on the subject.—His marriage with Miss Strong.—Increasing ambition.—Application to Tate Wilkinson, the York Patentee.—The Manager's letters in reply.—Mr. Mathews's visit to his family in London.—His reception.—Mr. and Mrs. John Litchfield.—Mr. Mathews's engagement with Tate Wilkinson, and journey into Yorkshire.

In the summer of 1797 Mr. Mathews met, at the house of a mutual friend, a young lady about his own age, of very prepossessing manners and of superior mind. It was said that the " gods had made her poetical," and that she was otherwise a person of elegant attainments. These young people became very intimate ; and, though friendship in such cases is not believed in by people of experience, I have been assured by both of the parties in question, that their acquaintance began and continued upon that basis alone, for some time. One day, however, the young man, in a *tété-à-téte* with the interesting orphan (for such she was), in a pensive mood, was drawn into a hearing of her history. She was the daughter of a physician, Doctor Strong, of Exeter, who, by a concurrence of wayward events, became embarrassed, and died almost penniless, leaving his only child upon the compassion of friends. She, however, was too proud to lead a life of dependence, and settled herself in a school, instructing a limited number of young ladies from the stores acquired by her education, laid up by her parents as resources for her own happiness in the position in society she was originally intended to take. With this best dowery that a child can boast of, she was enabled to obtain some of the comforts which it was at first hoped she might enjoy, without applying her mental gains for their purchase; and at this period she was labouring in her vocation, and highly esteemed by all who knew her. The story of her helpless youth and her honourable struggles, which allowed her a bare support, made an impression upon the somewhat romantic youth. He was not in any degree heart-touched; but *pity* is confessedly akin to love, if not nearly related. He had merely called upon Miss Strong for an hour's lounge on a day of non-rehearsal, without more intention or expectation than civility and kindness created; but, after an hour's stay, he left her presence as her *affianced husband!* As he walked towards his lodging, he asked himself what could have induced the offer he had made to this amiable girl?—and he found no answer in his *heart*. He was neither "in love," nor "pleased with ruin;" and yet he had plunged into the one without any of the sweet inducements of the other! Well, what was done could not be undone. He had listened to her woes, and admired her character; and, in the enthusiasm of youth and the moment, he had offered to protect the young creature against further toil and care. He had settled to marry a person without sixpence, and undertaken to provide for her upon the splendid expectancy of— twelve shillings per week! and this without what is called *being in love!*

That his intended wife was at that period deeply attached to him, every moment of her after-life indisputably evinced; and it is no mean praise of her husband, under the circumstances of their union, that he not only never divulged the delicate secret of his having inconsiderately and inadvertently made her the offer of his hand, but throughout her married life he treated her with every kindness and attention. Nor do I believe that, except to his second wife, (whom he *really* loved,) he ever committed the truth of his dispassionate feelings towards his devoted Eliza.

It will be seen, by the following sensible letter from his excellent father, that the bridegroom elect had written for that permission, which he felt to be a necessary form and preliminary to a determined act.

TO MR. CHARLES MATHEWS

Dear Charles, London, Sept. 11th, 1797.

I received yours of the 5th instant, which brought strange news unto my ears. You introduce a subject in your letter which rather surprised me, although you seem to think it would give me pleasure.

It will always give me pleasure to hear that you are doing well; but I cannot think that even success in your present pursuit is doing well; as I am convinced it will eventually turn out for evil, independently of the disgrace that attaches to your character while you continue in so disgraceful an employ. You say, that, with my concurrence and approbation, you are going to be married; and so you would, I suppose, whether I approved of it or not. You say that the lady has been introduced to me in a distant way — distant, indeed! I suppose with an express design to give me some intimation of her mental qualification, and to prove that her mind as well as her name was *Strong*, you have presented me with the figurability of her mind, and left me to guess at that of her body, which I suppose to be but small of stature by your own description of her, when you say, 'But the dear little girl,' &c. But I am satisfied though she be little, if that little be but good.

You have given me no account of her age, situation, or manner of life, or by what means she has hitherto subsisted. How can I form a just decision in my mind so as to give you advice, or grant my concurrence in an affair of such great importance as a cast for the life of one of the parties, without any premises to decide on? Has Miss Strong any probability, either by fortune or talents, of maintaining you? If she has not, what must be her conception of your being able to maintain her? Is your present income able to do it? or, have you any better prospects in life, to enable you to support her with honour and decency in future? I hate all Smithfield bargains in matrimonial contracts, and always esteem love-matches as the best, when entered into with " real discretion;" but " wisdom ought to dwell with prudence." If Miss Strong has no better prospect than to *live* and *starve* with you upon your present income, it plainly proves to me that her passion for your person, or the endowments of your mind, is very far stronger than the strength of her mind, and has overpowered her understanding in the present instance; and your love to her person, and particularly to her mental endowments, has shot beyond the mark, and will rather degenerate into a cruelty towards her, if you are not capable at present, or in prospect, of making provision for her future comfort.

The essential ingredient in the marriage-state, to render the parties happy, is mutual affection; where that is wanting, all is discord: but that, abstractedly considered, will not feed the body, clothe the back, or provide for the exigencies of an increasing family. Therefore, look before you leap, lest you leap into ruin, and involve the object of your delight in ruin with you, which I should be sorry to be the case with dear Miss Strong, whom I esteem, although a stranger to her, because you seem to esteem her upon valuable grounds.

I do not know enough of Miss Strong to put my negative to your union with her, whether it would be decisive or not; or to give my consent, from any conviction that she possesses known virtues and talents, to qualify her to make you a good, industrious, or an economical wife. Therefore both myself and your mother are at a loss to know how to act consistently with our duty and love to you, in regard to a question of such importance, and to give our decision upon a case, which we have only a prejudiced witness to testify of the party who is the beloved object of his wishes. I must own frankly, that had Miss Strong been one of your company, I should have shuddered at the idea of your union with such a person; but, as to all that appears concerning Miss Strong, your mother agrees with me that, upon mature deliberation between you, as your love is reciprocal, if you care for each other's welfare, enter into this union, so as not to involve yourselves in disgrace, and us in trouble,—you, being of age to judge for yourselves, have our *consent;* and God grant you his blessing, and much real happiness! But, let me remind you both, that, while I wish God's blessing on you in the rich provision of his hand, and social happiness with each other, you cannot be really or eventually happy, without you are found walking in his fear, and devoted to his service; and this, I think, my dear Charles, you are far from doing in your present situation. Your mother, sister, brother, and Mrs. Maitland, whom I saw yesterday, with all your other friends, &c. join in best wishes to you and Miss Strong.

I am, dear Charles, yours affectionately,

JAMES MATHEWS.

P.S.—Pray write to me soon about all particulars. William wrote to you last week.

In eight days after the date of the foregoing letter, the extract from the parish register now before me declares, that " Charles Mathews and Eliza Kirkham Strong were married by ' bans' on the 19th day of September, in the year one thousand seven hundred and ninety-seven, in the presence of John Wynne and Evan Francis, at Swansea;" and it may be hoped that the young husband found the society of his bride so sufficient, as to supersede for several months any *communion of soul* with distant friends; for, till the time that his ambition stirred him to remove to "new climes," all correspondence appears to have ceased with his friend Mr. Litchfield.

Human desires are ever onward,
"Man never *is*, but always *to be* blessed."

Mr. Mathews, it is true, was possessed of all the *fame* that a Welsh circuit had to bestow upon a favourite comedian, and all that esteem in private which attends upon an honest man in every part of the world. But he had married, and his dowerless wife was a daily though " sweet re- membrancer" that some addition to his income was urgently necessary to make up the sum of content and comfort. His *salary* did not exceed twelve shillings per week! but then he had be- nefits, *great* ones too, for the Lilliputian scheme he was engaged in; but all, alas! incompetent to that worldly ease which his active exertions and irreproachable habits seemed to deserve.

He had heard that *a* Mr. Emery, the principal comedian of the York company for some years past, was on the point of departure to London, and he immediately applied for his situation in a letter to Tate Wilkinson, which promptly pro- duced the following characteristic reply from that eccentric veteran. I shall subjoin those that followed, which luckily (as those of the applicant are not in existence) serve as explanation of the principal points of the comedian's rejoinders: I shall give them *verbatim*. It will be observed that they are written precisely as he would have spoken on the occasion to the same person.

Sir,   Hull, January 3rd, 1798.

Mr. Emery does *not* leave me until the end of October. Now you are an entire stranger to me, therefore it would be madness to engage a young man with a double-loaded company (as I really at present have), of whose abilities I am entirely ignorant. On the other hand, it would be madness for you next summer to come to Leeds on trial, at so heavy an expense. If you were near me, it would be practicable. What I want as Sneak, Oatland, Tom, &c. must be of great promise. Do you sing? for that is a great help in Hodge, &c. I am sir, yours, &c.

TATE WILKINSON.

Mr. Mathews, Theatre, Carmarthen.

Sir,   Hull, January 20th, 1798.

Your *cast* is a good one, but how you can perform that cast is a material question; for if you come here and are not equal to the task, why it will be a material disappointment. However, understand Mr. Emery does not leave me until the autumn, for Covent Garden Theatre; therefore, as you will have little to do but on trial, I will give you 18s. per week, from the first of June until the end of October, and double salaries at York assizes and races and Doncaster races. The journeys are nothing; and then I shall be able to judge whether you can sustain such an undertaking: if you can, it will be a fine opportunity. It

is a natural surmise, if clever, how you can be so lost in the mountains. I am sir, yours, &c.
TATE WILKINSON.

Shall be here until the 14th of February.

Mr. Mathews, Theatre, Carmarthen, Wales.

SIR, Hull, February 10th, 1798.

As a man in the mountains and not known on 'Change, added to y^r express desire of being here, convinces me you have misunderstood my meaning, for engaging you in June next. I shall want a comedian that can strike the audience well as to say, this will do, and *then* advance y^r situation; and as to coming into a first situation, and the business you wrote for, no such thing can be complied with. Mr. Emery is in full possession of fame and characters, so suit y^r convenience as to staying away. If you are with me at York 22nd of July, or August 18th, it will do. Mr. Emery will not quit me until the London theatre opens, therefore you can only play occasionally; but you will have full scope until the end of October, and then I can judge of continuance or raising of terms, according to y^r desert and success, for a good comedian only will do, if I can get him. Yours, &c.
TATE WILKINSON.

Open at York on Thursday next.

Mr. ~~Madox~~ Mathews, Theatre, Carmarthen, Wales.

One of Mr. Wilkinson's many peculiarities was that of confusing *names*. In conversation it generally happened, and the various modes of address which appear in these letters, though corrected, will show that he could not, even in writing, avoid an occasional mistake, directing his letters from memory in the first place, and, perhaps aware of his infirmity, afterwards referring to his correspondent's signature.

MR. MATHEWS, THEATRE, CARMARTHEN.

Sir, York, March 8th, 1798.

Your audience must have good stomachs to eat so long on your providings. It is the ruin of towns staying too long; but that, you will say, is not any business of mine. I can only say, be only as good as you hint, and you will be sure of my interest, and of course my will to assist you to every degree in my power. I am not prepared with any competitor; but, at present, my hopes and fears all rest on you and good behaviour. I must not make an engage^t so early as the first week in June, for, the parts being all supplied, you must be merely a cypher; consequently for y^r sake and mine, better not be here until York race-week, or the first week in September, at Leeds or Wakefield. You will then not only have an opportunity of trial, but almost immediately enter into a full field of business. And if you bring bills here that will pass at sight, they will be of much service to me, as they, if received as of true value, will do me much more essential service than my own notes, which are not always acceptable. I have heard y^r manager well spoken of as a gentleman; a happy and unusual praise to a manager. Beg he will accept my comp^{ts}. I assure you I often get into very disagreeable hobbles, by ladies and gentlemen unknown.

I have two ladies on my hands now that I wish at Carmarthen; yet the one not destitute of merit, a Mrs. Howard, daughter of a Mr. Maxwell,—a good education, good person, good wardrobe, good voice, and an income. She has played Mrs. Sullen, and neither with nor without approbation. She is in a few nights to play Calista, but I have thirteen ladies, and in that upper department much superior. The other lady came down as a lady of quality, but has not produced the certificate: it seems lost on the road. As to her abilities I know not, but she is to try in Letitia Hardy; don't think it an easy journey for her to reach Wales, if y^r manager wants such a person; but the other has rehearsed to Mr. Palmer, Wroughton, Hull,—is studied in a dozen parts in tragedy and comedy, and has played *often* at the private London Theatres, at Tottenham Court Road, and at White Chapel. Now I think such a person might serve y^r manager and herself, unless you have too many ladies. I am a great invalid, have been ill with new dislocations, strains, gout, &c. and am really poor old TATE WILKINSON.

Should Mr. Penson leave me end of May, shall be in want of service of some y^r parts: we are not on good but very bad terms; but it will not be determined until Sat. the week after Easter week. Will let you know. Let me know where to direct in April, and don't let the French again land in Wales.

This playful injunction related to a whimsical incident which took place, as I have heard my husband relate, about this period, when " the French" did actually land in Wales, but were induced to make a speedy retreat, from the conviction that the British troops were upon the spot in superior numbers, and prepared to repulse them; which conviction arose simply from the alarm of the female peasantry, who had congregated upon the mountains with a view to their safety; and their scarlet cloaks, wittles, and men's hats misled the enemy and induced them to fly.

After Mr. Mathews had determined to take his leave of his Welsh friends, (and but that "honour pricked him on," it would have been, nay, was a very painful effort,) he was naturally desirous, between the parting from one dramatic sovereign and swearing allegiance to another, to employ the interval in a visit to his family; to whom also he was anxious to present his amiable and clever wife.* The young couple, therefore, reached the paternal home—once so gloomy to Mr. Mathews —with feelings on his part which left no room for any other remembrance than the real affection he retained for his relations; while his father and mother, with as much good taste as goodness of heart, received their disobedient son in the true spirit of Christian forgiveness. It might have been supposed by the total oblivion of the past, which seemed to have been tacitly determined on, that he had been invited home by one of those

---

* At the close of Mr. Mathews's letters from Wales to Mr. Litchfield, that gentleman observes, in a note appended to the last—"There is a considerable gap in the correspondence. I suppose I must have lost some letters; but I remember during his Welsh engagement he paid a visit to London, and gratified all his friends with his vast stock (even then) of theatrical stories and imitations."

advertisements in which disconsolate parents promise, on the return of the fugitive, that no questions shall be asked: or, like one I once read in a country paper, which held out to a runaway spoiled boy the inducement, from his fond mother, that " if Richard would come back again, he should be allowed to sweeten his own tea, and not be *put upon* by his younger sister any longer."

Welcomed to London once more by his affectionate family, he had also the happiness of enjoying the society of his youthful friends—his earliest and dearest, Mr. John Litchfield, his first playmate in public, as well as in private. This gentleman's judgment he considered almost infallible; and he gave up to him his whole budget of mimic acquirements, which drew forth praise, and augury of future excellence, from the evidences given of present improvement. This opinion was a support to him in subsequent difficulties and drawbacks in his profession, and pointed out to him the road to future fame. Mr. Litchfield had also, like himself, married a young lady of great talents and engaging manners.*

With these friends the enthusiastic young couple visited all the theatres; and their pious pa-

* Mrs. Litchfield will be remembered as celebrated both in tragedy and comedy. She was some years a favourite and first-rate actress at Covent Garden, until her premature retirement from the profession she so ornamented, and which has since much missed her.

rents "asked no questions." His father saw that his son was unvitiated by *the walk* he had chosen. He found him respected by all his former friends; and those of his *new line,* who called at the house, were evidently *gentlemen,* though actors;—and, finding in his son every good quality unimpaired, (except that of bookselling,) he smiled with approbation upon him, perfectly satisfied "that nothing ill could dwell in such a temple." His wife, too, was a favourite with them, for they soon discovered a religious bent in her; and moreover rejoiced that, however poor, she had not been selected from that dreaded profession in which their son had enrolled himself;—a man might escape its contamination—a woman *could not:* so they had been told, and so they believed.

During this visit the dear kind people carefully excluded their more *serious* visiters, and no family could be happier. Mr. Mathews would even listen to "Charles's" songs and mimicry with complacency, nay, even with enjoyment; and Mrs. Mathews would give loose to a merriment she had before no idea she was capable of feeling. In short, when the time for separation arrived, it was as painful, though less bitter, to all parties, as it had been when, on the former occasion, the youth had resisted a father's will, and "rushed upon his fate."

The following letter (a little out of place here) had fixed his engagement with Tate Wilkinson;

and, at the appointed time, the young couple took their departure for Yorkshire.

May 20th, 1798.

Sir,—Don't let either of us place too great a reliance. I will engage you at 1*l.* per week, until the first Saturday in June 1799. But, to promise an increase of salary, and a certain line of business, where I have much at stake, would not be prudent on my part to give. Therefore, as to an additional salary, or a cast of parts—unseen, unknown—I cannot think of giving any such promise, as I must cast the parts as I judge. A Mr. Penson is going as well as Mr. Emery, and Mr. Penson possesses a very extensive comedy cast; so I must, with such an opening, try for the best. You may have great talents—moderate, or indifferent—all which must be judged by the manager and the public. Therefore, all the favour I have to ask is, whether you determine on being at York August the 18th. Don't neglect your interest; but don't let me rely on your coming and then *not* make your appearance:—may be disagreeable not only at the time, but as to other engagements. Mr. Penson leaves me in August.

I am, Sir, wishing you every success, yours, &c.

TATE WILKINSON.

If you possess near the merit you lead me to expect, you must not fear a good engagement *here*, *there*, or any *where*. You are sure I wish you to please. No managers part with favourite performers, but he must wish the new ones to succeed.

"MR. MATHEWS, JUN.

MATHEWS'S,

MR. MOUNTAINS, Bookseller,

No. 18, Strand,

London.

CHAPTER XI.

Arrival at Pontefract.—First interview with Tate Wilkinson.—The Manager's habit of confusing names.—Mr. Mathews's first appearance announced. — His début. —The result. — Emery. — Personal identity. —York.—Mr. Mathews's first appearance there. — Messrs. Melvin and Denman. — Mr. Rock.—Mr. T. Knight.

WITH new ardour, animated and strengthened by his present hopes, and reliances justified in some measure by the success of the last two years, this nevertheless undisciplined recruit entered somewhat rashly the front rank of the greatest dramatic general of England's provinces — the pupil of Foote—the personal friend of Garrick—and himself once a celebrated London actor. To be allowed admission was something; but to be pronounced, when there, able and worthy to maintain a prominent position in Tate Wilkinson's company was, all knew, a rapid step to advancement and promotion to the very summit of an actor's ambition; a London engagement making always the bright perspective in the view of a York favourite. That theatre was, in fact, considered a nursery and preparatory school for metropolitan performers at this period; and was, as it gave frequent proof, the very best (Bath excepted) that could be desired for the developement of incipient genius, and the maturity of rising talent.*

Early in August the young and sanguine comedian reached Pontefract, where the York company were " *located*" for a time, carrying with him all his worldly possessions — namely, a small trunk, containing his scanty wardrobe, about eight or ten comical wigs of various pretensions — a wife, and a stock of yet unsubdued animal spirits, promising better support to the young couple than the vast salary of twenty shillings per week — the extent of his expectations, even with the most brilliant success. But his partner loved him, and saw only the cheerful side of the question; and feeling how much he deserved, she could not doubt that his merits would be justly appreciated. Mrs. Mathews, however, had a mental reserve, when she expressed her conviction that they would "do very well" upon her husband's income. She was a candidate for literary gains, and relied upon her power to make

* The York and Bath theatres claim the thanks of the play-loving public, for having prepared and supplied some of the best performers that ever trod the London boards. In justification of this assertion I need only mention with reference to York, out of many, the names of Siddons, Jordan, Kemble, Cooke, Emery, and Fawcett, to show that it has " done the state some service."—A. M.

many additions to their comforts by the sweet labour of her pen; but she was timid, and would not whisper her plans until they were ripe for execution; so that her speculations were confined to her own bosom, and her husband was kept in ignorance of the mine of wealth in store for him when he least expected it.

In the mean time it was necessary, as his first duty, to present himself to his future master: accordingly, having spruced himself up in his *other* suit, he proceeded with a palpitating heart to the manager's house. After sending up his name, he was desired by the servant to walk up stairs, and in the shortest time possible found himself alone upon the first landing-place, with a choice of two doors. At a venture he tapped gently at the first, and he was immediately satisfied that it was the right one, for a drear yet authoritative voice bawled out, " Come in !" This command was reiterated with an increased force, before the palpitating heart of the person for whom it was meant would permit him to turn the lock. He thought of his interview with Macklin the terrible, and almost trembled as he entered. He had in some measure been prepared for something extraordinary in Tate's manner, by his own letters, and had endeavoured to make himself familiar with his character, by a careful perusal of " The Wandering Patentee," as this eccentric person styled himself in that entertaining work. The awe, however, felt by the aspirant at the idea of his first meeting with this celebrated man, and henceforth master of his fate, was in some measure relieved, if not removed, by his first glimpse of the figure before him, and its undignified occupation; neither of which realized any of Mr. Mathews's anticipations of the dignity of the old-school gentleman, or his preconceived notions of his consequence and superiority, and something approaching to self-possession was restored to him.

"Come in!"—the young man obeyed. Tate was shuffling about the room with a small ivory-handled brush in one hand, and a silver buckle in the other, in pretended industry, whistling during his employment after the fashion of a groom while currying and rubbing down a horse.* It was a minute at least before Tate took the least notice of the new-comer, who, in the short interval had opportunity to observe the ludicrous effect of Tate's appearance, which was indeed irresistibly droll. He was still in his morning's dishabille, which did not consist of the usual undress of men of his standing, who generally

* It appeared that it was his custom daily to polish his own buckles; for as these particular buckles (small silver shoe-buckles) were especial favourites, from having been the gift of his friend the immortal Garrick, and were worn constantly in his dress shoes, he was chary of allowing others the privilege of touching them; in fact, he never trusted them out of his own hands.—A. M.

indulged in a copious *robe de chambre*, easy slippers, and the Dilworth cap, to relieve the formality and confinement of a wig. Tate's early dress did not differ from the later one in which he appeared after the busy part of his day was finished. But "he wore his rue with a difference," that is, at this period, his coat collar was thrown back upon his shoulders, and his Brown George (a wig so called in compliment, I believe, to King George the Third, who set the fashion,) on one side, exposing the ear on the other, and cocked up behind so as to leave the bare nape of his neck open to observation. His hat was put on *side* foremost, and as forward and awry as his wig; both were perked on his head very insecurely, as it seemed to the observer. He presented altogether what might be called an *uncomfortable* appearance, and which to those who were in the habit of seeing him at other times, might be supposed to be contrived as a striking contrast to his precise and *smug* effect after he had made his toilette, when he was particularly neat.

When the young actor entered, he caught the back view of this strange figure, which made no movement either of courtesy or curiosity. Mr. Mathews, after an unsuccessful cough, and a few significant *hems*, which seemed to solicit welcome and attention, ventured at last upon an audible "Good morning, sir." This had its effect, and the following colloquy ensued. "Good morning, sir," said Mr. Mathews.—" Oh! good morning, *Mr. Meadows*," replied Tate very doggedly.— " My name is *Mathews*, sir,"—" Ay, I know," wheeling suddenly round, and looking at him for the first time with scrutinizing earnestness from head to foot. Winking his eyes and lifting his brows rapidly up and down, a habit with him when not pleased, he uttered a long drawn "U—gh!" and exclaimed, "What a maypole!— Sir, you 're too *tall* for low comedy."—" I 'm sorry, sir," said the poor disconcerted youth; but Tate did not seem to hear him, for dropping his eyes and resuming the brushing of his buckles, he continued as if in soliloquy: " But I don't know why a tall man shouldn't be a very comical fellow." Then again turning sharply for a reinvestigation of the slender figure before him, he added with gathering discontent, "You 're too *thin*, sir, for anything but the Apothecary in 'Romeo and Juliet;' and you would want stuffing for *that*."—" I am *very* sorry, sir," rejoined the mortified actor, who was immediately interrupted by the growing distaste and manifest ill humour of the disappointed manager.

"What 's the use of being *sorry?* You speak too *quick*." The accused anxiously assured him that he would endeavour to mend that habit. " What," said Tate snappishly, " by speaking *quicker*, I suppose." Then, looking at Mr. Mathews, he, as if again in soliloquy, added, " I never saw anybody so thin to be *alive!!* Why, sir, one hiss would blow you off the stage." This remark sounding more like good humour than anything he had uttered, the comedian ventured, with a faint smile, to observe, that he *hoped he should not get that one* — when Tate, with affected or real anger, replied, " You'll get a great many, sir. Why sir, *I've* been hissed—the great Mr. Garrick has been hissed; it's not very modest in *you* to expect to escape, Mr. Mountain."—"*Mathews,* sir," interposed the miscalled. " Well, Matthew *Mountain.*"—" No, sir—" — " Have you a quick study, Mr. Maddox ?" asked Tate, interrupting him once more. Mathews gave up the ineffectual attempt to preserve his proper name, and replied at once to the last question, " I *hope* so, sir," " Why" (in a voice of thunder) "arn't you *sure?*" "Ye-e-es, sir," asserted his terrified and harassed victim. Tate shuffled up and down the room, whistling and brushing rapidly, looking from time to time with evident dissatisfaction, if not disgust, at the object of his scrutiny ; and, after several of these furtive glances, he suddenly desisted from his occupation, and once more stopped abruptly before him.

It must be understood, that in Tate's first surprise he had neglected to offer his visiter a seat; therefore Mr. Mathews had remained standing near the door, relieving his weariness, after a long journey, by alternately shifting his position, like a pupil taking his first lesson from a dancing-master;

and leaning sometimes upon one foot and then upon the other, in awkward embarrassment. Tate, as I have observed, stopped and inquired if he was a single man? Of course, he replied in the negative. "I'm sorry for it, *Mr. Montague;* a wife's a dead weight without a salary, and I don't choose my actors to run in debt."—"I hope you will have no cause to complain of me in that respect, sir." Tate was again busy with his buckle; an obstinate tarnish, "a damned spot," called for his most vehement exertion; yet he spared a look or two at his visiter's face. At last, he seemed to have collected all his moral force, and, after another pause, he demanded, "Pray, when did you have that paralytic stroke, Mr. Maddox?" "I—I never had one at all, sir," said the now completely mortified youth, with difficulty restraining the tears which were making their way to his eyes; when Tate, giving him another earnest look, and as if unconsciously drawing his own mouth awry in imitation of the one which had suggested the last question, answered dryly and significantly, in Mr. Mathews's tone of voice, as he turned away, "Oh! I thought you *had!*"

All this was inauspicious; and, after the interview had lasted a few minutes longer, Tate strongly recommending the young man's return to his father, and an "honest trade," as he said, all that could be gained by Mr. Mathews was the manager's slow leave to let him enter upon his probation, and at least have a trial before final condemnation. Thus dispirited, he returned to his anxious wife, with the saddest impressions and anticipations. However, after a few days, his morning observations of the play-bills were cheered by the sight of his own name—*really* his name. *Mr. Mathews, from the Theatre Royal, Dublin,* (for Tate would not own a "man from the mountains,") was announced to appear in the character of *Silky,* in " The Road to Ruin," and *Lingo,* in " The Agreeable Surprise."

Mr. Mathews's first appearance was unattended with any of that "pomp and circumstance" usually so inspiring to the debutant. Nothing before or behind the curtain marked him as being considered an object of importance: besides, the town was one of no consequence, and could neither make nor mar the reputation of an actor—not even critical. Tate called it the *Montpellier* of Yorkshire; and I believe the air of the place, and other local prejudices, unconnected with his managerial interests, induced his annual remove to Pomfret with his company, so that no sensation was created for or against the new performer. If any feeling was produced by his appearance, it was probably to his disadvantage, their established favourite, Emery, having satisfied them that no other actor could exceed, few equal him; and probably the recollection of their brightest star rendered that of the night dim in comparison. His self-possession, too, shaken as it was by Tate's evident mean opinion of his talents, and predisposition, as it seemed, to crush his efforts, possibly and naturally affected his exertions, and made them fiat. In short, he retired from the scene of his first public trial without any definite impression of whether he had succeeded or not. Tate shunned him, the actors silently pitied him, but none praised him; and, in a few nights after, he was to be seen performing *Kenrick,* an old sentimental Irishman, in " The Heir at Law," and an *interesting* bespangled page in a serious *ballet* — the gentle *Theodore,* in " Raymond and Agnes!"

Mr. Emery, whom he fondly hoped to succeed, treated him, however, in the most friendly manner. He was playing a round of his favourite characters, previously to his departure for London; his successor, therefore, could not expect much to do before that gentleman's term had expired. This conviction, and the gratification he felt in nightly witnessing that great artist's performances, (though in many parts utterly unsuited to his talents,) in a great measure soothed and supported him; and the part of *Rundy,* in " The Farmer," in which Emery performed *Jemmy Jumps,* elated him with the hope that he might, by these small opportunities, at least prepare the audience for greater things. In that day " The Flaxen-headed Cow-boy" was a popular song;

and Mr. Mathews took great pains with it, and literally *whistled* " O'er the Lea," as symphony.* Still all was "stale, flat, and unprofitable ;" and he calmed his wounded self-love by the fact, that while Emery stayed no one else would be noticed. He was obliged to repeat his insipid *ballet* character, for which he always dressed with a heavy heart, notwithstanding the splendid jewel and plume of feathers which Miss Duncan had kindly lent him for his hat!

In this way matters proceeded : the young actor, for the most part, dragging on his time in most inglorious ease, (not of mind, it may be believed,) but free from personal exertion. His spirits, however, remained, and hope was kept alive by their aid; though, when he remembered the favouritism he enjoyed in his late situation, the perfect delight with which he was received by his Welsh friends, their good-hearted warm support and regard, and contrasted his feelings at that time with his present state, he could hardly

* Those who have seen these actors in their respective lines in London, will smile at the idea of Emery, the *Rustic*, performing a light foppish character, of rather burlesque humour, in a dandy dress of that period, and attempting rapid enunciation and singing, while Mathews, in a *countryman*, trying to give effect to a merely *pretty air*, and whistling to it with sentimental precision, must amuse all who were in later years acquainted with him. Had these actors changed characters in the piece, each would have been fitted to their best line of acting, as it was afterwards proved.—A. M.

at times believe in his own identity; and, indeed, a startling evidence happened about this time, to place him in further doubt upon this subject, and afford the company some amusement. One morning, when in a nothing-to-do lounging humour, he had joined a knot of the actors at the door of the theatre, (a custom they indulged in in hot weather during rehearsal, between their particular scenes, the green-room being close and sombre in such small buildings,) he perceived Emery standing at a short distance, talking to a large, gaunt figure of a man, who, from time to time, seemed to eye Mr. Mathews with interest, and at last even with anger! His glances were significant of much surprise at first, and ultimately of defiance. At length, Emery took leave of his companion, who departed with a severe look at the object of his interest; and the cause of the excitement manifested by the stranger was explained. The man, it seems, was a Sheffield knife-maker, a person of respectability in his way, who had some previous acquaintance with Emery, whom he addressed in a broad Yorkshire dialect, as follows, after the first greeting:—

" Why, I see you ha' gotten a new hand come to your troop! How long has *he* been wi' you?"—" Which do you mean?" said Emery.—" Why, that lank chap i' t' brown coit." — " Oh," said Emery, " about a fortnight."—" Dom it, I niver should ha' expected to have seen him wi' a coompany of *lakers*."*—" What, then," replied Emery, with surprise, " you *know* him?"—" To be sure I do," said the man sharply —" he's *hugged* † goods for me in Sheffield market mony's the time."— " Oh," said Emery, " you're mistaken; it couldn't be him."—" Not him!" (said the man indignantly) " as if I didn't know him!"—" Why," added Emery, " I don't believe he was ever in Sheffield or any part of Yorkshire, till he arrived here."— " No! Why, where does he *say* he came from?" —" From London, and his name is Mathews."— " Mathews be *dommed!* his name's Jemmy Laycock."—" Oh, no, indeed; his name is Mathews," replied Emery.—" His name is devil!" roared out the exasperated knife-dealer; " his name, I tell you, is Jemmy Laycock; and if he tells *me* it's not, I'll knock him down." So much for *identity*.

Mr. Mathews often saw the *hardware*-man after this; but, as may be imagined, kept a prudent distance from his *personal* greeting and his iron fist, which always appeared to his imagination ready clenched, in order to enforce his recognition. It was not, however, to be expected that so good a theme for jesting could be overlooked by the wags of the theatre, who were not disposed to let off poor " Jemmy" so easily as his Sheffield patron had done; so that many a practical joke

---

* *Lake* in the Yorkshire dialect means *play*. They say, " Wilt lake at cards?" &c.; so actors (players) are among the vulgar invariably termed " lakers."—A. M.   † *Carried.*

ensued, and the following was one of long continuance.

There was allowed to wander about the little town of Pomfret, to fright the eye (and ear) from its propriety, a half-crazed old woman of the most squalid and disgusting appearance, with a screaming cry after every stranger for money. "Gi' me ha'penny! gi' me ha'penny!" was her form of importunity; which in the event of refusal, was followed by—"Away wi' ye! away wi' ye!" in the most piercing tones, close to the ear of the unlucky person accosted, while she pursued him.

This woman, Emery induced to attack Mr. Mathews whenever she saw him, with the cry of "Jemmy Laycock, Jemmy Laycock, gi' me ha'penny! gi' me ha'penny!" reiterating the hateful name as often as time and occasion permitted: and every year after, her too tenacious memory (and the profit accruing therefrom,) prompted her to follow him with this tormenting cry. From the theatre at night, however late, it would accompany him on his way home; and even after he had closed his cottage-lodging door upon the beldam, "Jemmy Laycock! Jemmy Laycock!" filled the hollow of his ear. During supper it assailed him, and in bed and asleep, "Echo prolonged the tale," after the hag had disappeared, and shrieked the baneful sounds, which "made night hideous" to him.

The time having arrived when the company prepared to go to York for a week, the would-be comedian's hopes revived. *There* he *might* make some impression. *There* might be found judicious persons who might see his merit. Fortunately it happened that two new performers, who promised to be of importance to the concern, wished to open in " The Road to Ruin." Messrs. Melvin and Denman were to perform *Young* and *Old Dornton*, Emery, *Goldfinch!* This gave Mr. Mathews the advantage of appearing in his favourite part of *Silky*, in the same play; and, oh happiness! once more in *Lingo*. His efforts were more noticed and more successful than at Pontefract; his manner was more assured, and altogether his reception was very creditable to him: *that* night he and his poor wife retired to their humble home, elated and full of hope. The next day, however, showed him in capital letters *Mr. Rock's* name, announced in a principal comedian's character; with the boast that he came from the Theatre Royal, Edinburgh.* This was a blow. Two *Richmonds* in the field! What could Tate want with *him*, if he (Mathews) was to be retained? Well, Mr. Rock's success was not brilliant; yet enough to depress all Mathews's hope of succeeding to that portion of Emery's business

* Mr. Rock was afterwards a favourite performer in what is technically called the "low Irishmen," at Covent Garden Theatre.

he so much coveted, namely, the *old men;* and it was with an aching heart that he saw Rock advertised for his favourite, *Lord Duberly,* in " The Heir at Law." It is true that he did not regret to see the part of *Kenrick* transferred (though without consulting him,) to a more fitting representative (Denman); yet he sighed when he beheld himself again in green and gold, figuring away in the odious ballet, which, as if to torture him, was a favourite everywhere; and the measure of his discontent was full. He now appeared amongst the *chorus* in " The Castle Spectre," too; but to atone for this, *Rundy* was repeated: though the York audience seemed as little impressed with his plough-boy song and whistled symphony, as the Pontefract folk had been. At this time Mr. T. Knight, then a celebrated London actor, (who married a sister of Miss Farren, afterwards Countess of Derby,) came to perform as a star; so that having nothing given him to do with this gentleman but the respective Governors in " The Chapter of Accidents," and " The Critic," the poor young actor's hope was so deferred, as to make his heart sick indeed.

CHAPTER XII.

Dispiriting treatment.—Ill health.—Emery's departure to fulfil his engagement at Covent Garden Theatre.—Mr. Mathews's letter introducing him to Mr. Litchfield. — Hull. — Mr. Mathews's opening character.—Fresh mortifications.—Mr. Hatton's arrival.—Another disappointment.—The consequences. — Mr. Mathews's letter of remonstrance to the manager. — Tate Wilkinson's reply.—Increasing success of Mr. Mathews. — His letter to Mr. Litchfield announcing Hatton's discharge.—Triumph of industry and integrity.—Letter to Mr. Litchfield from Doncaster.

THUS matters went on. Not a gleam of sunshine to clear his clouded way. Emery, feeling for the young actor's situation, had lent him *Lingo* for his opening part at York; but, as a matter of course, resumed it when the piece was again played, by the manager's command. Emery, indeed, was consistent in his kindness to him from the moment they met; and I believe tried to induce him either to return to Wales, or to resign the profession altogether. The first part of his advice he would not follow, for he knew even then, inexperienced as he was in such matters, that to return to a place where he had been a favourite, to confess his utter failure in a higher sphere, would be folly, and utterly to lose caste in his former scene of triumph. The second he *could* not follow; for his only alternative would have been to throw himself and his wife helpless into his father's arms for shelter and provision. This thought was not to be entertained. His health continued weakly; symptoms of consumption, the fatal malady of his family, and which had swept away eleven of his brothers and sisters, now seemed to show themselves decidedly, and added to his difficulties; his chest was confined, his lungs precarious; in the morning he felt all exertion of them painful, often impossible, and seldom found himself able to sing at rehearsals.

He would spit blood upon the slightest bodily exertion, and was subject to fits: I do not know what they were called, but they would cause him to fall upon the ground senseless, after a slight convulsion, to the terror of all present. I understood that these seldom assailed him except under circumstances of mental agitation. To this infliction he had been subject from his birth; and, as he mentions in the early part of this book, they were the occasion of his distorted mouth. Strange to say, in the year 1802 they ceased for ever. I once witnessed the effect of his misfortune, when the sufferer remained unconscious for at least a quarter of an hour. Yet with all these drawbacks, he somehow, by the force of his constitutional buoyancy of spirit, sustained himself; and when not controlled by some recent check to his favourite wishes as an actor, was the life and soul of the green-room; enlivening by his vivacity all those who, unlike himself, had all the means of cheerfulness without his aid, yet wanted and sought it. In fact, his mercurial spirits, high principles, and good conduct, recommended and endeared him to all those whose regard was worth securing, and made imperceptible, but progressive way with Tate himself, who often praised the *man*, while he disliked the *actor*. In the company there were several well-educated gentlemen, with whom he formed a pleasant association, and with one or two of them, a sincere and lasting friendship. He wanted nothing more to content him, but a little wholesome encouragement in his darling pursuit, but this he seemed destined to be denied. In September, Emery took his departure for London, bearing with him the following letter, which I insert, because it shows the friendly disposition which these two comedians cherished towards each other, under such unequal circumstances. It also gives additional evidence of the candour and judgment of the one, of the talents of others, when his own were doubted, and his experience new.

TO MR. JOHN LITCHFIELD.

Dear Litchfield, Wakefield, Sept. 12th, 1798.

I know how willing you are to oblige me; and that you cannot do more effectually than by once more showing civility where I request it. The bearer of this is Mr. Emery. He is come up to take — no, make his trial in London. I know him well; and I assure you he is every way worthy of your notice. We have been very intimate; and I have found him a very worthy fellow. As he is an entire stranger in London, if you will ask him to call, *en passant*, at Tavistock Row, and direct him to the streets he may wish to find, I will thank you. Of his merit as a comedian, I think very highly; but as you must and will, ay, and can judge for yourself, it is needless for me to enter into a detail of his abilities. His best line of acting, in my opinion, is " countrymen;" *Zekiel Homespun*, *Frank Oatland*, &c. He is fond of " old men," of which *Crazy*, *Nicholas*, and such feeble men, are best. He is advised to open, if he can, in *Zekiel;* and I hope he may succeed, at least, in time, as very few actors have been established at once. A bad voice is his only disadvantage. Do what you can to assist him, for he has merit, if you will but find it out.

Be assured I am unalterably yours,
C. Mathews.

P. S. Thank you for your good word in " The Mirror."* The manager thinks I write the accounts myself, nay, told me so.

We move from hence to Doncaster in a fortnight.

---

* A magazine devoted exclusively to theatricals, of which Mr. Litchfield was editor at this time.—A. M.

Direct to me here, at Mrs. Boon's, New Street, Wakefield, Yorkshire.

Mr. John Litchfield, Tavistock Row, Covent Garden.

Emery was gone, (one thorn was thus plucked out,) but Rock remained, firm as his very name. He was not, indeed, a great favourite; yet he retained all the parts of weight and worth; and if the young actor occasionally had one of consequence intrusted to him, it was under unfavourable circumstances, and because there was no one else to be preferred. On the company's arrival in Hull (the next principal town to York in the circuit), poor Mr. Mathews saw himself announced (his first appearance) for *Cymon,* in the farce of "The Irishman in London," a most insignificant character of a few lines, and generally given to third or fourth-rate comedians, in order to present Mr. Rock in a favourite character to the Hull audience. This act at once showed the young man how little progress he had made in the manager's favour in a professional point of view; and that annoying ballet again exhibited him in action before, probably, the ridicule of audiences who witnessed his untaught attempts at serious pantomime. All this degradation, all the rubs and hinderances he had encountered, had however hitherto failed to depress his spirits, till, all at once, the dreadful cause of his having had so insignificant a part assigned him for his first appearance, presented itself to him in the palpable form of a Mr. Hatton,* ostentatiously announced to appear in characters which at once *tolled* to the heart of poor Mathews the death-knell of all his expectations. Mr. Hatton was evidently sent for on his presumed failure.

This person was a man of no genius, but of a certain theatrical tact, possessed by those brought up behind the scenes. His perceptions were coarse, but often effective. Hatton had probably heard that the non-success of Mathews was the basis of his own engagement; and he immediately made vigorous use of his advantage. His opening part was *Lenitive* in " The Prize." Mathews thought himself lucky to have *Label* " intrusted" to him; and when the time came, the coarse features of Hatton's florid style completely threw into shade the delicate outline of the timid and depressed young man he had come to supersede. Yet, there seemed on this occasion something more like good humour in the audience towards the stripling *Label* than the performer of it had before experienced; which being perceived by Hatton, he maliciously resolved to check; for, in the scene where *Label* lays claim to individual merit in having procured patients for his master, and boasts of having succeeded in making the

* Afterwards a subordinate performer at the Haymarket Theatre, when Mr. Mathews was an established first comedian there in 1805.—A. M.

mayor's family sick, Hatton, with great dexterity of purpose, observed, that "Such a fellow was enough to make anybody sick!" This sally turned the whole temper of the audience, which, with a simultaneous shout of assent to *Lenitive's* assertion, upset the small degree of confidence which Mr. Mathews had acquired, and the rest of the part fell under the weight of Hatton's boisterous efforts, which met with the approbation of the vulgar, however the judicious might grieve.

Hatton had the best parts in Emery's line, (which, as is customary in country theatres, included all the principal parts of "low-comedy,") and for a time they kept him up; but he was a careless, thoughtless actor, whose habits in private life were not calculated to enable him to keep his hold in a circuit where character was as much noticed off as on the stage. Not possessing ability for the first-rate station in which he had placed himself, he naturally fell lower by degrees in favour with the audience, while the hitherto unsuccessful candidate for dramatic fame, by patience, good conduct, and inherent merit, as gradually asserted his powers, and, depressed as they had been, and driven back, at last made themselves felt and appreciated. Genius, like murder, "will out." In fact, his humble perseverance, his watchful readiness to do any and everything required, eventually overcame all obstructions.

His trials, however, were not yet over. He had not yet a release from Mr. Hatton's overbearing triumphs, which he endured with most gentlemanlike forbearance. At length a provocation, an injustice, as he conceived, in the face of his manifest deservings, occurred. *Frank Oatland* was assigned to Mr. Hatton; a part in which Mr. Mathews had really gained some credit since Emery's departure; and his favourite *Rundy* was also wrested from him, without any reason being given. In lieu of these he was obliged to exercise his genius in comic as well as serious pantomime, and to play the clown to Mr. Hatton's harlequin; who announced his intention, for his own benefit, to leap through an oven of fire and a brilliant sun. Alas! the sun of the poor clown seemed set for ever by this degradation. These accumulated causes induced him to address a letter of remonstrance to "the manager," (as Tate was called *par excellence,*) who was at the time "ill at ease, and would admit no visitors." This produced the following reply, which may be deemed a fair specimen of the critic's temper towards the person addressed, remaining at the same time as a warning instance of prejudiced opinion and perverted judgment. It must be considered a rarity of its kind, and was preserved by Mr. Mathews ever after with the most guarded care.

TO MR. MATHEWS.

I am dangerously ill, therefore unable to attend to theatrical grievances. After a 2^d and a 3^d time seeing y^r performance, I *aver'd*, and *do aver* that *Misfortune* has placed an insurmountable bar as to the possibility of y^r *ever* being capable of sustaining the first line of comic business. Mr. Emery I requested to inform you of the same at Wakefield, who was entirely of my opinion. For the *paralytic* stroke,* so far from a comic effect, renders y^r performance *seriously disagreeable*. I told Mr. Hill† that not all the Mirrors in the kingdom, in print or in glass, ever can establish you for a first comedian. If God wills it, it will be so, but no other order or interest can effect such a miracle. If you were to hear how you are spoken of (ask Mr. Jarman‡), you would not rely too much on y^r unbounded applause at Hull. If you had ask'd at Wakefield if you were to play the characters you mention, Mr. Jarman would readily have told you, No. If you think the company is in general approv'd, you are mistaken; am sorry to be told, quite the contrary. Y^r *Rundy* is very bad indeed; so is *Motley*. *Rundy* they have been used to see really well acted. As to *Jabal* for Mr. Hatton, it was his first request which I granted, as Mr.

---

* It appears that the writer's impression on his first interview with Mr. Mathews, that the irregularity of his features was occasioned by a paralytic attack, had not been removed, although Mr. Mathews at the time denied that he had ever been visited by such a misfortune.—A. M.

† Mr. Hill was the proprietor of "The Monthly Mirror," the magazine mentioned by Mr. Mathews as having praised his acting.

‡ Mr. Jarman was the prompter of the theatre.

Jarman can testify. Do you think I engaged Mr. Hatton to hurt you? On my honor, *no*. If you say, why add to my expense? I answ^r, *necessity*, and full conviction stared me in the face. Try by degrees to be useful, and by such means get into respect. Y$_r$ worth as a man (as far as I know) I much esteem; but as a first-rate actor, you must try some more discerning leader, and officer some other troop. I think " Feeble Old Men" is a cast you are most likely to be *useful* in. The pain I have suffered at my breast in scratching these lines is more piercing than what you feel at the loss of *Frank*. You have youth, sobriety, and assiduity, which sometimes does wonders. Wish Emery had been more open with you. I recommended the shop, as suited to you and Mrs. M.; but he said you were so stage-bitten it would only vex you. I can only say, Stay and be happy, or Go and be happy; and ever be happy; and wishing myself better, am y^{rs} in great pain,

Tate Wilkinson.

Notwithstanding this letter, poor Mr. Mathews remained submissive to his fate, which he may truly be said to have thus ultimately conquered; for before the close of that year he saw the departure of his rivals, and found himself in possession of all the parts so long withheld from him. Mr. Hatton, overbearing in his fancied security, became negligent of his duty, and careless in the execution of it. At such times Mr. Mathews was ever ready to come forward and undertake anything necessary to the manager's interest. His study was miraculous, and he could always be *depended upon;* his principle, in all he did, to be just to his employer and fair to his brethren, gradually made his way. By degrees he acquired confidence from trust, and his powers became more and more apparent; so that, in the autumn of this year, on my arrival in Hull, I found him the principal comedian of the company, and a prodigious favourite with his audience and the manager. I had not, to be sure, much judgment, or the least experience in dramatic excellence, but I can remember thinking him "a very funny young man," though, as Tate said, the "thinnest" I had ever seen "to be alive." I suspect, his *Sentinel* in the play of "Pizarro" made little impression upon me, for I do not now remember seeing him at all till he appeared in the farce of "The Rival Soldiers," as *Nipperkin;* and in that his performance convulsed me with laughter from the beginning to the end.*

His overbearing rival gradually fell off in the manager's opinion, and in the estimation of the public. Mr. Mathews rose in proportion as Hatton fell, who, as the following letter will explain, was eventually compelled to leave the field open to his worthy competitor.

* Those who have seen him perform at the Adelphi, the first year he became part proprietor of that theatre, the Tinker (*Caleb Pipkin,*) in Mr. Buckstone's drama of "The May Queen," may form some notion of him in the part of *Nipperkin*, both characters requiring the same sort of humour.

TO MR. JOHN LITCHFIELD.

Dear Jack, York, April 28th, 1799.

I think I am still gaining ground with audience and manager. We have had a very good and pleasant season here; and close on the 12th of May. Then to Leeds. Kemble comes here in August, for the race-week. Hatton and Miss Comellys are both discharged; and I have been more comfortable since the critics have been quiet. I would not be praised again for a double salary. Senex's remarks were Denman's. Adieu. Remembrance to Mrs. L.

Yours sincerely,
Charles Mathews.

It is worthy of remark, how simply the above announcement is given to his friend and confident. It might have been expected that, after all the insults and overbearing conduct of his successful rival, something like triumph on his defeat would be expressed by the person who had so long suffered under his vulgar tyranny, and at length risen superior to him. But his nature was mild and forgiving, however irritable his temper might have become by repeated trials and bodily pain in later years; and his easily-appeased dislike to any one who had annoyed him, was as admirable as his known forgiveness of injuries.

From this time Mr. Mathews kept undisputed possession of his advantage. His comic singing was most particularly admired, though confined in those days merely to songs of epigrammatic point, or humorous detail; all mainly dependent for their effect upon the quaintness and oddity of his style in singing them: thus, as a local writer once observed in reference to his early struggles, " Mr. Mathews became a living instance of what may be effected by perseverance. It rendered him one of the most popular actors that ever appeared in the Yorkshire theatres."

Mr. Mathews, it may be imagined, became another creature from the time he found himself raised from the depressing position of a third-rate actor to that of the first; and had any increase to his income accompanied his success, he would have had no alloy to his satisfaction.

Poor Mrs. Mathews's projects of gain by her publications had all terminated in disappointment. She, like her husband, had been a triton among the minnows, and flattered into vanity by the partiality of her friends, who thought her poetry agreeable, and not being disposed to be critical upon a young lady's verses, written, as it appeared, for private circulation, had said more in commendation than they might have done had she then meditated the publication of her efforts. It was not to be expected that two people, even with habits of the most provident kind, could possibly exist upon eighteen shillings per week; and the non-success of Mr. Mathews having precluded any profits from his benefit, of any consequence,* it was not extraordinary that some debts had been contracted, especially as he had firmly abstained from applying to his family for aid. But still he worked on; and still Mrs. Mathews wrote: neither of them to any increase of their pecuniary means.

These considerations began now to make him restless; and the state of his feelings may be gleaned from the following letter to his friend and confident in London.

TO MR. LITCHFIELD.

Dear Jack,   Doncaster, Oct. 6th, 1799.

How you manage to get through the different concerns of office and "Mirror,"† I cannot understand, particularly as the last must require so much *reflection*. I wish it had been in your power to accept of good old Tate's invitation. I need not say what pleasure it would have afforded me and Mrs. M.; but I must submit. It is the only drawback I ever feel from the pleasures of my profession, that I am at such a distance from relations, friends, and companions of my youth. Ah! Jack, if ever I should be invited to London by either of those gentlemen you men-

---

* Tate's provident wisdom and humane consideration for his actors, had established terms for the "benefits," which preserved those who ventured to take them, from loss: the York plan being, for the performer to share with the manager all exceeding 5*l*. It therefore could scarcely happen but that something must be gained, however small the total receipts might turn out.—A. M.

† The Monthly Mirror before spoken of.

tion, and could only obtain a tolerable footing in either of the theatres, I should indeed be happy! If I could but once be established in London, no inducement on earth could possibly make me even wish to quit the profession. I am fonder of it than ever. I begin to consider it more of a science than I ever have done before. Since I came to Yorkshire I have been convinced of the necessity of great study, even in low comedy, which many actors I meet with think unnecessary; and that study endears me to the profession. But " London, dear London!" as *Archer* says, I look forward to as the reward of all the struggles and labours I have experienced. When you recollect some little *trifles* I endured under the management of Daly, you must allow that I did not begin my career very propitiously, and that I ought to be allowed some little merit for perseverance.

I have now every reason to be satisfied, for, next to London, this is one of the best situations. Wilkinson is one of the most generous men, and *certainly* the most generous *manager* in the world; yet, though I must allow I am very comfortably situated, I should not like to pass all my life in a country theatre. The most material objection must strike you in a moment to be, the small salary which they can afford in such a situation. Though it is true there are many that save money, I am very sure I never shall here; and that is a great object after all. Every actor hopes to go to London, who has any love of fame. I think, my dear Jack, that I have now some rational hopes that I may one day pay a visit there; but this is *entre nous*, for I would not be accused of vanity. My success here has flattered me. I was pleased with the approbation of my Welsh friends; but I could not place proper dependence on the judgment of people who admired my predecessor, who was a most miserable dog. Here, however, it is otherwise; they have been used to see good acting; and the company has always been excellent. The manager too, from experience, must be capable of judging; and his approbation is to me worth " a whole theatre of others!"—Shakspeare! hem!

If I could but take three or four inches from my height, I should fear nothing; but it is useless to lament; and of this I am sure, that perseverance and industry will accomplish wonders. If Suett would but tipple harder, and tip off in three or four years, I should like to hazard an appearance. That is certainly the line I must succeed in, in the opinion of the manager, after the " feeble old men," which, he swears, are fifty degrees beyond everything else; and I think so myself, fortunately; such as *Silky, Kecksey, Crazy,** &c. I almost feel happy in *Endless, Stave,* &c. in which, as they were written for Suett, my unfortunate figure cannot be thrown in my teeth.

Heaven defend me from getting fat—that is all! If that should be the case, there will be an end of everything—all my hopes in Suett will be destroyed. Though I should be a scarecrow in my old age, I hope I may still continue to be able to count my ribs with my fingers. That is the only chance of my looking comical. A great fat *low* comedian—oh, Lord! oh, Lord! †— all I should have left for my comfort would be, to be, as old Hurst said of me, " an imitating rascal; a tall, cut-down, taking-off scoundrel!" Do you remember the Bull's eye, Cox's museum, and Daly in his box? I

---

* *Silky,* in " The Road to Ruin;" *Kecksey,* in " The Irish Widow;" and *Crazy,* in " Peeping Tom;" all admirable performances of his.—A. M.

† Mr. John Reeve gave him a new view of the subject.—A. M.

had the satisfaction of making you laugh at that — and my greatest pleasure is, in being laughed at. Do not think me sanguine and vain. I should not have said thus much to you, but the names of Sheridan and Harris roused me, and I may say, provoked me to it. We shall rob you of Mrs. Siddons, I fancy, for a month or two yet.. She played here six nights, and concluded her engagement on Friday, for her "benefit," when she played the two Catherines, as at York.* At present, she is gone to Sheffield, to Macready; and opens to-morrow night. We do not see her again till we go to Hull, where she will again join us. But, if I recollect, the manager told me yesterday, he had enclosed you a bill—it was either to you or " Levi the Jew," I don't know which.† *Rolla*, Mr. Macready.‡ I entreat you to procure me that same scene of *Quotem's*, if it is to be got, without delay.

Mrs. M. is corresponding with Ben Thompson, though she never saw him. She had to alter Adelaide of Walfingen, for my "benefit" at Hull; and wrote to him for approbation; submitting her plan. He has behaved very politely, and has sent two or three other pieces, which he thinks better adapted for representation; and he recommends one called "The Indian Exiles," which, I think, will be the piece. I build great hopes upon it, as he is a native of Hull, and may probably interest himself for us. Do you know him? If you do, and if you

* *Queen Catherine*, and *Catherine* in "Catherine and Petruchio."—A. M.

† This refers to the manager's habit of wandering in conversation and confounding one subject with another.—A. M.

‡ Father of the present great tragedian, the original actor in London of *Murtock Delany*, a comic Irishman, in his own farce of "The Irishman in London."—A. M.

could, without any awkward sensations, just say that there is a person in the York company whom you know, and that any service or notice, &c.—that if he should visit Hull—you understand me.

Does Suett look well? Does he drink much? hey? comfort me. We stay here six weeks; then to Hull for the winter. Remember me to Hill, Grove, &c. and be assured I am unalterably yours,

CHARLES MATHEWS.

CHAPTER XIII.

Haunted Room.—Eccentrics of Tate Wilkinson's company.—Johnny Winter, the wardrobe-keeper and tailor.—Kemble and Shakspeare.—Dress for a bishop.—Johnny and a dramatic aspirant.—Mr. Mathews in *Caleb Quotem.*—" Charlie Wood's" benefit.—Winter's ambition for a horse.—Johnny and the manager.—Marriage of Johnny's daughter.—Stephen Kemble's new dress.—Mrs. Siddons.

ONE of the most uncomfortable results from the poor income of Mr. Mathews was the almost impossibility of obtaining, upon the terms to which he was compelled to limit himself, a lodging for himself and Mrs. Mathews of a respectable and comfortable kind. In York this was a more difficult thing than at the smaller places, where cottage effect and summer atoned for more solid recommendations. It was necessary that he should live in the immediate vicinity of the theatre, and here was the difficulty, for it stood in the heart of the town and its gentility. He was told that a very good and reasonable lodging was to be had in Stonegate (the very spot he would have chosen), but that a recent report of the rooms being *haunted,* and which formed the ground of their cheapness, would probably deter him from thinking of it as a residence. It was the house which Sterne had inhabited, and a particular room in it, the one in which he was said to have written his *Tristram Shandy*, was shown as a temptation. No one, however, would stay there; many had tried, but a few days saw them depart, all going for the same reason—namely, that the rooms were *certainly haunted*. Mrs. Mathews was not superstitious, neither was she weak upon such points; and the very idea of sitting where Sterne sat, of writing where he wrote, was quite enough for her to induce her husband to enter upon these rooms immediately. This he was most glad to do; for the advantages they presented above all others as to price and situation, as well as superiority of comfort, rendered him anxious to overlook the affirmed drawback, which touched him not a jot.

The young couple straightway took possession. The landlady, a widow woman, "well to do," yet glad to do better than well by receiving a portion of her rent from the use of the rooms she had no occasion for, received her lodgers with marked attention, and did all in her power to render them content, made light of the cause of the house being so shunned, and frankly told them that she lived in it herself because she found it impossible to get a tenant who would take it altogether off her hands; but, if there was a ghost it was a harmless one, as her sojourn of years had proved, for it had done no injury to her or any one. (Indeed, *she* had not been disturbed by it, as it was a ghost of taste and discernment, and only visited the best bedroom of the house, which she did not occupy.) To this she added many arguments, with the view of strengthening the young couple's resolution not to be "afeard," as she said, of whatever they might hear, for it was an invisible spirit. Well, night came, and being fatigued with the removal, the new lodgers retired earlier to rest than was consistent with the husband's habits, whose custom, from his earliest years up to the last year of his life, was to sit up reading (whatever his fatigue during the day and exhaustion during the evening,) until two or three in the morning, when every other person had retired to bed; and as the clock struck twelve (for ghosts are proverbially punctual,) the sleepers were awoke by three several blows (as they, half awake, and tired as they were, believed,) *upon their heads!* Both started up in a state of affright, notwithstanding all their daylight resolutions. Their eyes wandered about the apartment, which a rush-light dimly illumined. It was an old-fashioned room, with furniture apparently coeval with its form, heavy and dark, and calculated to excite every association favourable to the abode of spirits, dark as Erebus. But neither spirit of light nor darkness seemed disposed to show itself; and, after a breathless watchfulness for some time, the newcomers tried to forget the interruption, and forget it they did; for they sunk into a deep sleep, which lasted without interruption till morning.

When they again saw their hostess, she was curious to observe how the night's alarm had affected them. They told her what had happened; and she assured them they had experienced all that would occur, for that everybody's account was precisely the same: and, in fact, she tried to persuade her lodgers, that it was "nothing when they were *used* to it." Mr. Mathews consulted his wife, who was in favour of another night's trial; but she afterwards confessed that her heart quivered at the anticipation of the awful noise. They, however, resolved to sit up with plenty of light in the room, until it was over; and an expedient occurred to Mr. Mathews, which he carried into effect—namely, to deceive his wife as to the hour, out-talk the "iron tongue of time," and drown the monster's note whenever he heard it sounding. At eleven o'clock, he told her that it was twelve, and she went to bed in consequence, quite tranquil in the belief that the ghost was giving way to their comfort, her husband affecting to go down stairs to read, as was his custom, after she had retired.

About five minutes before twelve he crept softly up stairs, and went into the bed-room, where Mrs. Mathews was soundly asleep, and there waited armed at all points for the expected shock—

or rather, as he expected, to detect some imposture, as he fully supposed the whole affair would turn out. The Minster was on the last stroke of the appointed hour, when the startling noises of the preceding night were repeated, and poor Mrs. Mathews started up from her sleep in dreadful agitation! The sounds evidently came from the head of the bed, but were heard no more during that night. Mr. Mathews, however, desired his wife to lie still, while he drew away the bedstead from the wainscot, in order to examine whether any hollow or panel contained the cause of these annoyances: yet, how could it be anything living, that had for so long a time past carried on this scheme?—It was not to be supposed that a *trick* could have been prosecuted for a series of years, whatever its intent might be. It was very strange—'twas passing strange! for there was no reason to believe anybody could be secreted where the noise invariably came from.

The next day and the next they had to tell the same tale;—whether they were asleep, or whether they were awake, in or out of bed, the same *three* blows were struck at the same hour. After a time, (though certainly not without much suffering on the part of Mrs. Mathews, and some occasional trepidation on the part of her husband, who felt at times a vague apprehension and shudder at the mysterious recurrence,) custom, and certain arithmetical calculations, induced by the summing up of the weekly receipts, reconciled the poor young couple to their nightly visitant's *rule of three*. They had, in fact, screwed their courage to the "sticking (and knocking) place," and the season ended with their promise to return to their apartments on their next arrival in York.

Accordingly, the following season again saw them in possession of their cheap and commodious lodgings, the episode to which had served often for conversation in the green-room, though the subject had become somewhat "musty." The bed, which they had formerly removed from the particular spot where it had first stood, remained where they had placed it; and its occupants were seldom annoyed by the cause of terror, as their habits were late. Moreover, as the *knocker* was as regular as time itself, the young couple sat out the ghost, who, however, went on, "never-minding;" and, before the cock had crowed, performed his accustomed task, which at last became a mere matter of course and indifference to those who listened. Many came to hear and marvel, when the residents had ceased to feel any emotion whatever.

Suddenly, a new cause for wonder and speculation presented itself, in the total cessation of these noises! The visitation, once so awful, had ceased! It almost seemed as if the power that had so long exercised itself for the terror of the inhabitants, had withdrawn itself from pique at the total disregard and apathy with which it was now endured. The effect of this, strange to say, was almost as fearful as the terror originally felt at the unaccountable sounds. The customary knocking was missed; and the silence which took its place seemed even more awful!

The result was much talked of, it may be believed, in and out of the theatre, and Mr. and Mrs. Mathews began to fear that they would be obliged to resign their apartments from increased demands, and to remove to others alike uninviting to corporeal as to spiritual inhabitants; for they could never again reasonably expect, with their present income, to live so comfortably where the landlady was less *spirituelle* and, therefore, disposed to remit a portion of her rent. In the mean time, they had no intimation to quit, and, of course, said nothing of their surmises or fears.

Some weeks after this, Mrs. Leng, an old lady, who with her husband had grown from youth to age in Tate Wilkinson's company, (Mr. Leng having retired for many years from great infirmity, and recently died,) was sitting in her widow's dress in the green-room, when the strange business of the *Stonegate Ghost* was canvassed; its many years' invariable custom, and its sudden disappearance, or rather silence. Mrs. Leng, whose cares for her dying husband, whose illness had been of long continuance, had kept her for a long while out of the habit of mixing much with the performers, or with any one out of the sick room, had not heard any description of the particular manner in which the original alarm was given; her notion of the story being a general one of *unaccountable and dreadful noises*, sending away in turn all who attempted to live in the apartments. She therefore was struck by the account given by Mr. Mathews, (for the hundredth time at least,) and his imitations of the sounds which had been invariably heard at the same hour. At length the old lady exclaimed, —" Why that was my dear Billy Leng!" A general cry of astonishment was heard, and an explanation eagerly demanded; and as soon as the excitement occasioned by her words had subsided, she readily gave it, to the following effect:

Mrs. Leng and her husband had occupied for several years the adjoining floor of the next house. Leng being almost entirely confined during that time; so great an invalid was he indeed, that he seldom quitted his bed-room. His constant ill health required regularity of hours, and his system had become in fact, from being such a home-stayer, most rigid. He had little else to do but to watch the minutes as they " dragged their slow length along." So particular was he in all things which regarded time and manner, that had he heard anything of the lumps and bumps of later times, he would have *boasted* of the *organ of order*, which he possessed to a teazing degree, his *bump* prompting a periodical set of habits, which no consideration or chance ever interfered with. One of these arose from a terror of thieves, which time had augmented to a childish extent since he had been confined to the house; he had consequently adopted a mode of satisfying his doubts before he slept, which at once assured him of his security. This was, after he was in bed, (where he might be found at a precise moment every night,) just as he heard the Minster *give warning* of the midnight hour, to employ a crutch-handled stick, which supported his steps when up, in striking three blows along the head of his bed, in order to satisfy himself that no lurker stood "behind the arras," to "murder sleep," or Billy Leng!

Here then was the mystery of several years explained by a simple relation. Poor Mr. Leng, having once performed this operation upon the three breadths of calico at the head of his bed, must needs keep up for ever after such a custom. The only wonder left now, was how Mrs. Leng could so often listen to the account of her neighbour's haunted room, without being struck with the fact that she herself possessed the key of the mystery. But she declared she had never before heard *particulars;* or, if she had, she was not impressed by them in a way to cause her to suppose her "Billy" had anything to do with the affair. In short, the ghost was laid, as many other ghosts might have been, had a natural solution, like the present, been given to the seekers of truth.

It is justice to the memory of the owner of the haunted house to record, that she allowed the young couple to occupy her rooms after this, without any increase of rent.

It is not to be supposed that with Mr. Mathews's active observation of character, and the leisure he had to contemplate any amusing specimens, he could have been so long in Tate Wilkinson's company without noting down much. In fact, when he reached the theatre, a volume of eccentricity laid wide open before him, to which the manager might be called the title-page. In the index might be found the names of Swalwel, the treasurer; French, the leader of the band—rich subjects for Mr. Mathews; and last, not least, in our dear love, John, or Johnny Winter, wardrobe-keeper and tailor. He was more than pen can do justice to, or living tongue *now* describe. Amongst his numerous prejudices, he hated a new-comer, from whom he rationally reckoned on new arrangements, new demands, and a complete change of habits (literally), which his predecessor had by custom made easy to him; and though the person succeeded had never partaken more liberally either of Johnny's regard or attentions than his successor was likely to do, yet he seemed, now that he was gone, to have been less troublesome than he of the present time, and his name was sure to be dragged forward on every occasion, to the disparagement of the later known.

Previously to Mr. Mathews's arrival, an actor of the name of Southgate had played some of the parts intrusted to the former, when he first appeared; such as *Rundy*, and others of that class. Southgate's death had left these parts open. He had been a careless, slovenly person in his profession, and unstudied in it further than to make the unskilful laugh. His *hits* were at the galleries; his life was dissipated, and he took the least possible time in selecting his dresses, and putting them on. These characteristics won Johnny Winter's good will after Southgate's death, if not before; for then he learned to appreciate him, when a more fastidious and careful professor stood in his place. The rejection of the "smock frock," by Mr. Mathews, for all manner of countrymen, which had satisfied his predecessor, disgusted Johnny at once " wi' t' conceited chap coom'd ta' t' coompany. Eh, I reckon ye bain't a better actor than poor *Soothgate*, though ye ha' your mouth soomut crooked like. Ah, Soothgate *was* an actor! *I* shall niver see anoother like him in *my* time! *He* niver gave trooble to a poor tailor. No, he wad run in to t' wardrobe at t' last minute, tak' a Hob's frock from t' pin (*i. e.* peg), clap a bit o' red upon t' nose, and folks would *shout!* Eh, Soothgate *was* an actor!"

All manner of spectacle was Johnny's particular dread and detestation, and Shakspeare's plays were classed and confounded by him with all pieces requiring show, dress, and numbers. In fact, all that gave him trouble, was certain to meet with Winter's hearty condemnation. Above all, he hated to look out dresses for the supernumeraries, whom he called *superneedlesses*, without considering the propriety of such auxiliaries, or whether " by opposing" he could " end them." He argued against and resisted their aid, in the most senseless, selfish manner he was master of; and when the night came, he would abuse the people and obstruct their preparations. Whenever the manager ordered the revival of any of Shakspeare's plays, (which gave him additional trouble from the number of dresses he had to select and prepare, not only for the actors, but the odious "superneedlesses,") his abhorrence of them was proportioned to their processions, and he was almost frantic during John Kemble's engagement, when the play of " Coriolanus" was revived. " *That* John Kemble and Shakspeare," Mr. Mathews heard him say, " have given me more trooble than all t' other people in t' world put together, and my spouse into t' bargain." He especially hated " Henry the Eighth," and others of the historical plays that required numbers to be dressed; and he set down every dramatic piece to our immortal bard, which consisted of anything like show, spectacle, and procession. "Well, John," said Mr. Mathews one day, in order to draw him out; "there is a grand piece coming out spick and span from London."—"What, 'Blue Beard,' I reckon? Eh! it's more of that fond Shakspeare's stuff. I wish he was drowned i' t' river Ouse. I shall have no peace while he's alive, I see. What with his 'Henry t' Eighth,' and 'Perouse,' and 'Pizarro,' and 'Robinson Crusoe,' and 'Coriolanus,' and his 'Jubilee,' and such fond stuff, I'd better be a galley slave, I's sure. D—n the chap! why doesn't he get his bread by some honest trade, or if he must write plays, why can't he write 'em without so many folk in 'em? he niver thinks of the trooble he gives t' poor tailors and wardrobe-keepers."

When one of the "superneedlesses" applied to him for a dress, he would throw it at him, and reply to the request of, "Please, Mr. Winter, give me a dress for a herald?"—"Eh! choke thee, I could like to gi' thee a bit of sponge, and mak' thee eat it, thou nasty, idle hound! Why don't thee stop at home wi' thy wife and bairns, and not come neglecting thy business to black thy face for a shilling a-night."

Winter had prejudices and opinions too about church and state; and, amongst other complaints against the existing constitution, the enormous incomes, as he deemed them, of high churchmen, formed a matter of great dissatisfaction to "a poor tailor, who could only earn sixteen shillings a week."

It was one of Tate's whims, that his principal comedian should perform Bishop Gardiner in "Henry the Eighth;" and, according to long usage, this part was given to the low-comedy man of the company. Mr. Mathews applied early for a dress, anxious not to add ridicule to his representation of such a part by an imperfect costume. Therefore, on the first intimation of the manager's desire that he should appear in a character so obviously unfit for him, he went to the wardrobe to ascertain what was usually found for it. As usual, whenever Shakspeare's "fond stuff" was in preparation, Johnny Winter was seen in exceedingly insolent ill-humour, and senselessly opposing every application relating to the occasion. Mr. Mathews began:— "Winter, I want to see what dress you can give me for a bishop?"—"A dress for a bishop!" quoth John, his political ire rising: "Eh! if I had *my* will, there shouldn't be a bishop i' the world."—"Well," replied Mr. Mathews, "that has nothing to do with my request; I want a dress fit for the part."—"Well, then," rejoined the incorrigible John, "tak ony thing you see!"— "Nonsense!" said the actor; "I desire you'll look me out a proper dress for a bishop."—"Well, then," persevered Johnny, "there's a soldier's coit (coat) upon t' pin, quite good enough for ony bishop *I* ever knew!" and he actually threw across the room to him a common soldier's coat, adding, " I'll gi' thee nought else, I's sure."

In this manner his impertinent ill-humour would contend with his duty; but of course he was at last compelled to yield. Johnny was a wit too in his way, and often said amusing if not always good things. The professors of tragedy, of course, he hated more than others. Once a very *fine* dandy sort of young man came from London "to play for an engagement," as it is called, but in other words to be allowed to prove himself unworthy of one (as it generally happens): being evidently a novice in theatricals, and totally ignorant of the usages of country theatres in particular, and above all, quite unaware of how *great* a man he had to deal with, in the loose-gartered, sleek-headed person before him, (whose coolness and indifference did not seem to strike the would-be actor with any awe,) he ordered various dresses to be taken from "t' pins," in order to choose a Romeo's suit. The wardrobe-keeper at first slily watched the examination, as if waiting for his time to tease the "chap," as he would have called him. The novice being undecided, kept Winter in attendance a long while; and it was pretty evident that Johnny's ire was only half smothered, and waiting till a happy opportunity should enable him to pour it forth on the devoted head of the young man. At last having settled his dresses he asked, in a drawling yet confident tone, always, by the way, addressing Johnny by the title of "Tailor," (the most offensive term he could have hit upon,) "You, of course, find feathers, gloves, and shoes, in your theatre?" —"Oh, yes," said Winter, with affected acquiescence, "oh, yes, yes; feathers, gloves, silk stockings, *port wine;* all *them* sort o' things; and plenty of them!"

When Mr. Mathews had overcome his first professional difficulties, and was established as the representative of the parts for which he had so long struggled, he observed that Winter studiously avoided any notice of his success or his performances, although it was not his habit to abstain either from blame or commendation generally, and Mr. Mathews could never draw out his opinion of his acting, though he often "fished" for it. After the successful result of "The Wags of Windsor," in which Mr. Mathews's *Caleb Quotem* (one of his first original parts in York,) was an immense hit, he threw out all sorts of hints to Johnny to go to the side-scenes, but he seemed deaf to them all. At last, to *Caleb Quotem's* surprise, one night, during his principal scene, he saw Johnny at the front entrance, absolutely grinning, and intently watching him.

Elated at this, he could not resist, as he undressed, endeavouring to ascertan Winter's impression of his acting.* He knew that a direct question would be a failure. So, after waiting a short time in the hope that Johnny would volunteer something, and finding him not disposed to open, the actor carelessly observed, " So, Winter, I think I saw you behind the scenes during the farce to-night: how did you like it?" Winter replied, as carelessly, — " Eh ! *vary much* indeed, what *I saw* of it." Mr. Mathews was " very glad to hear it." On which Winter smiled slyly, and reiterated his approbation:—" Nay, without flattery, I niver saw a prettier bit o' acting than Mr. Hope's *Dubbs* i' my life!" — a character of about two lines, and played of course by one of the nobodies of the company. But John would have his humour.

John Winter detested Leeds. It was a favourite assertion of his, that they never would have had occasion to build a gallows at York except "to hang Leids-folk upon." When the company were there, he would count the time, after the first few days of the period they were destined to remain, and cheat himself thus:— " Ah! hey! it's one coomfort, that at t' end o' t' week after next, I reckon, we shall ha' only five weeks to stay !"

* It must be explained, that " Dresser" was added to the titles of Wardrobe-keeper and Tailor, in this theatre.

An actor of the name of Wood, a native of the county, an excellent man, and who had been a great favourite in his youth, had grown old in the service, with a wife and large family; yet, though much respected, he never could command anything like a good "benefit" in that town. On the occasion now alluded to, there was little more than a sprinkling in pit, boxes, and gallery; certainly, not receipts enough to pay the expenses of the night. Poor "Charlie Wood," as he was affectionately called, was a man of the most invincible good humour, and imperturbable temper. He peeped through the hole in the green curtain previously to its rising, and with unruffled voice and a half chuckle, in a tone of course not audible to the public, he exclaimed, "Ah, ha! very pretty indeed! Your servant, ladies and gentlemen!" Then turning away laughing, he added —"A very select party, upon my word!" The performers, at the conclusion of the evening, while undressing, remarked upon Mr. Wood's calmness upon an occasion of such disappointment and mortification. Mr. Mathews observing, that "he must have the patience of Job himself," Winter replied sharply, "Job! Job be d—d! Job never had ten bairns and a Leids benefit!"

Winter entertained the most miserable discontent at his calling; which arose less from the dislike of what he was, than an overweening preference for what he was not. He would say—

"Eh! I wish my poor father had been dead and gone before he made a tailor o' me; but, howiver, there's one thing they never shall say of me. I niver *did* sit cross-legged, and I niver *will*. Eh! Mr. Mathus, I wish I had been summut i' t' horse line. I could like to hunt ivery day of my life." (Johnny had been frequently known to follow the hounds on foot, so fond was he of the sport.) "Eh! I wish I had a horse, Mister Mathus. I've been looking out all my life to the time when I should keep a horse. I've gotten a vary neat bridle and saddle; I want nought but a horse to mak it complete. But what's a poor lazy loppy tailor to do, with a sick wife and sixteen shillings a-week? Eh!" with a sigh, "horses are out o' t' question where there are bairns, I reckon."

Mr. Mathews, who by this conversation may be guessed to have advanced in some degree into Winter's good graces, inquired how his wife really was?—"Eh! she's badly, I reckon; *vary* badly. I suppose* she's in t' consumption line. T' doctor says, she mun ha' port-wine allowed her. Wha's to pay for it? says I. Nay, nay, Mr. Mathus, when women begin to drink wine, it's time they were out o' t' way."

Not only were the performers subject to the humorous impertinences of Winter, but even

* "Suppose" does not, in Yorkshire, imply a doubt, but a certainty.

Tate himself, who unresistingly suffered his familiarities and retorts.

One day when John came to the manager's daily levee, upon which occasion his treasurer, tailor, leader of the band, and ladies' wardrobe-keeper, all had their half-hour, John appeared in his slip-shod shop-board costume, unshaven, and unseemly in all respects. This was unusual and displeasing to his master, who reproved him for such negligence of his person; more especially for not having used his razor that morning. John received this half good-humoured reproof in silence, and when he had transacted the business of the morning, he retreated. The next day his appearance was altered—he had reformed it altogether; and he presented himself in his neatest attire; his dress being a groom-like frock, striped waistcoat, with drab " continuations," buttoned knowingly at the front of the knee, and tied with strings, which were allowed to hang down upon a very neat pair of top-boots; his hair, light and sleek, under a narrow-brimmed hat; altogether presenting what now would be called a full-blown, *tigerish* appearance. Mr. Mathews happened to be present on this occasion, when Winter, armed and invulnerable at all points, came confidently into the presence of his master, who had been severely ill all night, and who presented a striking contrast by his careless neglect of himself under suffering, to Johnny's well *got up* person. As he entered, he looked steadily in the manager's face, and advancing in his usual way, rising upon tip-toe as if going to dance, and rubbing (I should say snapping, but that no sound was heard,) the thumb and second finger of either hand together, came close to his master; then placing his hand with a feeling action under the old gentleman's chin, he asked in the coolest manner imaginable — "Eh! wha wants shaving *now*, I woonder?" and he danced himself back again to his usual stand, near the door. The manager took no notice of this liberty, but resumed his talk upon the business of the morning.

John was indeed sadly spoiled, both by manager and actors; and, truth to say, he was sometimes unbearable: yet he had his agreeable hours, and was at heart a pleasant as well as good sort of fellow. Mr. Mathews, and the other principal actors, who enjoyed his humours, would often lounge near his shop-board, (upon which, as he boasted, he never crossed his legs,) and draw forth and listen to his oddities, while he proceeded with his work.

Winter had married young, and had a large family; and losing the mother of his children, he married again. He was equally unlucky in his second choice, for she proved to be as ailing in constitution as his first; and instead of being a helpmate to poor Johnny, added to his expenses and cares, without in the least contributing to the comfort of his family, chiefly daughters. While he was dressing, and smoothing down the coats of the performers, he would sometimes in pensive mood give vent to his softly uttered complaints: " Eh, Mr. Mathus, you're a lucky man; your spouse (Mr. Mathews's first wife) has no bairns to provide for. Eh, I've just getten one wedded, *that's* a good thing, one mouth less to feed: she's married to Mr. Whitely; I suppose, a very good match, as times go."—" What!" asked Mr. Mathews, " Whitely, who plays in the orchestra? Impossible! that pretty daughter of yours, married to that frightful, disgusting-looking man! She can't like him, I'm sure."—" Eh, Mr. Mathus," said Johnny, a little put down by this remark: " I know nothing aboot *that;* a poor lazy loppy tailor's bairn musn't be vary particular in such things." — " Yes, but," continued Mr. Mathews, " yes, but he is so *very* ugly; why, he has hardly a nose upon his face."—" Eh, ah! as you say, Mr. Mathus, he's no beauty to be sure; he hasn't much of a *nose*, but then he has a large garden at Leids."

Mr. Mathews one day found Johnny at work upon a pair of Brobdignag " inexpressibles," which evidently were intended for Stephen Kemble, then performing for a few nights in York. John was drawing out his needle with a hurried distaste of his job:—" What, Winter!" said Mr. " Mathus," as he called him who wished to draw forth John's discontent; "you are obliged, I suppose, to make up everything *new* for Mr. Kemble?"—" Eh," sighed the tailor, " eh, it's vary hard, I reckon, to be obliged to work for such a great fat sow as that, just at t'race time, when t' horses are running. I was obliged yesterday to hire six men, to sit round his waistcoit, (one man could not mak' it in time,) and I'm now working at one o' his fat knees mysel'. Eh, it's bad to 'bide! when I've done all *his* work, I reckon I've getten only another job to match."—" And what's that?" said the querist. "Eh, ha! to make a great-coit for t' York Minster."

Mrs. Siddons had, in September, just concluded her engagement at York and Leeds, which had proved a rich treat to Mr. Mathews, who had only once before seen this magnificent woman and actress. In a letter to his friend Mr. Litchfield, dated September 2nd, he describes with enthusiasm the delight he had felt in witnessing her performances:—" Mrs. Siddons is with us, and will be for the summer: you may judge what a feast this is for me. I am out of most of her plays, of course. I think she looks more beautiful than ever, and never could have played better. I never saw her to such advantage as now, as the London theatres are too large for her powers."

In the city of York, her splendid talents had been attentively enjoyed and appreciated; but at Leeds, " Bonny Leids," as John Winter, with *bitter irony*, termed it, she encountered much annoyance and interruption from that part of the spectators whom it was not possible to exclude. The gentry who came from the surrounding neighbourhood, shared with the performers the drawback of whatever conduct the respective humours of the frequenters of pit and gallery chose to exhibit. These parts of the theatre were generally occupied with what were called " croppers," and their wives and sweethearts, (namely, the working people in the cloth manufactories of the town,) who were at this time semi-barbarous in their manners and habits, and who moreover held in the most supreme contempt, if not abhorrence, the professors of the art they willingly paid to be amused by. The men would not hesitate, like the Irish, to make their comments audibly, though, *un*like the Irish, they were destitute of humour to compensate for their interruptions. It was very painful to the admirers of Mrs. Siddons to witness her involuntary submission to such brutal treatment. It was not surprising that the majestic and refined style of her performances should not be appreciated by such people; they would have prized far higher the efforts of a good wear-and-tear pair of lungs, that could " split the ears of the groundlings," than the beautiful subdued tones, for which this accomplished mistress of her art was so celebrated in particular scenes, and which reached the heart by their tenderness.*

One night when she had been acting Jane Shore, Mr. Mathews, who had been rooted to the spot, watching her every look and word, until the curtain fell, was quitting the front of the house, when a man hurrying towards the gallery-door, rather late for the half-price, was accosted by another who was leaving it. "Eh, Tommy, where beest thou ganging?"—"I's ganging to t' play," replied the comer. "Well, then, thou may'st ha' my place if thou can'st get it, for I's ganging hame again."—"Why," asked 'Tommy' with anxiety; "is t' play over?" (meaning the whole night's performance.) "Nay," said the other, "I know not; but I's tired o't all."—"Well," said his friend; "but thou 'st seed the great Lunnon laker, Missis Siddins, I reckon?"—"Eh, I know not," quoth the malcontent; "Aw 've been there this holf-hour, and I seed

* When John Kemble left the York company for a London engagement, there was much difference of opinion in Leeds as to the relative merits of Mr. Cummins, his brother tragedian, whom his admirers considered ill-used, in not having been selected by the London manager as worthy of distinction. Two Leeds blues (*i.e.* croppers) discussing the matter, one of them observed that "It was merely a toss-up of luck whether Kemble or Coommins wa' engaged; for though Kemble was a vary good laker, yet Coommins could shout twice as loud as he could."

nought but a fond woman ligging o' top o' t' fleer."*

Another night, when Mrs. Siddons had occasion to drain " the poisoned cup," a ruffian bawled out, to the overthrow of all order in the rest of the house, " That's right, Molly, soop it opp, ma lass!" And in one of her most beautiful scenes of pathos, a cropper arrested the attention of one of his fellows, seated in a distant part of the theatre, by inquiring in the voice of a Stentor, though at the same time with an affectation of sentiment, — " Aw say, Sammy!" — " Well!" — " How's thy poor moother?"

On one memorable night, however, during her engagement, a *contretems* of a ludicrous nature occurred, for which no part of the audience was answerable. The evening was excessively hot, and Mrs. Siddons was tempted by a torturing thirst to consent to avail herself of the only obtainable relief proposed to her at the moment. Her dresser, therefore, despatched a boy in great haste to "fetch a pint of beer for Mrs. Siddons," at the same time charging him to be quick, as Mrs. Siddons was in a hurry for it. Meanwhile the play proceeded, and on the boy's return with the frothed pitcher, he looked about for the person who had sent him on his errand; and not seeing

* A foolish woman lying upon the floor; in other words, Jane Shore in her dying scene.

her, inquired " Where is Mrs. Siddons?" The scene-shifter whom he questioned, pointing his finger to the stage where she was performing the sleeping scene of Lady Macbeth, replied—" There she is." To the surprise and horror of all the performers, the boy promptly walked on the stage close up to Mrs. Siddons, and with a total unconsciousness of the impropriety he was committing, presented the porter! Her distress may be imagined; she waved the boy away in her grand manner several times, without effect; at last the people behind the scenes by dint of beckoning, stamping, and calling in half-audible whispers, succeeded in getting him off with the beer, part of which in his exit he spilled on the stage; while the audience were in an uproar of laughter, which the dignity of the actress was unable to quell for several minutes.

When the night's performance had closed, the boy was taken aside and severely lectured by the prompter, upon his stupid conduct. Winter, who was a sort of patron to him, was present during his correction, and when it was over, patted the boy upon the shoulder mildly, saying, in mock solemnity of tone,—" Eh, Moses, ma bairn, let me gi' thee a piece of advice, and be sure ye recollect it all the days o' thy life. Niver go upon t' stage, Moses, ma lad, without thy name 's i' t' bill."

With so many annoyances from the vulgar part of the audience, it was natural that Mrs.

Siddons should be disgusted with her engagement in Leeds; and on the dropping of the curtain at the close of her last night's performance, she clasped her hands in thankfulness, ejaculating, in her most tragic tones, "Farewell, ye brutes! and for ever, I trust: ye shall never torture me again, be assured." And it certainly was her last appearance there.

CHAPTER XIV.

Leeds.—Prejudice entertained there against actors.—Rudeness to female performers.—Outrage upon Mr. Holman, and upon Miss Gough.—Feeling towards actors in Hull.—Anecdote. —Denman and the landlady.—Johnny Winter and Dwyer. —Winter's disdain of "mock modesty."—Lady W—ne and her family.—Miss Topham.—Major Topham.—Mrs. Townend.—Idiots.—Tommy Myers.—Journey from York to London and back for a shilling.—" Fond Barney."

LEEDS was at this period considered little better than the Botany Bay of actors. Their dread of the season was in proportion to the inconveniences and disagreeables they experienced during its course. The extraordinary, nay frightful, prejudice cherished by the people I have spoken of in that day, made this periodical stay amongst them a matter of serious dread, especially to the females of the theatre. It appeared as if even the lives of the performers were held in no consideration amongst a certain portion of the natives, whose estimation of "lakers" seemed to agree with ours in relation to the most insignificant animals created only for our use. These people carried their opinions still farther, for they deemed it no sin to torture, or even destroy (could they have done so with impunity) any one of the profession. If an actress had occasion to cross a certain *brig* (bridge), at a period of the day when the croppers were "sunning themselves" in each other's eyes, (in other words, taking their lounge between their working hours,) she was obliged to provide herself with an escort to protect her from the rough jokes and assaults of even the most gallant, whose kindness was as much dreaded as their brutalities.

Mr. Holman once came to Leeds to act, and not liking the dressing-room assigned him in the theatre, performed his theatrical toilette at home. On the first night of his appearance, he was proceeding in a sedan-chair, dressed for *Lord Townley* in "The Provoked Husband," in the customary court-suit, &c. and otherwise ready to appear upon the stage. In order to escape notice, the scanty curtains of the chair were drawn, it being still day-light. Unluckily, "'t brig" was lined on either side with its dusky visitants. The sedan, unluckily also, happened to be a novelty to these barbarians, and was hailed as an event—an object of excitement and curiosity. "Eh, dom't! what's cooming o'er t' brig? A leather box wi' two chaps a carrying o' t'! What divil o' thing! Well, I niver seed sooch in all moy loife!" Then stopping the chairmen, who were proceeding gravely along, and crowding round the chair, they uttered many suggestions as to its nature and use; while Mr. Holman, in some trepidation, endeavoured to draw the little curtains still closer about him. The foremost of the croppers, however, insisted upon the chairmen setting "the thing" down, for his particular inspection; and then peering through a small line of uncovered glass into the interior, he caught an obscure view of poor *Lord Townley*, who, deeming it now best to speak, and awe them into forbearance, undrew the curtain, and by this act almost sealed his fate. The comedy in which he was going to take part became in great danger of being exchanged for a tragedy; for no sooner did the men obtain a full view of his lordship in his embroidered coat, powdered head, and rouged face, than with a cry of horror (natural enough), they shouted — "A mon wi' his face painted!" "It's a laker!" was the simultaneous cry, and an order from the crowd to "toss him o'er t' brig" was the consequence of this discovery.

Whether such a suggestion would have been carried into execution or not is uncertain; but the timely interference of several gentlemen of weight and authority luckily put the matter beyond the control of Mr. Holman's assailants. The sedan was ordered on, accompanied by his deliverers, (who were going to see him perform,) to the very great relief of the actor; who, as he was carried out of the mob, heard one of the ruffians exclaim to another,—" Well, I'm vexed we didn't topple him into t' water. Where 'd been t' harm i' drowning a laker?"

I remember hearing another instance, which occurred about a year previously to the foregoing. A Miss Gough, wishing during the period of her sister's performance at the theatre to enjoy an evening's stroll by the canal-side, found herself suddenly caught up in the arms of an enormous man-monster, of a stone-blue colour from head to feet, dress and complexion. She struggled for freedom, which he declared he " wad na gi' her till she told him wha she was wi' sooch few claithes on" (the fashion at that period being to wear very scanty petticoats, and of thin texture). Too glad to give him the first part of the information required, in hopes of release, she told him that she belonged to the theatre. " Ah! a laker!" cried the brute, setting her down upon her feet, but holding her securely. " Here! here! here's a laker!" he bawled out triumphantly, as it seemed, to some of his companions who were employed dressing cloth at a distance. " Coom hither, aw tell thee, here's a domned laker! aw 've getten a laker!" Away they came, leaving their occupation, and running with as much eagerness as might be supposed to have been excited by an announcement of a unicorn, or any other unknown or rare monster. Men, women, and children came thronging round the unfortunate girl; and after having commented upon her dress and profession with coarse jests and insulting words, they soaked in the canal a quantity of brown paper, (which they appeared to use in their occupation,) and wrapped it round her slight form, till she looked like a mummy. They then turned her forth towards the town, driving and chasing her before them with yells of delight, until she came in view of some human beings, who compassionated and relieved her from her pursuers and her damp habiliments.

But it was not only with such as these that an actor's profession was despised, but even amongst the majority of the inhabitants. With them, actors, showmen, or any other exhibitors, were synonymous, since they had but one word in common for all; and Garrick, and Richardson of " Bartlemy Fair," the hero of Wilkinson's company, and the trumpeter for Punch, would be all included and confounded in the term " laker."

Wakefield, as far as related to the lower orders, was in the same state of refinement. Mr. Mathews was walking there by the river-side one day, with a pet puppy at his heels, when one cropper said to another, " Aw say, kick that dug; topple him into t' river; he's nought but a laker's dug, thou knowst?"

At Pontefract and Doncaster such things were out of the question; and at the latter place, to be a " laker" was to ensure a welcome with all the kind and agreeable inhabitants of that town; whilst Hull was the genuine seat of hospitality. Even there, however, might be found amongst the middle orders people who at the best looked upon an actor as an object of commiseration. In the winter of 1799 Mr. Mathews dined, in company with one of the performers (Mr. Denman), at a respectable tradesman's house, where two neighbours joined the party after dinner. When the glass had enlivened the party, and every one became chatty and sociable, the two friends who had "dropped in" (and who were evidently not theatrical,) were desirous to know who the new visiters were. On receiving from their host the intimation in a whisper, one of them expressed his astonishment aloud, and both indeed seemed incredulous. Mr. Mathews's thin, spare form was a striking contrast to the John-Bull look of Denman, who was ruddy and plump. "Nay, nay, I cannot stand that," exclaimed one of the worthies, when mine host reiterated his assurance that "the gentlemen were of Mr. Wilkinson's company."—"Why not?" asked Mr. Mathews, with some pique in his tone and manner. "Why," replied the puzzled Yorkshireman, "I's sure you're both such nice-looking men, and so well-dressed, that I can't believe you can be players. You," continued he, looking at Mr. Mathews, "*do* look a little bit hungered, but your friend there, I warrant, gets a good meal's meat every day of his life." Denman, much amused, drily observed, "You're quite right, sir, I certainly do; but my poor friend there seldom gets a dinner above once in a fortnight!"

The following anecdote will serve as a closing illustration of the prejudices entertained by the lower ranks in Leeds against the profession. Mr. Mathews was one night sitting in the upper part of the theatre to witness a pantomime, when a young creature entered the adjoining box, evidently in the last stage of consumption, squalid and wasted from the effects of an irregular life. She had been pretty, and, of course, was finely dressed in her way, with gaudy taste. Her extreme youth, and miserable condition, excited the observer's notice and commiseration. A party of supposed gipsies and beggars, who came upon the stage, dressed in appropriate costume, fixed her attention. When they made their exit, the poor unfortunate lifted up her head, which had been leaning pensively upon her hand, and observed to the person sitting next to her: "What wretched creatures players are! Well, that's the *last* thing I should take to!"

Besides a large proportion of Quakers, Leeds abounded in a variety of religious sects; and as they were generally of the lower and middle order, and made up the majority of people who let lodgings, the performers (" t' lakers") found it difficult to obtain accommodation during the season of the theatre. Mr. Denman on his first arrival in the town, when in quest of a lodging, was much struck with the quiet neatness of a house which boasted of " an apartment for a single gentleman." Now Mr. Denman answered this description about as well as Will Waddle, who looked "like *two* single gentlemen rolled into one;" yet he ventured to apply to the landlady for her room, which was speedily agreed upon; she undertaking to " do for him." All in fact was finally arranged, and Mr. Denman was turning away, with his broad expanse of face benevolently beaming with satisfaction towards his good-humoured landlady (a widow), when it occurred to him as prudent to mention his necessarily late hours, occasioned by his profession. A demur now arose from religious scruples to the admission of one of the " devil's imps" under the pure roof which had sheltered the serious departed. It seemed like profanation in his loving relict to think even of such a thing. "No," at last she said; "it was out of the question; impossible!" The dame looked, however, as much chagrined and disappointed as Denman was. He nevertheless would not at once be so put off; he had set his heart upon the lodging, and he talked sentimentally and perseveringly to her; quoting several of Shakspeare's moral and religious aphorisms as arguments against the lady's prejudices. She was struck; and she once more gazed earnestly at his good-looking face and portly figure. "His port she liked;" and her true discernment saw an honest meaning in his eye, which readily caught encouragement from the expression of hers to prosecute his advantage. Again he pleaded; and though the name and writings of Shakspeare were alike unknown to the "serious" widow, she little doubted what Denman told her, when he said that the words he uttered were those of "a divine" author. She was overcome; and, with a latent hope that she might gather a stray sheep into the fold, she at length consented to receive the actor as her lodger; and took him in accordingly — not an uncommon result of such arrangements.

All went well. Denman continued cheerful and contented, and his landlady from day to day grew more *serious* in her attentions to him, often taking occasion to throw out hints how much her lodger would become the pulpit; talked warmly of the advantages of "*Jumping*"— (the dear departed was a "*Jumper;*") offered to initiate him into its sacred mysteries; and, in short, she carried this feeling so far as at length to convert the very dinners she provided for him in her own parlour into pure *love-feasts.* Thus this widow — like her of Ephesus — mourned her love! Denman, in truth, had unintentionally made a conquest, and the lady had "seriously" set her heart upon making a convert of him. This discovery was very emharrassing to the actor. It was a difficult point—a delicate and dangerous one—to tarry after the knowledge of these sentiments; however he was a shrewd as well as facetious person, valued the comforts of his lodging, and contrived to remain in it till the season terminated, without exposing himself to a direct disclosure of his landlady's hopes and inclinations. At last the feelings of the poor woman could no longer be controlled; and, on the eve of his departure, she frankly made him an offer of her hand and house, on the conditions that he would forsake the "*Devil's walk*," and take to "*Jumping.*" How he resisted this three-fold temptation, I cannot tell; but it is certain that he evaded it with so much tact, dexterity, and good feeling, that his enamoured landlady parted from him — not without many pious tears, yet without one reproach. In truth, more in sorrow than in anger, finally sobbing out the following pathetic speech at parting :—

"Well, if thee cannot fancy to marry me and become a saint, as thou surely wouldst, instead of remaining a sinner, by walking in thy awful line o' life, I must gi' thee up. Oh !" (and here her sobs were redoubled) " to think o' such a man to be a laker! when he might be the leader and pattern to his flock !" Here the afflicted widow looked up in his face with increased agony of expression whilst she concluded —" And to ha' thy precious carcass hawked about from town to town by a gang of lakers, is worse to think on than if thou wert carried off by the gipsies!"

To return to Johnny Winter. About this time Mr. Dwyer, a very handsome, but evidently vain young man, joined the York company; and Winter immediately conceived a more than common dislike to him; for, though he required no character-dresses and found his own for the line he acted, (which was, what is called first comedy, parts such as *Ranger, Belcour, Charles Surface,* &c.) yet Winter saw more of him than he admired in the dressing-room. Here he had earned much of his unpopularity by an ostentatious care in setting off his really fine person and handsome face. John's natural perception of the weakness of vanity, and his quick insight into human character, immediately enabled him to penetrate that of Mr. Dwyer. He felt a wish to put down anything like rising or confirmed conceit in those who came under his thumb, and the off-hand manner in which Winter was treated by this gentleman rankled in his mind; while Dwyer, evidently annoyed at not being able to impress Johnny with his general importance, foolishly replied to his impertinences, and thus gave Winter fresh opportunities of mortifying him. Amongst Mr. Dwyer's successes, he most piqued himself upon his performance of *The Liar;* and it was, in fact, one of great merit. On a particular night, after having played this part for the first time in York, he entered the dressing-room when the piece was over. He had received immense applause, and thought he had a right to lay some stress upon his great exertions before those who had not had an opportunity of witnessing them. Therefore, when he reached the chair at his dressing-table, he sank, as if exhausted, into it, rather, as John Winter thought, in an affected attitude, at the same moment declaring his fatigue excessive—his exhaustion complete. Winter allowed him to proceed, without showing the least feeling for Mr. Dwyer's exertions; but when, at last, he said something which sounded like a call upon his dresser's sympathy, Johnny took the liberty of observing, in his cool provoking manner and tone, "Ah! you should see Mr. Bennett, after he has played *harlequin*. That *is* fatigue, I reckon!" To this Dwyer wisely offered no reply, affecting not to have noticed this degrading parallel with the harlequin of the theatre. An inquiry from impudent John, whether he did not mean to undress, induced the actor to declare that the excess of *heat* he was in rendered it impossible for him to undress *yet*. Now, *Mister* Winter was desirous to get home to supper, and this (as he thought) unnecessary delay exasperated his predisposed spite towards the "*conceited* chap," who reiterated his declaration of fatigue, at the same time congratulating Mr. Melvin (who had performed Papillion in the same piece with him,) upon his power to get home before him. Winter's temper at this waxed almost as warm as Mr. Dwyer's person, who still dwelling upon the heat from which he suffered, Winter observed, " Eh! I reckon you're not half as hot as Mr. Bennett, and *he* tak's t' claithes off as soon as he leaves t' stage." " Yes," persisted Dwyer, " but he never played *The Liar!* No *harlequin* can make a man as hot as the performance of *The Liar*." " Eh!" said Johnny, " it's quite a mistake, I tell thee; if you were to tell a *thousand* lies, you wouldn't be so hot as Mr. Bennett!"

In truth, Johnny Winter liked to put down what appeared affectation, either in man or woman. A very young lady performing for the first time in male attire, was called upon by Winter with his measures, as a matter of course; but her delicacy shrunk from the idea of submitting to any experiment of the kind, and she blushingly intimated that she preferred trying on a ready-made dress, the requisite alterations in which her maid would be able afterwards to describe. Johnny, who from custom could not enter into such fastidious feelings, where business was in question, considered the poor girl as affected, that she disdained his aid, and he determined to " tak' t' conceat" out of her. He, therefore, coolly replied that she might do as she liked, observing that it was no treat to him to measure any lady, after the many *he* had measured. " Eh! I've measured a vast mony! a *vast!* Eh! I reckon you know Mrs. Crouch? Eh! well, what a figure *she* had! I've measured *her* from hip to heel—she nivir objected; but then she had a figure! Eh! she was a perfect beauty without ony airs or mock modesty! Ah!" he exclaimed with a deep sigh as he made his exit, " I reckon I shan't see such another leg as hers for one while!"

Winter was not, as I have observed, the only person of eccentric character in York; it abounded, in and out of the theatre, with the most extraordinary people. There existed at this period a Lady W—ne, the widow of a baronet, whose habits turned night into day, as it were, —a habit of many years, and for which conjecture assigned some hidden sin as the cause. She never allowed herself to behold daylight; but, as soon as it departed, she arose from the bed in her no-windowed room, and pursued her customary occupations, until the hour again warned her that her night had set in. This unnatural and wretched life proved, as might be supposed, ruinous to the comfort, and indeed to the interests, of her children, whose education was quite neglected. Her daughter, consequently, if she did not, like *Miss Hoyden,* think of " running off with the baker," did not make a much better match, I believe, in order to escape from the gloom and misery of her mother's mansion. Her brother, Sir

R— W—ne, was a handsome bluff boy, uneducated for his condition, and for want of proper direction in his tastes and pursuits, was like an unlicked cub — or at best a rough country squire, a perfect Tony Lumpkin; his appearance, dress, and manner, forming a " concatenation accordingly." Mrs. Bennett, in her novel of the "Beggar Girl," so popular at that time, described him exactly under the title of " Sir Jacob." He was perfectly handsome, had a fine voice, and sang with untaught taste: but was as perfectly uncouth in his behaviour as if he had been born the clown he looked. For want of something to do, he was often to be found under the window of some pretty actress, and was madly in love at the time I speak of with one whom it required all Tate's precautions (under whose care she happened to be) to preserve her from being forcibly carried off by this youthful Tarquin. Poor Sir R., happily, I think, was gathered to his ancestors while young.

Then there was Miss Topham, sister to Major Topham, noticeable in his day as editor of a popular paper called " The World," the particular friend of Miles Peter Andrews, and like him, known as the writer of many pleasant epilogues. Miss Topham was charitably styled " an eccentric lady." She used to stalk about the city of York and its suburbs in all the exaggerated pomp of Tilburina, and like her, had a " *confi-*

dante in white linen," treading dutifully in her steps. Miss Topham's figure was tall and gaunt; sometimes she dressed like an Arcadian shepherdess, as we find her represented in Dresden china upon our mantel-pieces; her hair profusely pomatumed and powdered, and dressed high and wide, in large curls and bows, surmounted by a little flat-crowned hat, stuck up on end (the edge of its brim resting upon her forehead,) and decorated with a wreath of artificial flowers, not remarkable for their freshness of tint, with long ribbons of various colours appended. Festoons of faded flowers, of the same material and date as those upon her hat, were fancifully hung round about her lank, withered form; and high-heeled white satin shoes and diamond buckles graced her feet. Her *sacque* and petticoat of fine flowered brocade would one day assert its independence; on another you would behold her attired in light gauzy, unstiffened drapery, which clung tenaciously to her limbs, forming a sudden and striking contrast to the previous fussiness of her silk dress. Sometimes she carried a very tall cane, somewhat resembling a crook; on another day, a parasol, held high above her head, with studied care so as not to touch or hide her head-dress from admiring gazers; her smiling countenance invariably bearing evidence of self-approval and satisfaction. Her " confidante" had a short plump person, and, I suspect, like Sheridan's " gentle Nora," shrewdly accommodated her pursuits and behaviour most gravely to all the varieties of her mistress's moods. She also " wore *her* rue with a difference," and varied her dress as often as her superior did. Whether she lent herself as an artful accessary for her own private ends, or was prudently placed by her friends near Miss Topham for her security, no one seemed to know. These two equally extraordinary beings walked, as I have said, about York and its vicinity with little or no notice from the natives, mostly "to their manner born." They were perfectly harmless; and, from the station Miss Topham held, being a woman of family and fortune, they were never molested or inconvenienced by any one. Miss Topham was supposed to have been " crossed in love," the unvarying mode formerly of accounting for the lost wits of unmarried ladies. Her home-eccentricities were very amusing, but cannot be related.

Major Topham, although a man of the world in one sense more than the usual acceptation of the term, had a slight shade of his sister's eccentricities when he appeared in the streets of York (where he was not a resident) during the public weeks, races, or assizes. He was, at the period alluded to, an elderly man, whose figure appeared to have been once slight, but whose body seemed to have increased without allowing his limbs to share in the accumulated bulk, for his legs and arms retained their first slimness; and he was tall and very upright. His dress and manner were hardly less extraordinary than his sister's, (by the by, he and Miss Topham were never seen abroad together,) though he was without the same excuse for singularity. He wore a suit of grass-green cloth, made precisely in the fashion of a schoolboy's dress of that day, namely, a short-tail jacket with outside pockets; trousers, short enough to show his slender ankle cased in a white silk stocking; and a short-waisted vest, with yellow sugar-loaf metal buttons. Altogether, his appearance suggested the idea of a huge Brobdignag lad of ten or twelve years old; differing in one respect, inasmuch as his bushy, powdered whiskers might be seen on either side of his large cheeks by the person following him.*

As far as regarded oddity in dress, and in some other trivial particulars, Mrs. Townend (wife of the town-clerk, a great patroness of the theatre, and a musical amateur,) was remarkable in her way. The reigning fashion being Grecian, it was startling to see a woman, certainly not old, enter the stage-box with her head built up like the ruin of some ancient tower; a large frizzled head of dark hair, supporting gauze enough to have made an entire dress in that day, to say nothing of the fanciful additions of ribbons, bows, flowers, &c. I can fancy this lady now before me, as she was ac-

* This description forms a curious contrast with the dress described by Mr. Mathews as that worn some years before by the same person in London, when editor of " The World."

customed to be handed out of the box upon an intimation, (which her weak nerves rendered necessary,) that a gun or pistol was about to be fired on or behind the stage. Mrs. Townend's rising, after a respectful whisper from the box-keeper, or some other person deputed by the prompter, and her departure from the box, was the signal for every timid female in the theatre to place her fingers to her ears. It would have puzzled a stranger to guess what could occasion so simultaneous an action, where no outward visible sign appeared of the intended explosion.

Besides the persons recorded as noticeable in " my time" for singularity, there was a lady of noble family, who generally appeared in a riding-dress during the morning, under which, for the convenience of hunting, she invariably wore buckskin inexpressibles and top-boots. She had, however, a delicate-looking feminine figure, and was so essentially womanly in manner, that unless she had occasion in shopping to take her purse from her pocket, the suspicion would never have crossed any one that her outer dress covered any masculine habiliments. I think I see her now in her " habit as she lived," lifting up her cloth petticoat to cross a dirty kennel, and exposing her pretty little boot, with its white top, which excited my especial wonder at the time.

About the streets of York might be seen, in another grade of life, and less agreeable, several objects which might be called *natural* curiosities. Idiotcy is generally a painful object to contemplate; but it was not so with some idiots at this time in York, who might be supposed to suffer but a palpable obscure, a darkness visible, rather than that dark void, that total eclipse of thought, that want of comprehension, which renders them generally shocking to others, and joyless to themselves. It seemed the peculiar privilege of the poor half-witted beings of this place to be both cheerful and good-humoured. They were universal favourites; and I never saw the least indication of cruelty or unkindness towards them even from the most uncivilized. On the contrary, these simple creatures appeared to be considered under the especial care of every person who knew them, and to be essentially a part of the community,—a trust from Providence, placed in the hands of their more gifted brethren. No scoffing, no repulse ever scared or distressed these poor half-endowed, helpless beings, who smiled with a full and cordial reliance upon their protectors, and were treated by them as a portion of human nature intended to be exempt from the responsibilities of life, and therefore unprovided with powers to meet them. They were nevertheless mixed up, though inactively, in all their city's privileges and immunities, and, above all, were included in its most charitable and humane exercises. They were, in fact, but "children of a larger growth" in the eyes of their fellow-citizens, and as such played about the streets in harmless gaiety. They seemed as if they could not be spared; they were a daily interest to the spots to which they were attached; a something to be periodically kind to, that would have been missed. Indeed, I remember, after I was settled in London, paying a visit to York, and feeling a temporary depression at not finding these former appendages to the ancient city. My poor " fond" friends were all dead, and I could not help fancying that their absence had left a gloom, an uncomfortable stillness, in the streets in which I had been accustomed to see them. My husband always took a very great interest in all such people; and I believe I imbibed from his feeling and affecting representations of them, an impression I might not otherwise have entertained.

First, there was Tommy Myers, a devotee (no one could tell why,) to the outer precincts of the theatre. There might he be seen during the chief part of the day, moving, in a sidelong trot, backwards and forwards, talking in a rapid style upon small matters, which made up his narrow stock of reasoning. He was about five and twenty years of age, and was a most comfortable, comely personage. His affectionate mother, an industrious hard-working creature, took the nicest care of the person of her half-witted " bairn;" who, in fact, was a somewhat generally interesting being, whose few lucid ideas were sufficient for his own enjoyment, good-humour, and cheerfulness. He had an intuitive perception of the Yorkshireman's born-love of a race, and a perfect understanding of the necessity of having money *to lose*—the notion of winning, fortunately, never entered his head. His dress was always neat, consisting of a coarse but entire suit of blue cloth; and it was his constant boast, that he had, besides that in wear, a beautiful " new suit of blue claithes, wi' six pockets."

Tommy's constant approximation to the theatre was probably induced by the encouraging bribes of " the manager's" servants; for Tate's dwelling-house made part of the building, and they employed him in any way that his services could be made available. This had enabled him to become very well acquainted with the performers; but Emery was his chosen friend and crony; he knew his name, and called him by it—the only person he so distinguished; and Emery gave him money " to lose at the next York races." When spoken to by strangers, or persons indifferent to him, he would run to and fro playfully, crying out, with good-tempered gaiety,—" Get away, get away wi' ye! My name's Tommy Myers, wi' new blue claithes, wi' six pockets. I getten a sixpence. Mr. Emery gi' me penny to lose at t' races. Get away, I tell ye; get away wi' ye!" He would then affect to sing a new tune, (knowing really only a fragment of one,) boasting of the acquisition, which amounted to the last line of any popular song at the time, which he would tack to the close of his *one* air, "Margery Grinder," in the following manner;—"Tira la la la, tira la la la, tira la la la, God save the King," &c.

Tommy had a great love, as I have said, for money, without any specific notion of its value, unless to get rid of it at York races; not that he ever went to them, but that at that period he believed it to be his bounden duty to allow any cunning clown to rob him of all he had, under the pretext of winning it; and he then relinquished his long savings with all possible cheerfulness, as a matter of course. When his great friend, Emery, went to London, he had impressed upon Tommy with his parting sixpence, that he should return on the first of May following, and give him another. Tommy never forgot this, but often boasted that Mr. Emery would come back the "One of May," and give him more money. This poor fellow was a universal favourite with the actors. One day he came up to a party of them as they stood near the theatre door, in great affliction, sobbing and crying like an infant: when questioned, he exclaimed,—" Get away wi' ye! Get away wi' ye!

Tommy Myers has lost his moother, poor Mrs. Myers, Tommy's moother! They've put her in the pit-hole, and covered her all over wi' muck. Poor Tommy Myers has no moother! He must sleep alone now! Poor Tommy Myers!" In this way he made what was in effect a pathetic lament. He had indeed lost his best friend; and it was long before poor Tommy recovered his cheerfulness, or cared to lose his money at race-time.

When Tate's servants were somewhat pressed for time by their master's frequent hospitalities, they employed Tommy, at small cost, to clean their knives; the scene of action being a large square area, situated under Mr. Wilkinson's library. The manager's valetudinary habits had for several years confined his movements from home to carriage exercise, and therefore kept him partially unacquainted with his local out-door interests; consequently he knew little of "Tommy Myers" personally, or had perhaps forgotten him. On one occasion, Mr. Mathews enjoyed an amusing scene from his own dressing-room window, which also overlooked the said area where Tommy was diligently fulfilling the behests of his patrons of the scullery, just at the period of the manager's evening nap, and the actor's preparation for the night's performance. Tommy, it will be seen, was not familiar with Tate's person, although he had been taught to hold his name and authority in great respect. Having stationed himself at the board with his knives, he beguiled his employment with the last new song. — " Tira la lira, tira la lira, Nong tong paw!" while, by way of accompaniment, he clattered and rubbed the knives in time with his discordant recreation. Tate, roused by these inharmonious and unwonted sounds, put his head out of window in great wrath at such disturbance, and commanded the " noisy fellow" to go away. Tommy, totally unsuspicious who the person was who addressed him, and intent upon his duty to his employers, refused in his own peculiar manner to give up either his vocal or instrumental pursuits; and only laughed at the impertinent interference of the " fond auld man," telling him that " Mr. Wilkinson gave him a penny to clean his knives, and he would not leave off to please a fond auld chap like him." At the same time he invited his friends Betty and Molly, to " come and laff at a funny auld man out o' t' window, wi' a red nightcap." The servants heard nothing of this. In vain Tate raged, and Tommy persevered with his " Get away, get away wi 'ye!" telling him that he must earn all the money he could, because the " One o' May would soon come for him to lose it on," &c.

Another fond (*i. e.* foolish) man, whose name I think was Emanuel, was remarkable for his power of locomotion, and one spark of intelligence which prompted him on the first suggestion to set off on any given errand, whatever the distance might be. He had frequently been known to undertake, for the consideration of one shilling, to carry a letter to London, and bring back an answer, going off *instanter*, as if the point of distance lay only in the next street, and required neither preparation nor consideration of any kind. Many wagers had been laid and won in proof of his manner of undertaking his task, and his punctual fulfilment of it. It was supposed that he begged his way up to town and back. On delivering the fruit of his mission in evidence of his faithful performance of it, he would receive the stipulated shilling, and walk away with it perfectly satisfied and apparently pleased. He generally took about three weeks or a month to execute his journey to town and back.

" Fond Barney," was another of the same class, " more potent," but certainly less agreeable than the two former; for he was very ugly, and besides, had vices in common with his more rational brethren. Barney was fond of drink. His principal pursuit and means of support arose from selling the racing calendars, and " last dying speeches" of executed criminals; and from his intemperate habits he so blended his alternate tasks, that, not knowing how to read, there were times when he was wholly at a loss to separate the subjects. It was the pleasure of certain wags, who were aware of poor Barney's failing, to make him drink more ale than his weak brain could bear, and then take their fill of amusement from the result which was sure to be a complete confusion of matter, from a doubtful understanding of his that day's *calling*. Thus, in race-time, he would mix up the mournful chronicle of the assize with the inspiriting details of the race; jumbling judges and jockeys, horses and housebreakers together in " most admired disorder." Stalking onwards on tiptoe, (his peculiar way of walking,) with his papers held at arm's length to attract attention, he would begin with a very long —" Here—'s! a right and true list of all the running horses, who are to take their trial before my lord judge—" (here a mischievous correction from one of his *friends*, would in some measure make him conscious of error).—" No. Here's! a right and true list of all the malefactors, who are to start to-morrow at Knaresmire, for the plate; with the names of their owners, and the colour of their riders, now in York Castle,—and how they came in these three days. Buy a list?" After another stupified pause he would resume. " Here—'s! a right and true list of all the running horses—now confined in Ouse-bridge gaol, — who are to take their trial on Monday next—at the grand stand, for the gold cup: and a right, true and particular account of the life, character, and behaviour, of the celebrated horse Hambletonian, — who was executed in chains at the new drop, yesterday, pursuant to his sentence; with a copy of the letter which he wrote to his wife the night before his execution," &c.

This man was a favourite study of Mr. Mathews, and was introduced into the Harlowe Picture, which represents my husband in five characters; the last head in the back-ground is intended for " Fond Barney," which it completely describes. The centre and principal figure, catching a fly, was also a study from another of these harmless beings, who had no very striking peculiarity, and died early while we were in York.

CHAPTER XV.

Unpopularity of the Income-tax. — Mr. Mathews's whimsical remonstrance to the Commissioners.—Anecdote of Quick.— Letter of Mr. Litchfield to Mr. Mathews.—Mrs. Litchfield as *Lady Macbeth.* — Cooke's success at Covent Garden. — Mrs. Mathews a novelist. — Straitened circumstances of Mr. Mathews.— Mrs. Mathews's literary projects for defraying the claims upon her husband.—Letter to Mr. Litchfield.—Tate Wilkinson's opinion of Mr. Mathews. — Mr. William Mathews's departure for the West Indies, and letter to his brother.—Letter to Mr. Litchfield.—Tate Wilkinson's opinion of Murphy's Life of Garrick. — Mr. Mathews's success at York.—His fondness for attending trials.—Action for killing a donkey. — Witness interrogated by Counsellors Raine and Cockle.— Simplicity of the witness.—Letter of Mr. William Mathews to his brother.

AMONGST other reminiscences of my husband's Yorkshire engagement, I remember, when the Income-tax occasioned such commotion and heart-burning amongst people of small means, the actors belonging to the York theatre felt the hardship of its lessening the little they received; which, at the utmost, was barely sufficient to maintain them. Mr. Mathews, just then rising into notice, and his humour getting pretty well understood in private as well as in public, took it into his head to resist this claim upon his little pittance, with all the power of his droll fancy; and he hit upon an expedient as original as it was eccentric, in order to evade the tax. To induce a mitigation of its enforcement, he drew out a long and tedious list of all the professional drawbacks upon his limited receipts, and in a lengthened string of absurd items, enumerated with ingenious minuteness his " stock in trade;" something in the following manner, but extended beyond my limits to give entire. A specimen will suffice.

At " the head and front" of his inventory, we will suppose " *wigs*," which were described in all their infinite variety : such as, " Black wigs, white wigs, brown wigs, red wigs; bush wigs, tye wigs, bob wigs, bishops' wigs; wigs with a tail, wigs without a tail; lawyers' wigs, judges' wigs, parsons' wigs, powdered wigs; old men's wigs, young men's wigs, &c.

" Natural heads of hair: namely, Red hair, grey hair, flaxen hair, brown hair, black hair, Quakers' hair, countrymen's hair, and bald heads of every description. Beards, whiskers, mustachios, eye-brows," &c.

Stockings of every colour were then enumerated. " White, black, brown, yellow, grey, blue, green. White stockings with red clocks, red stockings with white clocks, white stockings with blue clocks, blue stockings with white clocks. Silk stockings, worsted ditto. Black stockings with scarlet clocks, scarlet stockings with black clocks, yellow stockings with green clocks, red stockings with no clocks, &c.

" Old men's shoes, young men's shoes, velvet

shoes, leather shoes, gouty shoes, dancing shoes, hob-nail shoes, square-toed shoes, round-toed shoes," &c. After which, boots of every quality and shape were described. Then shoe and knee-buckles of every size and fashion : " diamond-buckles, paste-buckles, gold-buckles, silver-buckles, stock-buckles, belt-buckles, hat-buckles," &c. &c. .After these regular requisites were given, came the miscellaneous part of his stock; such as, " Hats, feathers, caps, cravats, stocks, ruffles, frills, neckerchiefs, handkerchiefs, pens, books, ink, paper, music paper, red-ochre, rouge, carmine, hair-powder, wax candles, Indian ink, camel's hair pencils, hare's feet, whiting, burnt corks, cold cream, Windsor-soap, and huckaback towels."

The above abridgment of this almost interminable list, which covered many sheets of paper, will give some idea of the whole, which was drawn out with the most scrupulous exactness. The author of this piece of absurdity was told that the commissioners listened to the account of the comedian's expenses, which was read aloud to them, and which they thought would last until the " crack of doom," with matter-of-fact attention and gravity for a few minutes. This was succeeded by peals of laughter and perfect good humour to the close; and though it is to be feared that this laughable appeal did not exempt his theatrical brethren from the tax, it is quite certain that Mr. Mathews was never called upon in York, from that time forth, to contribute to it.

Nothing particular now occurred to break "the even tenor of his way," for some time, but the arrival of Mr. Quick from London, in the autumn of 1800, to perform a certain number of nights. In a letter to Mr. Litchfield will be found a notice of that circumstance, in the writer's characteristic style.

Quick has played five nights: *The Miser, Sir Benjamin Dove, Scrub, Little Isaac, Cockletop,* &c. Last night, his benefit, *Solus* and *Old Doiley.* He leaves us to-day for Sheffield. He is a pleasant little fellow, and, barring that he plays my business, I wish his stay with us was much longer. He has not an atom of improper consequence in his composition.

On the day of Mr. Quick's departure just mentioned, Mr. Mathews accompanied him to the inn, whence the Sheffield coach was to start; and as they arrived before the time for leaving, and the weather was very damp and cold, (it was the middle of November,) they entered the kitchen, where there was a blazing fire, at which a large goose was being roasted. Quick, who was very cold, walking up to the chimney-corner, rubbed and warmed his hands until the arrival of the coach, when Mr. Mathews took leave of him. As the coach drove off, my husband observed two men, who had been in the kitchen while they were there, looking after Mr. Quick with some interest; one of whom immediately asked the landlord if he knew who that "comical-looking little chap" was. The landlord informed them that it was Mr. Quick, the great London actor; on which the questioner, clapping his hands together with great knowingness, exclaimed to his friend,—" Dom it, I *thought* he was a player! Didn't ye see how he eyed the goose?"

TO MR. CHARLES MATHEWS.

DEAR STICK,* 13th January 1801.

I am a sad dog, Charles; scorn me, buffet me, but utter not one syllable against either my punctuality or my consistency; for of fifty letters received from you, Mrs. Mathews, Harley the actor, and other friends, not one have I answered. But now you write to me on business, I am compelled to return an answer; "You tie me to the stake, I cannot fly;" Shakspeare, hem! Briefly then, the "Wags of Windsor" I never saw, so I can tell you nothing about Fawcett's dress;—"are you answered?" But I will make inquiry, and you shall have an account of it; "What, are you answered yet?"

15th January 1801. I had got thus far on Tuesday last, when I was interrupted, and have not had an opportunity of proceeding till this moment. My dear fellow, I have a thousand things to say when I see you, which I hope will be shortly, either as a visiter to the metropolis or as a star in one of our theatres. By the by, Mrs. Litchfield is getting on: she has played *Lady Macbeth* four times to Cooke's *Macbeth*, with great credit and applause; and the critics are very high in their diurnal commendations. She is engaged at the Haymarket. I am ashamed of myself for neglecting to acknowledge the receipt of Mrs. Ma-

* Mr. Litchfield applied this name to him when a boy, from his very slender figure, and it was generally adopted by Mr. Mathews's early friends.—A. M.

thews's letter; but my gallantry was ever as conspicuous as my punctuality. I am anxious to read her new novel, the sale of which I shall do all in my power to promote, and the reputation of its author. Happy, most happy, to hear of your successful benefit, and of your increasing theatrical fame. Cooke has brought a mine of wealth to Covent Garden. He is a curious actor; often great, often surprising, with some whimsical defects that act as a foil to his excellences. Mrs. Litchfield, since we saw you, has been very dangerously ill in consequence of the loss of a beautiful little girl, our last; the particulars I cannot relate—they are too horrible! Time has somewhat mitigated our affliction, but the recollection of our loss frequently embitters our happiest moments.

My best respects to Mrs. Mathews; calm the indignation which I know she must feel at my conduct. Mrs. Litchfield desires her remembrance to both.

Dear Stick,

Ever your sincere friend, and regular correspondent,

JOHN LITCHFIELD.

Council Office, 15th January, 1801.

The novel alluded to in Mr. Litchfield's letter was one out of several which Mrs. Mathews wrote, and the only one she confessed to her husband. During the hours he was engaged in his profession, she would, to the injury of her health, employ herself at her pen, with a hope (which proved fallacious in the end,) of acquiring so much money unknown to him as might discharge arrears for living, of the existence of which her uncalculating husband was wholly unconscious.

It may, however, be easily understood, that the

small salary of five-and-twenty shillings per week* was insufficient for the support of two persons even of the most frugal habits. Unfortunately, Mrs. Mathews loved well, but not wisely. She saw the weekly means fall short of just demands; but dreading to distress her husband, and being sanguine as to her own resources, upon which she reckoned to defray the excess unpaid, she allowed an accumulating care to corrode her heart, and in effect to place her well-meant reserve in the light of criminal deceit, when the revelation must necessarily be made. In short, she had not courage to tell her husband in the first instance that their means were inadequate to their wants. On his part, he gave up weekly the whole of his receipts to his little housekeeper, and never doubted or questioned that the amount sufficed for their narrow plan of life; while their wardrobe and every extra expense was met (as he supposed) by the profits from his benefits. Poor Mrs. Mathews, however, still went on writing, and offering her works for sale (novels, sonnets, elegies, love-songs, &c.); and, as may be imagined, she never received that which her hopes led her to expect from their sale. Her debts (I say *hers*, because she had in a manner made them such by concealing them from her husband,) became harassing, and the poor anxious, amiable girl worked

---

* Mr. Mathews's salary had been increased to this amount since his success.—A. M.

early and late to earn the amount required to defray them, denying herself rest and happiness. Still was she unsuccessful; but she contrived to keep her husband free from care, and that comforted her. In truth, there was little power in her writings. She knew nothing of society or of the world. Her reading had been slender, and confined to the generally mawkish style of the novels of that day. From them she gave faint impressions of nature; and no publisher thought them worth much more than the cost of printing. Disappointment followed disappointment. She suffered deeply, and, I have sometimes suspected, dangerously. Naturally delicate, this constant state of secret anxiety must have injured a constitution which required constant ease to support it.

The novel of "What has been" was her best, and was published with her name; but without augmenting much the pecuniary resources of the young couple. Still Mrs. Mathews was indefatigable in her pursuit of fame and profit; and her husband, wholly intent upon his profession, "laboured in his vocation," without suspecting the covered pitfall which was every hour deepening for his reception, by one who, to save him from one minute's pain, would have bound herself to years of torture; in fact, she had done so.

It became eventually necessary that the sad

truth should be told. Creditors applied to the husband for that which the wife had so long evaded; and just before her death the truth disclosed to him embarrassments which sufficed to interfere with his comfort for several years after he came to London. The poor weak, but well-meaning cause of them, however, was never afflicted by one moment's reproach; indeed, a less benevolent spirit than that to which she confessed her fault, must have pardoned an error caused solely by her unbounded though mistaken love for him she so unintentionally injured. This early enthralment was the basis, as I have said, of much after-difficulty.

TO JOHN LITCHFIELD, Esq.

DEAR JACK, Hull, January 25th, 1801.

" Give me your hand, you dog. I forgive you. Your last letter has made your peace for you,"—Sheridan—hem! "Confound you, you shall be Jack again." Indeed, my dear *regular* correspondent, your letter gave me pleasure, and I am sincerely glad that I hit on an expedient at last to induce you to write. I have heard of your tricks. Halpin, who has joined us, tells me that Harley informed him of his having sent you a packet, and that he received no answer, and was apprehensive that he had offended you. " But I forgive all."

I think it will be worth while to come to town to hear your "thousand things." Indeed I long to see you; but it will be as a visiter. As for " a star," why, indeed, Jack, the idea of a London audience will ever terrify me, though *here* I get on —I do—I will. Seriously, my dear fellow, if it is possible for a man to judge of himself, I do not think it unlikely that in time I may meet with an offer from London. But I have made up my mind, and think that, my figure and everything considered, it would be imprudent to accept of any offer, without Heaven should take Dicky Suett. That is the situation which is set down for me here, and any other I should be very, very cautious of accepting. To be shelfed would break my heart. *Aut Cæsar, aut nullus,* for me! Am I not right? ha!

By the by, Tate once said, " All the Mirrors* in the world could not make me a first-rate actor, nor his principal low comedian." The other day he said, " I'll never judge hastily again," speaking of a lady. " Now, there's Mathews; when he came, I said it never could be —thought it was not in the cards; now, I do not hesitate to say, Meadows is a good comedian" (meaning me). " Good morning to you, Mr. Maddox; you played your part in 'The Disaster' very well" (meaning me again, in " The Deserter"). When I come to London, which, by the by, I hope to do in Passion Week, but, mum! I think I can make you laugh by an imitation of our worthy old manager, and his incoherent manner of talking. I have played *Quotem* with great applause; and on Friday last, *Frederick,* in " Of Age To-morrow," with great applause also; two very valuable original parts. The old man thanked me in the green-room for my support to the piece, and said he never laughed more in his life I know, Jack, that in the pleasure you will receive at hearing of my success you will forget that I am an egotist, or, if you should not, you will forgive my vanity.

I am happy to hear Mrs. Litchfield is successful. I have heard of her fame before. It did not surprise me at

* The Monthly Mirror.

all, as I was convinced, when I saw her play *Calista* and *Aura*,* that she was a good actress, and merit everywhere will in time be found out, and rewarded. Cooke's success, to be sure, has been wonderful. Your account of him, in a few words, is just and clever. I know him well; played with him in Ireland, and, I believe, mentioned him to you with enthusiasm. And now, my old boy, one more favour, though I almost tremble to ask it. But as you say you will inquire about *Quotem's* dress, and will let me know, you certainly mean to write another letter, and one subject is as good as another. I have played *Quotem*, and therefore do not wish to know the dress, (as I had part of it made from my own fancy,) and it would now be too late; therefore, if you will be kind enough to let me know the dress of *Gabriel Lackbrain* in " Life," you will serve me much. I do not know that I should trouble you, Jack, but for your own declaration. I can no more. Excuse the *brevity* of this. Do not impute my abrupt conclusion to " want of regard," and be assured

    I am unalterably yours,
       CHARLES MATHEWS.

(From another correspondent):—

Allow me to thank you for your kind mention of me, and friendly intentions with regard to my novel. It has been a long time in the press, and I hope will soon be out. An early review will be of great service to me. If Charles's great modesty would permit him to be as warm in his own praises as the audience are, he would have said much more of his success here. I truly rejoice at the justly acquired fame of Mrs. Litchfield. With sincere wishes that she may each day increase in fame and fortune, I remain yours sincerely,   E. K. MATHEWS.

* In " The Farm-House."

For the insertion of the following letter, and one of a later date, which will appear in its place, I make no apology. The highly-gifted writer was so nearly allied, and so intimately dear to my husband, that were his letters less worthy in themselves, or not connected with future details, I should feel the omission of them unnatural, in the pages of his brother's history. Mr. William Mathews is remembered by a numerous list of his early associates, men of first-rate talent; amongst whom may be mentioned Mr. Wordsworth, who was his most intimate friend and correspondent.

TO MR. CHARLES MATHEWS.

Feb. 10th, 1801, on board the Beckford,
My dear Brother, Stokes' Bay, Portsmouth.

Here I am on board a fine West Indiaman, expecting to sail to-morrow morning for St. Kitts. I wrote to your father this morning; and being then much hurried, and expecting to sail in two or three hours, I desired him to inform you that I was fearful I should not be able to write to you before we weighed anchor. Fortunately, I have an opportunity, which I embrace with much satisfaction, as it gives me the pleasure of communicating with you once more before I may fairly be said to have quitted my native country. My dear fellow, I have been a very remiss correspondent; but, as I have frequently told you, you may always rest assured that it never has proceeded from any want of affection.

For several years, as you know, I have felt myself a

disappointed man. The depression this has given my spirits has disqualified me for any exertion, and in this lies the whole secret of my neglect towards you. For the future, however, you will have no reason to complain. I am now embarking on a speculation, which, in all human probability, will be in the highest degree advantageous to me. Every individual of my acquaintance assures me I am certain of making a considerable fortune. This of course will, after I have recovered the shock of parting with my natural friends, and some very tender connexions, restore me to my natural character, which most undoubtedly is not disposed to melancholy.

Though I have not written to you, believe me, I have not felt the less disposed to the heartiest wishes for your welfare, and have had constant opportunities of gaining intelligence of your proceedings from our respectable father, with whom your communication has been more frequent than with me.

I can assure you that the greatest pleasure I have ever received in my life has been the constant and uniform testimony of all who know you, to the excellence of your character and the amiability of your manners. That you are beloved by all who have the happiness of your acquaintance, is the highest gratification to me. The very favourable and flattering accounts I have heard of your talents and diligence in your profession, have also contributed to my happiness, accompanied however by a considerable drawback, when I have understood that your exertions have an unfavourable effect upon your health. I applaud your diligence and attention much, but for the love of us all, do not suffer it to injure your health; your life is too precious to us to be sacrificed, even for the acquisition of fame and fortune.

Give my most affectionate love to Eliza, and tell her

I hope to hear of her success as an author; but she must allow me to suggest, that if she wishes to be eminent, she must not write quite in such a hurry as she has been accustomed to do. Let me beg of her, as yet, not to put her name to her novels; and, above all things, let me recommend her to write every one of her productions over at least twice, and very carefully to correct the little inaccuracies which will escape even the most experienced eye. Very few indeed, if any, of our writers of celebrity, have gained their fame except by incessant labour; and perhaps there are not more than one or two who ever have sent any of their productions into the world without a revisal at the least, and that not by barely reading them over, but by re-writing them; for there is no mode so effectual for correcting mistakes. The authors who have occasionally omitted this, (for none have done it except occasionally,) have been persons of such transcendant genius, combined with such an exquisite accuracy of mind, as to render it the extreme of arrogance for any one seriously to suppose that they may venture to neglect this most useful precaution. Tell Eliza, that during my residence in London I have looked to the corrections of her proofs, and have altered parts of the novel which Lane has been printing, according to some sensible suggestions of Mrs. Lane. I hope it has improved it. I have also added some mottoes to those chapters where they had been omitted. To some others appropriate ones did not suggest themselves; I was therefore compelled to suffer them to stand as they did.

Now, my dear Charles, I shall bid you adieu, wishing you every possible happiness. Continue as you have begun, and I am confident you will do well. Above all things, strive to preserve the station you have gained as a man and a gentleman. Cultivate the habits of gentlemanly life, and an amiability of temper and manners. This small change of the world is that which gains affection; and benevolence towards each other, exhibited in mutual good humour, is by far the most gratifying spectacle human nature can exhibit, excepting only real conjugal affection. Adieu. Live happy till I see you.

Yours most affectionately,
W. MATHEWS.*

To Mr. Charles Mathews, Theatre Royal,
    Hull, Yorkshire.

TO MR. JOHN LITCHFIELD.

DEAR JACK,   York, March 7th, 1801.

Murphy's Life of Garrick has done our worthy old manager such mischief that he cannot eat, drink, or sleep. He was in eager expectation of this publication, and hoped to derive much amusement from it; but his disappointment has been such, that he attributes an illness under which he now labours to that cause. Certainly it is not what might have been expected from so clever a man as Murphy. It was natural to look for some anecdotes of Garrick hitherto unpublished, from a man who was on the stage himself in his time. This circumstance he never mentions. In fact, there is nothing to be met with but that which we have already seen in Davies, Wilkinson, &c.; and the prologues may be had for a shilling, in the Spouters' Companion. We are *much obliged* to him, cer-

---

* The admonitory tone of this letter may remind the reader that Mr. William Mathews was some years the senior of his brother.—A. M.

tainly, for his account of the plot, characters, &c. in
" Venice Preserved," " Orphan," &c.

However, to my business. Mr. Wilkinson has detected some gross errors, particularly that of the King not having seen Garrick for many years after he came to London; and that Garrick solicited to play before him. He has the play-bills of those times by him, and has proved him to be wrong. He is anxious to publish his discovery of Murphy's mistake, and requests to know if you can oblige him with about six pages in your next Mirror; or should it be more, to be continued. He says he wants neither fame nor profit, but he could not resist correcting such gross mistakes as Murphy has made, and he likes the truth to be spoken. Now, supposing a theatrical controversy to be rather valuable to a periodical publication, I flattered him with hopes of your acceding to his request. Do not fail to let him know by return of post, and if it be possible, pray grant it to him; for his perturbed spirit will not rest till his sentiments are known. He has interlarded all his conversation these eight or nine days past, with this subject: Question, " What play, sir, have you fixed for Monday?"—Answer, " Why, Mr. Richer dances, and the farce is ———, and as to his saying that the King did not see Garrick, it is all nonsense; because my Memoirs will tell," &c. Question — " Good day, sir; any news? How is the King?" " Why, they say that ——— For my part, I have no patience, because now the 'Chinese Festival,' was played when the King bespoke," &c. Question — " What will you have for dinner, my dear?" Answer—" Dinner! Oh, that mutton yesterday, was — and then you know, Murphy not giving any account of his own playing, and giving us all the prologues that we know by heart," &c. Ha! ha! ha! Oh Jack, I wish you could hear him.

Yours, unalterably,
CHARLES MATHEWS.

Mrs. Simpson's, Stonegate.

DEAR JACK, York, 22nd March, 1801.

I have waited several days in expectation of Mr. "Williamskin's"* remarks on Murphy's life, but he at last has declared that he cannot finish them till Passion Week, so of course they cannot be inserted in the Mirror till the number for April. I am very sorry, my dear Jack, that I shall not be able to see you as I proposed, in Passion Week. I am so engaged in the business, that I was fearful of getting excused from a night or two's plays, without which, it would have been but little pleasure to me, as I should have had so short a time to stay; but I found from the arrangements that I could not be spared. I then had some idea of accepting an invitation from Ben Thompson, to whom I was introduced, and with whom I spent some pleasant hours in Hull. I had made up my mind to spend a part of the week at Nottingham, but even of that I am disappointed, for the manager has his benefit on Easter Tuesday, and gets up " Deaf and Dumb," and " Il Bonducani;" and having *Dominique*, and the *Cadi*, to study, with rehearsals, &c. it will be impossible. You may judge of my disappointment.

I am getting on in York very fast, and am told by the inhabitants that I am a great favourite, which I did not think was the case last year, my benefit being only 25*l*.

* The name Mr. Wilkinson called himself occasionally.

To be sure, that is no absolute proof, though Mr. Richer had 96*l*.; and one of his houses, his last night, in the assize week, amounted, at advanced prices, to 143*l*.; so much for heels! However, they promise me better things this year; but Hull is our best town, for a favourite in Hull cannot have a bad house. But they are so cursedly fashionable in York, that we have either concerts, routs, and parties, or assemblies, every night in the week. However, I have had " Counsellor's opinion" of my acting this week, and *Serjeant Cockle* awarded great praise to it. I had the pleasure of making him laugh heartily in *Caleb Quotem*. I have delayed saying anything about the novel, and am now writing to you in a hurry; if you have, therefore, leisure to make any alterations, or improvements, in the following title, I will be obliged—" What has been."

I find it so lame, and I am so unused to anything of the sort, that I will thank you to write something in its stead. Adieu.

Yours unalterably,
CHARLES MATHEWS.

Mr. Mathews was always exceedingly fond of hearing trials; and during the assize-weeks at York was a frequent attendant in the courts of justice, whence he derived much of that vast stock of observation of life and character of which he so successfully availed himself in after years.

He felt great enjoyment from the frequently ludicrous trials at which he was present in the civil courts, where originals abounded, and where the passions, in all their varieties and shades, are displayed, and characteristic traits are unfolded to the observer, by the "cunning of the scene." My husband felt that much was to be gathered from the contemplation of human nature under the conflicting and self-deluding position of plaintiff and defendant. He often related cases of deep interest, but more commonly those of a ridiculous nature.

The mention of Serjeant Cockle recals the recollection of a trivial but amusing fact, which he related to me on the day it occurred, and which had convulsed the court with laughter. It was an instance of naïveté in a witness whom he saw examined at York. An action was brought against the owner of a waggon, which by the reckless driving of the waggoner had forced a poor donkey against a wall, and there pressed the poor creature to death. Compensation was therefore sought by its proprietor for the loss of the animal and its services. This trial caused much mirth in its progress. The principal witness for the plaintiff was the driver of the donkey, who, feeling himself very much "brow-beat" by the defendant's counsel, Mr. Raine, became exceedingly nervous and confused in his evidence, which he gave with his eyes upon the ground. He was several times reprimanded by the judge for not looking in the faces of those by whom he was interrogated, and desired to hold up his head. The poor timid fellow's embarrassment increased upon every reproof, and the opposing counsel, Mr. Raine, (who had a powerful cast in his eyes,) was particularly severe with him, repeating the judge's injunction several times, saying, " Hold up your head, witness; look up; why don't you look up, I say? Can't you hold up your head, fellow? Can't you look as I do?"—" Nay, sir," replied the countryman with perfect simplicity, " I can't—you squint."

The laughter of the court now gave the supporting counsel, Serjeant Cockle, (who was also a sharp questioner, but, luckily for the poor witness, on his side,) opportunity of calling upon the man to describe the local situations of the several parties concerned, their relative positions at the time of the accident and death of the poor donkey — where the waggon was — and where the animal, &c. The poor harassed witness paused for a minute, standing with his eyes again downcast, as if he saw no possibility, by words, of giving the required explanation. Objects palpable seemed necessary to describe the scene referred to. However, looking stealthily round at the parties present, as he scratched his head, the image of perplexity, while Serjeant Cockle mildly urged him to obey orders, he at length seemed to have arranged the means in his mind's eye of giving the required information. Hesitatingly he began,—" Weel, my Lord Joodge, I'll tell ye how it happened, as well as I can.

First of all," turning to Cockle, " you'll suppose you are the wall."—" Very good," said Cockle. " Ay, you are the wall," repeated the witness, and the counsel, rather impatient at the repetition, replied, " Yes, yes; now proceed. I am the wall. Well?"—" Yees, sir," reiterated the man, " you are the wall." Then changing his own position in the court to another spot, he added, " And now, I am the waggon."—" Very well," observed the judge, in token of his understanding him; "proceed."—" Yees," again asserted the tedious but earnest witness, " I am the waggon." — " Well, well," said the now impatient judge; " you've told us that before. Go on; you're the waggon."—" Yees, I'm the waggon; —and," with a low bow, " your lordship's the *Ass*."

This evidence, though not perhaps quite satisfactory to the judge, was conclusive.

TO MR. CHARLES MATHEWS.

My dear Charles,   Barbadoes, June 5th, 1801.

There is a melancholy pleasure in communicating our thoughts to the objects of our best regards, when at an immense distance from us, which is not to be conceived by those who pass their lives in the dull uniformity of a settled existence, and without even an occasional separation from those they love. When I could hear every day of your proceedings, I acknowledge that you had some reason to complain of my indolence, though never of my love to you and yours. The case is now altered, and the desire of hearing from you, and communicating with you, becomes a passion of great force in my breast. Your happiness is a great object with me, and it is with much impatience I am waiting to have a communication of good news from you or your wife. Do not, I entreat you, suffer any notion of my former negligence to prevent your writing to me by every opportunity. There are two pair of hands in your family fully capable of contributing to the pleasure of an absent friend and brother; and you will be really inexcusable, if one or other of you do not frequently let me know how you pass your time, and give me full information of the amelioration of your prospects in life, and your progress towards the higher situations in the liberal profession in which you are engaged. I have been in this island two months, and have met with the greatest hospitality and friendship. A better prospect, however, offering itself for the acquisition of money in Tobago, I am about to quit this place for the latter, and as there are only two lawyers in the island, I make no doubt, with the recommendations I shall have, of soon acquiring a considerable share of business.

Hitherto ill-fortune has pursued me in every shape; but I hope that her persecution is nearly over; and I trust that hereafter I shall be enabled to spend a tranquil life in the society of my friends in England in ease and affluence. Whatever may be my fate, I shall still have the consolation of having exerted myself, and of having acquired in every situation the esteem of men of sense and worth. There has never occurred in the course of my life any circumstance so flattering to me as the estimation in which I have the honour to be held by some of the first people in point of consequence and liberality of sentiment in this island, to whom I had not even the slight introduction of a letter. Success, therefore, in my object will be the highest gratification of my self-love, as I shall in that case with propriety call myself the fabricator of my own fortunes.

You also, my dear brother, will have a similar gratification. You have uniformly gained the esteem of strangers; and by a continuance of the same good conduct you may be certain of a final termination of all your wants, and satisfaction of every wish of your heart. I hope Eliza continues to employ her pen, and still more, that she takes pains to improve her style. Her invention and powers are good; and by a constant perusal of the best writers, and a sedulous attention to their errors, and the defects of her own compositions, she may hereafter expect both fame and fortune from her exertions; but without labour neither can be acquired.

I hope you both continue to enjoy good health. My own is better than ever it was in England. Heat is the element in which I live. In cold weather I have a bare, comfortless existence. Tell Eliza from me, that I sincerely wish her well in body and mind; but that to secure the latter from disease, she must carefully watch that the seeds of superstition, which some one has plentifully sown in her heart, do not bring forth the fruit it generally does, illiberality of sentiment, and that worst of all fiends, religious bigotry. The whole history of mankind is but a relation of the fatal and mischievous effects of this diabolical tyrant, who has uniformly preyed upon the enlightened few that have dared to lift up their heads against the oppressor of their afflicted brethren, and has gnawed the very vitals of social existence. There is no part of the globe that is not even now groaning beneath her baneful pressure; and whatever form she assumes, she still arrogates to herself the claim of infallibility, and her votaries, of whatever sect they may be, damn by wholesale all the rest of the world.

A freedom from superstition is the first blessing we can enjoy. Religion in some shape seems necessary to political existence. The wise man laughs at the follies of the vulgar, and in the pure contemplation of a benevolent Author of all Beings, finds that happiness which others in vain look for amid the load of trumpery and ceremonies with which they think the Creator is gratified. If He can be gratified by any exertion of feeble mortals, it must be when they imitate His perfection by mutual benevolence and kindness. That you may long enjoy these blessings is the sincere prayer of your brother and friend,

W. MATHEWS.

With the above remarks the writer's early experience had something to do; and his feelings naturally took alarm at a mistaken tendency, evident to all who knew the amiable person to whom he alludes. Mr. William Mathews had in his boyhood felt the gloom and rigours of fanaticism under his father's roof, where he had ceased to reside for some years, although he frequently visited it, and was on the most affectionate terms with all his family, who might be said to idolize him. But in these visits he resisted with all the energies of his strong mind every after-association with the ignorant and illiberal portion of his father's " brethren."

CHAPTER XVI.

Mr. Mathews's accident while performing at York.—Death of his brother.—Letter to Mr. Litchfield.—Mrs. Mathews's illness and dying wishes.—Letter to Mr. Litchfield.—Death of Mrs. Mathews.—A remarkable dream.—Letter from Mr. Colman, offering Mr. Mathews an engagement in London.—Correspondence on the subject.

THE September of this year (1801) brought with it much calamity and sorrow. Mr. Mathews, while performing the Obi-Woman in "Three-fingered Jack," (in compliance with a whim of his master,) was crouching under a heavy platform, when the whole of it suddenly gave way and fell upon him! The audience and all present were much alarmed, and believed that he was killed, but after the tedious process of removing the whole of the apparatus, he was found alive, but senseless; nor was he restored to consciousness for a long time, when his bruises were found to be severe. He was then put to bed in a wretched state of suffering, covered with plaisters and bandages; and as " one sorrow seldom comes, but brings an heir that may succeed," a letter by the next morning's post filled his heart with the deepest anguish. The cause of this will be explained in the following bill, issued from the theatre the same day:

Theatre, Wakefield, Sept. 19th, 1801.

The unfortunate accident which Mr. Mathews met with last night in the entertainment of " Obi," and in addition to that misfortune, the melancholy news received this day of the sudden death of his brother, has so affected him as to render it utterly impossible for him to make his appearance on the stage this evening. Mr. Wilkinson is therefore under the absolute necessity of changing the play and farce to Dr. Goldsmith's favourite comedy of " She stoops to Conquer," and " The Poor Soldier."

Thus, wounded alike in body and mind, Mr. Mathews continued incapable of any exertion of either for some time, as the annexed letter, dated a month after, to his kind friend Mr. Litchfield, (by whom his brother's death had been communicated to him) will show.

TO MR. JOHN LITCHFIELD.

Doncaster, October 18th, 1801.

I know, my dear friend, that you will not attribute my silence to neglect, or imagine that I have not a proper sense of your kindness; but you are of course aware, from " sad experience," what must have been my feelings on the receipt of your melancholy though kind and sensible letter. I never received such a shock before. I have since found that it was mentioned in the Yorkshire papers three days before I received the unhappy news from you.

I seldom miss reading the papers, but it so happened that just at that time we were travelling, and I had no opportunity of seeing them. To have received the intelligence in such a way would have been, if possible, a worse shock to my spirits. I feel many obligations to you, my dear and valued friend, for the manly and sensible consolation you offered in your letter.

Poor William! never were two brothers more enthusiastically attached to each other than that noble fellow and myself. Why would he be persuaded to go to that fatal country? I think it not at all irrational to say, that whoever goes voluntarily to that cursed climate is in some degree guilty of suicide; and if otherwise, those who persuade him are in some degree guilty of murder. How many thousand Europeans have found their graves in that destructive spot. But it is in vain to lament! The grief one naturally feels, however, at the loss of friends is considerably augmented when they die at a distance; for there is a melancholy satisfaction in reflecting that we had it in our power to soothe and comfort the last moments of a departed friend. Poor lamented William! what must have been his sensations! How must his sufferings have been aggravated by anticipating the severe shock his death must occasion to his beloved parents and family. I think it somewhat singular that the person who wrote on the subject should not mention the cause of his death.*

Yours unalterably,
Charles Mathews.

Mr. Mathews had scarcely time allowed him to recover from the effects of this severe blow upon

---

* It was afterwards ascertained that he died of the yellow fever.—A. M.

his affections, when another threatened to lay prostrate his domestic happiness and " desolate his hearth."

For many months past the natural delicacy of Mrs. Mathews's constitution had increased, and at length a more serious result seemed impending than was at first apprehended. The symptoms of decline hourly gained ground; her habits of confinement, (for she still clung to the fallacious hope of gain by her pen, and was constantly devoted to its exercise,) and her anxiety to contribute to her husband's narrow and inadequate means was such, that she neither allowed herself air nor proper exercise; and everybody who saw her, except (as it generally happens) those who were most interested in her safety, clearly perceived her danger. She grew weaker and weaker, but the activity of her mind, and her naturally good spirits, not only deceived her husband, but even herself; and it was not until the winter of this year that he apprehended any serious catastrophe. Physicians were then called in, and the " coming event cast its shadow before;" for the shocked husband was candidly told that medical aid could not avert the premature doom which hung over the head of his amiable wife.

She daily grew worse, and at last was constantly confined to her bed. Her own convictions may be learned from the following circumstance, which I must introduce with a compliment necessarily implied to myself. Mrs. Mathews, from the first moment of our meeting, conceived a violent affection for me; and, though I was many years her junior, she sought my friendship and regard by every means in her power. I was hardly capahle of estimating her superiority of intellect, but I loved her sufficiently to think her society desirable; and I esteemed her husband as an honourable young man, and, to *my* perception, the most perfect comic actor in the world. In fact, I would stand at the side-scenes for a whole evening to see him act, so delighted was I with him; further than this, I was unconscious of partiality for him.

It happened that at one period during the winter of this year, I had not been so recently to see my poor friend as I wished. The weather was severe, and her habitation distant from my own: I was, besides, constantly occupied at the theatre, where I received daily accounts of her state from her husband, whose depression was evidently increasing; and messages of the kindest nature passed through him between the invalid and myself. One evening, Mr. Mathews told me that his wife was better, and was most desirous that I would go to see her the next day at a particular hour. Of course I obeyed her summons; and found her, as I had been led to expect, apparently much better. I complimented her upon the favourable change, which she told me was owing to a design she had conceived, and in the fulfilment of which she required me to aid her. I was delighted; but the invalid wished to postpone the explanation until her husband's return home, which she expected every moment. In the mean time, she chatted with cheerfulness, and would be propped up in bed, in order, as she said, to be able to look at us both while she revealed her project. Mr. Mathews at last entered the room, and uttered an exclamation of surprise and pleasure at seeing the poor sufferer able to be raised up as she had been. She repeated to him what she had told me, that the cause of her present comfort was that which she had called us together to reveal; and after a preface, which agitated all parties very much, (for she candidly avowed her conviction that it was out of the power of human skill to save her,) she pathetically deplored leaving her husband, particularly as he would naturally marry again — *possibly* a woman who would less understand his valuable qualities of heart and mind than she had done. She saw too, in that case, that he would be wretched, and this idea had preyed upon her feelings as her disease increased, and sharpened all her pains.

During a pause which her weakness rendered necessary, her hearers looked at each other with perplexity, and some suspicion that her intellects were wandering. She resumed, however, and after one or two affecting allusions to her own death, which she predicted must occur within a brief period from the time she was addressing us, turning to me, she began to expatiate upon her feelings and affection towards me, and deplored my partially unprotected state, which my extreme youth and inexperience rendered so dangerous. The thought of this, she declared, doubled her remaining cares in this world, and she conjured me, with her "dear husband," to take compassion upon her state, and the fears which so embittered her last days, by making a promise jointly with him, to fulfil her dying wishes. The poor sufferer then took her husband's hand in hers, and kissed it fervently, and asking for mine, and pressing it also to her feverish lips in a solemn manner, which I remember made me tremble all over, called upon us both to pledge ourselves to become man and wife after her dissolution!

It would be impossible to describe our surprise, embarrassment, and distress. The proposition was truly painful to me, and it was impossible not to feel for the equally delicate position of Mr. Mathews, who rather impetuously reproved the poor invalid, for having drawn him into so extraordinary a dilemma; whilst I, covered with confusion and drowned in tears, sobbed with agony at the necessity I felt of rejecting the proposal, in which she said she believed she provided for the mutual good of the two beings she loved best. Dreading the worst consequences from the agitation and disappointment of her romantic project, I fell upon my knees at her bed-side, beseeching her pardon at the impossibility I felt to comply with her desire, from a total absence of any feeling but that of friendship for her husband. As for poor Mr. Mathews, he seemed inexpressibly shocked and mortified at the situation into which he had been surprised, as well as for the distressing scene in which I had been implicated. After I had soothed her as far as possible, and reiterated my want of power to think of such an union, I quitted the chamber of my poor dying friend; her husband rushed after me, beseeching me not to harbour for one moment a suspicion that he had the remotest idea of the nature of his wife's intention, when he delivered her summons to me; and begging me to attribute her extraordinary conduct to a slight delirium, for such he felt assured it was.

However this might be, I ever after, during the remainder of her painful existence, dreaded and avoided any approach to confidential communication with her; and, I fear, saw less of her than a strict feeling of friendship would justify. It may also be imagined that Mr. Mathews and myself became more formal in our manners and intimacy than we otherwise should have been, until the painful impression gradually subsided.

The scene just described happened early in the

year, and still the poor sufferer lived on in pain and difficulty, such as only an implicit reliance upon the goodness of Heaven could lend her resignation to support. In May, however, it will be seen by the following letter of her husband to his friend in London, that hope was rapidly lessening; and his own words will best speak for his feelings, and the virtues of her whom he was about to lose, and will at the same time show his just appreciation of them.

DEAR JACK, York, May 16th, 1802.

Believe me, I am much gratified to find that you will not pass over an opportunity of writing to me; and that it is in my power to compliment you on your reformation in that respect, as your communications are much more frequent than they used to be. I assure you, my dear friend, that the sight of " Dear Stick" is one of the most pleasurable sensations I experience, and such sensations have of late been more than ever valuable.

I am in a most melancholy situation—six months' illness! Poor Eliza! she still continues lingering—the greatest of all sufferers, and one of the most patient. She coughs sometimes for nearly half an hour together, and this is succeeded by the most dreadful sight I ever saw—the vomiting of blood. Her bones are so nearly through the skin, that she can with difficulty turn in her bed. She rises for about half an hour in the day, and then can with difficulty crawl across the room. I have had the best advice I could procure; but all the medical men I have employed are of opinion she cannot recover, and it appears to me impossible that she can, for her lungs must certainly be very much injured, if not nearly decayed. I assure you it is a severe stroke upon me. Independently of the prospect of losing a valuable and intelligent companion, the dreadful expenses of her illness are nearly the ruin of me. You may judge yourself how heavily it must fall on a country actor—six months' apothecaries' bills, with the mortifying reflection that all such assistance is in vain. But this is a melancholy subject to intrude on you; you must excuse my dwelling on it; in fact, I am not fit to write. My mind and body are harassed. I have not had a sound night's sleep these three months.

You may judge I was much flattered at hearing the opinion of Pope. It is, indeed, valuable to hear of such praise, and to me of all people. No one has met with more difficulties than I have; but I have persevered, and when I find myself thus spoken of, it is an assurance that my efforts have not been in vain. When I came here, Wilkinson thought I never should make an actor; certainly he saw me frequently to disadvantage. Now he is proud of reading his recantation. He told Mrs. Chapman (who, by the by, is a wonderful favourite here,) that I was the most promising young man he ever remembered to have had—the most perfect and attentive to dress, and the greatest favourite he has had for many years, particularly in York. "Nay, ma'am, Fawcett was nothing to him" (meaning as a favourite). This, from him, you may imagine is highly gratifying. I must tell you that by his desire I studied, or rather restudied, *Falstaff;* I have played it twice, and have been highly complimented by him. He told Stephen Kemble, who played here four nights, and values himself much on *Falstaff*, that I played it better, and that he wanted humour. I have had the second best benefit here—96*l.* 15*s.* 0*d.* The manager only beat me, and he had a great bill—" Cabinet," and a Harlequin Pantomime. Mine is a plain bill —" The Beaux' Stratagem," and " The Lying Valet." Fifty pounds is reckoned a great house here. Emery, who was a great favourite, never got so high. I assure you I am most comfortably situated, and never expected to be so fortunate in the profession. I have the first business—first salary—first benefits—first acquaintance; and never had an unpleasant word with the manager, in the course of my engagement. I have before apologised to you for being guilty of egotism; but I am confident it is not unpleasant to you, and you are the only person to whom I could say so much. Thompson's opinion I am not a little proud of.* I disputed the point with him before he wrote, about *Ollapod's* jacket having the facing, and that I could not help. I maintain I dress it right. Fawcett's, from the description I have had of it, has nothing but extravagance to recommend it; I dress it as I see all apothecaries, in the cavalry, dress.

I was much disappointed at not coming to London in Passion week. I had made up my mind some time before, and nothing but Mrs. Mathews's dangerous state could have prevented me; however, it was impossible to leave her.

Have you seen Dwyer? I never doubted his first reception in London; he has the *knack* of striking at first; but, as John Moody says, " he canna haud it." If he become a favourite in London, I shall think our York audi-

---

* Benjamin Thompson, then well known for his literary and dramatic taste, and recognised as the translator and adapter of " The Stranger." He was also a person of great local influence, so that his favourable opinion was worth obtaining.— A. M.

ence " plaguy hard to please." His benefit was only 26*l*.; but, to be sure, that is not always a criterion of estimation. Oh! I forgot to tell you that I have discovered I am a famous ventriloquist—at least I have made the people believe so, and that is pretty nearly the same thing. I have done it on the stage in Hull and York with amazing applause, and am told I am a capital artist.

The poems are finished, and the printer only waits for subscribers' names. Now, my dear Jack, I think this long letter deserves an immediate answer. Do write; it will afford me peculiar consolation.

I am unalterably yours,
CHARLES MATHEWS.

Mrs. Mathews's disorder (pulmonary consumption) increased hourly, and her dissolution was daily expected during a painful period of six months. Her excessive sufferings were borne by her with an equal mind throughout, a strong religious reliance, which never wavered, supporting her; and on the 25th of May the following *affiche* at the door of the theatre, announced the release of this amiable young woman from her earthly trials, her illness having lasted upwards of a year and a half.

THEATRE ROYAL, YORK.

May 25th, 1802.

The sudden death of Mrs. Mathews this afternoon, rendering it impossible for Mr. Mathews to perform this evening, Mr. Wilkinson is under the absolute necessity of changing the opera of " The Cabinet," to Mr. Cumberland's comedy of " The Jew ; or a Peep at the Human Heart." The farce, Mr. W. is in hopes, can be done without the assistance of Mr. Mathews.

Although prepared—if expectation of the loss of those we love can be called preparation—for this mournful event, Mr. Mathews felt as if he had never contemplated the result of his wife's illness. The fits to which he had so long been occasionally subject assailed him with redoubled violence, and when he again appeared amongst us, he seemed almost as ill as his suffering wife had looked on the day of our distressing interview. When her death was announced to me by a mutual friend, I almost reproached myself that I had not sacrificed my own inclinations to her dying request. As it was, the recollection of it produced almost a coldness between the sad widower and myself for some time after, though in a few months both seemed to have recovered from it, and an easy friendship was resumed.

At the close of the summer a very remarkable instance occurred of a coincidence of dreams, befalling Mr. Mathews and myself, a circumstance which I am induced to relate, since it was attested by witnesses who severally and apart were informed of it, before the dreamers had power to communicate with each other, or their mutual friends.* Mr. Mathews's account of his impressions was as follows :—He had gone to rest, after a very late night's performance at the theatre, finding himself too fatigued to sit up to his usual hour to read; but after he was in bed he discovered—as will happen when persons attempt to sleep before their accustomed time, that to close his eyes was an impossibility. He had no light, nor the means of getting one, all the family being in bed; but the night was not absolutely dark—it was only too dark for the purpose of reading: indeed, every object was visible. Still he endeavoured to go to sleep, but his eyes refused to close, and in this state of restlessness he remained, when suddenly a slight rustling, as if of a hasty approach of something, induced him to turn his head to that side of the bed whence the noise seemed to proceed; and there he clearly beheld the figure of his late wife, "in her habit as she lived," who, smiling sweetly upon him, put forth her hand as if to take his, as she bent forward. This was all he could relate; for in shrinking from the contact with the figure he beheld, he threw himself out of bed upon the floor, where (the fall having alarmed his landlord) he was found in one

* Many of our familiar friends in London will remember with what earnestness and solemnity my husband related this account long after the period of its occurrence, when he thought his listeners were not disposed to scoff at such details, or be sceptical of their truth.

of those dreadful fits to which I have alluded. On his recovery from it he related the cause of the accident, and the whole of the following day he remained extremely ill, and unable to quit his room.

There is nothing surprising in all this; for admitting it not to be a dream, but one of those cases called nightmare, so frequently experienced, (when the sufferer always believes himself under real influences,) it was not a case to excite astonishment. The circumstance which rendered it remarkable, was that at the exact hour when this scene was taking place at a remote distance, a vision of the same kind caused me to be discovered precisely in the same situation. The same sleepless effect, the same cause of terror, had occasioned me to seize the bell-rope, in order to summon the people of the house, which, giving way at the moment, I fell with it in my hand upon the ground. My impressions of this visitation (as I persisted it was) were exactly similar to those of Mr. Mathews. The parties with whom we resided at the time were perfect strangers to each other, and living widely apart, and they recounted severally to those about them the extraordinary dream, for such I must call it, though my entire belief will never be shaken that I was as perfectly awake as at this moment. These persons repeated the story to many, before they were requested to meet and compare accounts; there could consequently be no doubt of the facts, and the circumstance became a matter of much general interest amongst all those who knew us.

That the scene at the bedside of the dying woman simultaneously recurred to the dreamers when awake was natural enough, and was afterwards confessed. How far the facts which I have here related tended to the serious result of our continued intimacy I will not determine; but it is certain that neither of us regarded it as an impediment at a future period, or a just reason why we should not at last fulfil the desire of her whose wishes were made known to us at a time when it would have been discreditable to both, had we supposed ourselves able to comply with it at any future period of our lives.

In the space of eight months, Mr. Mathews had been deprived of two of his dearest ties: for the first loss he was totally unprepared, and the shock was appalling in its effect upon him; but of the latter, he had been mercifully and gradually warned; and though he felt it deeply and sincerely, yet his grief naturally bore a milder aspect than it would otherwise have done. It might be said that his wife had been dead to him and the world long before the event of her actual dissolution. Notwithstanding this, his own malady, as I have said, returned with alarming force, for it always recurred when mental suffering existed. He had several severe fits, which weakened his strength and retarded the renewal of the composure of which he had so long been deprived.

Fortunately an event, as unexpected as it was gratifying, occurred, which was calculated to rouse his dormant energies and to raise his mind from its distressing depression and disability. The master-passion was again predominant, and though he sighed when he remembered that she, who would have so gloried in his triumph, was no longer a participator in his woe or weal, yet he could not conceal from himself or others the satisfaction which the offer now made to him gave his pride as well as his ambition. This offer, " big with the fate of" Mathews, shall speak for itself, in its original form.

TO MR. MATHEWS.

Sir, Theatre Royal, Haymarket, 14th Sept. 1802.

Your merits as an actor having been mentioned to me, give me leave to propose an engagement to you, for next year, in my theatre. It is my intention to commence the season positively on the 15th of next May; and to continue it to the 15th of the following September. Should you think it eligible to embrace the opportunity which I now offer to you, of performing for four months before a London audience, I beg you will be kind enough to inform me on what terms you will give me your assistance. At all events, I shall thank you for a speedy answer, directed to me, at Mr. Jewell's, 26, Suffolk Street, Charing Cross. I am, sir, your obedient servant,

G. Colman.

TO GEORGE COLMAN, ESQ.

Sir, Wakefield, September 23rd, 1802.

I feel much flattered by the offer of an engagement in your theatre, but cannot come to any determination on the subject till I understand more particularly what situation you propose to me. I must beg leave to decline mentioning terms, as I am entirely ignorant of the salaries you usually give. I am so fortunate as to be in great fame on this circuit, in possession of the first cast of characters, and on the best of terms with my manager. It is indeed in every respect a most valuable situation, and it is only on very advantageous terms that I shall be induced to quit it. I most undoubtedly wish to perform in London, but must look for an ample compensation for resigning a lucrative situation, for an engagement of only four months.

I shall be obliged to you, sir, to let me know what salaries you can afford to give, and if I accede to your wishes, what business will be allotted me. This is a very material consideration, and I entreat that you will be as explicit as possible. I have performed in the York theatre the entire range of principal low comedy, and am well studied.

Have the goodness to inform me, if at any part of the season any of the established London performers are to be engaged. I shall thank you for an answer as soon as possible. We leave this place on Tuesday the 28th, after which time, be kind enough to direct—Theatre, Doncaster.

I am, sir, your obedient servant,
Charles Mathews.

GEORGE COLMAN,

The next letter from Mr. Colman is lost, but Mr. Mathews's reply will explain its general tendency.

TO GEORGE COLMAN, ESQ.

Sir,　　　　　　　　　　Doncaster, Oct. 5th, 1802.

I agree with you, that my talents are my own property, and that I have a right to put a price on them; but I may set too high a value on those talents, and incur the charge of monstrous vanity. You offer handsomely, yet still I wish you had mentioned terms. However, as that seems the only bar to our coming to a final determination, I will, rather than be the cause of any farther delay, wave my objections, and speak decidedly on the subject. I must confess the style of your letter is so liberal and gentlemanly, that the desire I feel to engage with you is increased. With respect to my situation here, I can only repeat what I have already said. It will be tedious and uninteresting to you to particularize the many circumstances which make this circuit valuable to me. In leaving it, I make a great sacrifice both as to profit and pleasure; therefore, considering the advantages I resign, the shortness of your engagement, and the hazard of remaining out of a situation at the close of it, I cannot in justice to myself think of resigning my present certain income under 10*l.* per week. If your scheme will afford such a salary, I am willing immediately to close an engagement with you. I beg an answer as soon as possible, and am, sir, your obedient servant,

　　　　　　　　　　　　　　　Charles Mathews.

TO MR. MATHEWS.

Sir, Suffolk-street, Oct. 8, 1802.

The terms which you have proposed are certainly high, and perhaps unprecedented, for a performer who has not yet felt the pulse of a London audience; but the reasons stated for thus fixing your *ultimatum* appear to be founded on justice, to put vanity out of the question. I wave, therefore, all mention of any risk incurred on my part in my new speculation, and embrace your offer. But to prevent all mistakes, permit me to state precisely what I conceive to be the engagement. Ten pounds a week and a benefit, of which benefit you pay the usual charges. You will perform from the 15th May to the 15th September inclusive. If you engage in London after your appearance with me, you give me the preference in a re-engagement. If you think any short legal memorandum requisite between us, I am willing to enter into it. If you conceive the letters that pass between us as sufficient, I am quite content that it should remain an agreement *upon honour*. Pray send me two lines speedily, which will be conclusive. I will (when we meet in the summer) do everything in my power to contribute to your reputation with the public, and your comfort in my theatre.

I am, sir, your obedient humble servant,

G. Colman.

P.S.—Of course, your attendance will be expected in town a week or ten days (as I begin with novelties) previously to the opening of the theatre.

TO GEORGE COLMAN, ESQ.

Sir,   Doncaster, October 13, 1802.

I ought to apologise for neglecting to give you an immediate answer; but I was absent from Doncaster when your letter arrived, and hurry of business has since prevented me.

Nothing now remains but my final decision for your satisfaction. *I accept the terms, and will be with you at the time proposed.* On my part, I feel perfectly satisfied with the letters that have passed between us, and am content it should remain an agreement upon honour. I cannot for a moment think of the necessity for a legal agreement with a man who, in every part of our negotiation, has behaved so liberally. I thank you for your warm assurances of assistance, and hope I shall prove worthy of your kindness. The only anxiety I now feel is as to my appearance before the awful tribunal of the metropolis. Much depends on a judicious choice of character. Pray satisfy me (when you are at leisure) if you positively intend to open with new pieces. Original characters will be undoubtedly desirable; but it will be necessary for you to know my particular *forte*, and satisfactory to all to know in what kind of character you propose to introduce me. A few lines explaining your intentions on this subject will much oblige me. If I have the good fortune to succeed with the public, I feel a perfect reliance, from your general character for gentlemanly conduct to your performers, of comfort in your theatre.

I am, sir, your obedient servant,
CHARLES MATHEWS.

TO MR. MATHEWS.

Dear Sir,   October 23, 1802.

I am happy to find by your last letter of the 13th, that our agreement is completed. You see by the date of this that I take the latitude you offer, when you desire me to inform you of my plans for the opening of the theatre " at leisure." To give you this information (which I will as well as I now can, for you must naturally be anxious) I send you a parcel of crude hints and disjointed sentences, rather than a perfect system; but from these you will be able to make out a sketch of my general intentions. I will endeavour to be more particular in what most immediately regards yourself. Recollect however, that there are secrets in the most petty theatrical states, and that I send you the outline of my scheme in confidence.

New matter, as fast as possible, after the commencement of the season. Certainly an occasional prelude on the first night. A new grand *ballet* of action almost immediately on the opening. A new light drama (of dialogue) to add to it, after a few nights of its run. New matter to follow the above sooner or later, in proportion as the preceding novelties may hit or miss. The prelude I shall write myself, and shall endeavour to cast in it, or leave out of it, such new performers whose reputations might be served or hurt, by appearing thus abruptly (for the first time) before a London audience. New actors of whatever merit, cannot expect to be nursed so much (by giving intervals in their appearances) when they come into an established London company. The scheme is new—almost all the actors are new. If we wait for niceties, the stage will stand still—off we must go at once! ding dong! helter skelter! and the new troops must commence regular action like the veterans. Now, let us see how this plan will militate towards you, premising that I wish to do the best for you which such an undertaking will permit, and that I wish you to suggest anything to me which you think will contribute to your fame. The prelude you may be in or out of, as you please. I think certainly better out; for, as I wish to make you a great gun, it would be a pity to let you off like a squib (in a prelude) at first. When I say this, you need not fear having original characters enough, (just as they may turn out, for that rests with the town,) in the course of the season. The *ballet* on the opening (if it succeed) will be a favourable circumstance for you, for it will supply the place of many a light speaking drama, (into which you will naturally afterwards be thrown,) and give you breathing time. You will not thus be hurried from one character to another, night after night, as if the arrangement were otherwise. Here I begin to perceive (from the length of my letter) that I shall put you to the charge of double postage, but I shall make no apology; for, as you have unwittingly sold yourself to a Turk of a manager, I dare say you would willingly give half-a-crown to know what the tyrant means to do with you.

Let me now consider your first appearance. It must be immediately on the opening; but it shall be in whatever character you please. This is a subject which requires deliberation, and we have no time to deliberate. You tell me that you have performed in the " York theatre the entire range of low comedy." This is a very wide range indeed! But tell me also, in which part of that range you feel yourself to have succeeded most with the audience. Old men, country boys, dapper servants, mingled characters like those of Munden, of sentiment and fun, &c. In short, make out a list of what you like, and send it to me. I would advise you to avoid, if possible, in your first appearance, the difficulty (it is a great one to avoid) of encountering comparison.

First impressions often make or mar. I remember, soon after Munden's first appearance in London, he ate, with uncommon success, a hundred pounds' weight of plum-pudding in "Two Strings to your Bow." This feat was new to a London audience. He had a good character in it, in which nobody had been seen before. Do you recollect anything in which you might make your appearance, under the same favourable circumstances? When you have recovered from the fatigue of reading this ('tis worse than a part of twenty lengths) send me a line. Be assured that, from the reports I have heard of your merits, and from the candid, clear, manly style of your letters to me, I have your interests, abstracted from my own, fully at heart. I am, dear sir, yours sincerely,

G. COLMAN.

TO GEORGE COLMAN, ESQ. THEATRE ROYAL, HAYMARKET.

DEAR SIR, Hull, February 14th, 1803.

I have anxiously waited in expectation of the pleasure of a letter from you. I much wished to hear your further opinion with respect to the characters most proper to fix on for my first appearance. I wrote to you at some length upon this subject, which letter (together with the list of characters in which I am studied) I presume you received. However, I should not have troubled you again on this subject, as we have yet good time to deliberate; but I can no longer delay mentioning to you a circumstance of considerable importance to myself, and in which you may in some degree be hereafter interested. It is, therefore, necessary that I impart to you a secret, which none of my friends in London are in possession of. In all human probability, before I leave Yorkshire I shall take unto myself a wife. Now, sir, if you please you may, as I said before, be interested in this matter, as I write to you now to solicit an engagement for the lady. As (of course) you will not give me credit for impartiality, I shall forbear in this letter saying anything as to the merits of the one in question. If you have any room for a second singer, have the goodness to let me know, and I will be more particular in my next. Her name is Jackson, a pupil of Mr. Kelly; she has supported the first line of singing in the York company. I think she would be useful if you have a vacancy, as she is very young, and her appearance much in her favour. I do not wish you to make any positive engagement until you are satisfied whether she is worthy your notice. I make this early application, fearing that if I delayed it your arrangements might preclude the possibility of offering her a situation.

If you think it possible that you can make room for her, it will give me great pleasure.

I am, sir, your obedient servant,
C. MATHEWS.

It is scarcely necessary to explain that the announced bride in the foregoing letter, was the same person who, only twelvemonths previously, at the bedside of her dying friend, implicitly believed such an union impossible! May it not be, as Shakspeare has declared, that "Marriage comes of destiny?" I am sometimes disposed to think so.

TO JOHN LITCHFIELD, ESQ.

Dear Jack, York, Feb. 27th, 1803.

Why don't you write? Can you give me any information about the Haymarket scheme? Is it expected to succeed, or are we country actors to be sacrificed in the speculation? If it fails, I do not know what is to become of us. Do you know any performers engaged, that you have not given us in the Mirror? Why does Colman give his new comedy to Covent Garden? He has not written to me lately. Let me know, pray do.—If this does not provoke him to write, I know not what will (*Aside*).

By the by, I have taken half a sheet of paper to write to you, fearing to swell the packet; and had almost forgot that I had something to communicate to you of consequence. Then, to tell you a secret, which I wish all the world to know, I am going to be married, and that very shortly too. Therefore write to me directly, and say you rejoice at it, and wish me happy, or I shall think you are no friend to the married state. I have not room to enter into particulars; but say with Solus, "She is my choice." Who? you'll say. The first *letter* of her name is Jackson, of Wilkinson's company, a pupil of Kelly: you have heard of her before. I shall not enter into encomiums, as you will consider me partial, and not think it good evidence. Besides, I have neither time nor room to say any more. Give me your consent, that is all I ask. Club with my father this week for a frank, and let me hear from you. " Adieu, thou dreary pile."

Yours ever most truly,
C. Mathews.

CHAPTER XVII.

George Colman at York.—Tate Wilkinson's reception of him.—The York performers.—Mr. Colman's dramatic reading.—"Little Knight."—Mr. Liston.—Tate Wilkinson's letters to him.—Mr. Mathews's second marriage.—Wedding incidents.—Miss De Camp.—Mr. Colman's letter to Mr. Mathews.—The Yorkshire tailor and the mis-fit.—Parting interview between Mr. Mathews and Tate Wilkinson.

In March, Mr. Colman, accompanied by his son, Captain George Colman, arrived in York; probably induced by an anxiety to see the actor he had taken upon trust, and to satisfy himself, as he hoped to do, that his blind bargain was not likely to prove a lame one.

Here commenced a friendship between Mr. Colman and my husband, which never suffered a moment's interruption. During Mr. Colman's stay in York, he and his son supped nightly with the young actor at the close of the performance; and it would have been difficult on these occasions, when they separated, to determine which felt most pleased with the other; so that when the manager returned to London, he was prepared to welcome a friend, whom he had every expectation, at the same time, of establishing as a favourite with the town. In short, he was immediately impressed with Mr. Mathews's talents both on and off the stage; and those who have experienced the fascination of Mr. Colman's society may, without difficulty, understand how completely he charmed his new acquaintance. Mr. Mathews's application for an engagement for his intended wife was answered with cordial kindness. He had taken his future manager to see the young lady perform *Harriet*, in " The Guardian," and she was immediately engaged.

As might be expected, Mr. Wilkinson's gentlemanlike feeling and hospitable habits were displayed on the arrival of this distinguished visiter; to whom, notwithstanding he came to rob him of his trump card, he could not omit those attentions which a resident is expected to offer to strangers. Although he was at the time much more than usually an invalid, he requested Mr. Colman and his son to dine with him every day during their stay. On the first visit, there was scarcely more than a family party, Mr. Mathews and Mr. Cummins being the only persons invited to meet them; and it was an early dinner, in order to allow the two actors time to dress for their evening duties. Mr. Colman, who was desirous of enlisting some more recruits for his opening campaign, was naturally inquisitive as to who and what he might expect to see during his short stay, and asked for the bill of fare for the evening, this being his first opportunity of seeing the York performers. He was told that the play was to be " The School for Scandal." The London manager was pleased at this, and eagerly inquired what sort of a *Charles* they had? for at the time he wanted a dashing actor in that line. His attention was directed to a respectable gentleman who sat opposite to him, who had mumbled his dinner, and whose well-powdered head had a cauliflower appearance, and his face the visible impress of sixty winters. " Mr. Cummins is the *Charles*," said Tate. Mr. Cummins bowed to Mr. Colman with the precision of the old school, in confirmation of the manager's statement. Mr. Colman started, bowed in return with an unnatural grin of courtesy, and then took a pinch of snuff in nervous haste.

After a short pause, however, being desirous to do away the appearance of the embarrassed surprise he was too conscious of having shown, Mr. Colman made inquiries as to the ladies of the theatre. " Paul and Virginia" was mentioned as one of the novelties to be performed in the course of his visit, and he caught at this information in order to ask who was to play *Virginia* (expecting, as he afterwards told Mr. Mathews, that his intended wife, to whom he had been introduced in the morning, would be named); but his attention was directed again to one of the party present, and he was informed that " Mrs. John," so Mrs. J. Wilkinson was always called, would personify the youthful heroine. This lady was a bulky matron, who certainly had once been young, and still was handsome. Mr. Colman at the first glance again started, and again resorted to the friendly aid of his snuffbox, now fairly thrown off his balance. At length, turning round with something like an angry feeling, in despair of finding much rising talent for his purpose, he whispered, " Fore gad, Mathews, yours is a superannuated company!"

It was on this occasion that we first had the delight of hearing Mr. Colman read. The comedy of " John Bull" was on the point of being " got up" at York, and Tate requested as a favour that the author would give the performers the advantage of his instructions in their several characters, by reading the play in the green-room. This indeed proved a treat: those who were to act in the comedy, and those who were not, alike enjoyed it. It is for those only who have experienced the delight of hearing Mr. Colman read his dramatic productions, to guess the pleasure with which his perfect representation of every character was listened to by the performers; proving that one of the best dramatists of his day might also have been one of the finest actors.

It was now necessary for Mr. Wilkinson to look out for a comedian to supply his approaching loss; and the popularity to which Mr. Mathews had reached, rendered the choice of his successor a difficult and dangerous experiment. The manager rejoiced most liberally at his young friend's advancement; but his own wretched state of health made it irksome to him to encounter risks, and indeed he was almost unfit to contend with the chances attendant upon new faces and tempers.

It was no mean compliment to Mr. Mathews's versatility, (little as it was then known, compared with a later period,) that his manager thought it requisite to engage more than one actor to supply his place. During the winter, Mr. Knight ("Little Knight," as he good-humouredly designated himself,) had joined the company and made a successful *début;* but he was not allowed great scope till Mr. Mathews left the company. Besides this gentleman, Tate was in negotiation with *a* Mr. Liston (now *the* Mr. Liston), to whom the eccentric manager addressed the following letters, which will not be considered altogether irrelevant to the present subject, besides being in themselves curious and amusing in relation to that justly celebrated comedian, who has kindly furnished me with them.

TO MR. LISTON, THEATRE, DURHAM.

Sir,

Mr. Mathews plays full casts of comedy. I take it for granted in very full plays you will assist, and not object to pantomime utility, being a lord mayor, a witch, &c. Also not to do all y^r Newcastle parts, but Hodge, and Justice Woodcock—Sir Oliver Oldstock—Sir Peter, " More Ways than One ;"—E. Smooth — Solomon — Allspice—Renault*— Don Choleric — Don Manuel — Sir S. Flourish — Sir Walter Waring—Baron Duberly — Gabriel Lackbrain—Bonus—Shenkin—Dominique—Sir A. Absolute—Ollapod—Mr. Tempest—L. Puzzle—" Funeral ;" — Proteus — Sentinel in " Pizarro ;"—Moneytrap, " Confederacy ;"— Don Cæsar — Silky — Lord Ogleby — Sadi—John Moody—Ennui—Verdun. I am so ill, cannot recollect any more to-night. Mr. Melvin seems as dangerously ill as myself. Excuse me until to-morrow. Sunday night. Monday :—Lord Priory — Pedrillo — Sir F. Plagiary—Crazy, or P. Tom—Shacabac—Nipperkin—Trudge — Ralph — Frederick, " Of Age To-morrow," — Apathy ;—Lump you will do with Mr. Fawcett's Caleb. — Lingo — Shelty — Old Philpot — Kecksey — Osmyn, " Sultan"— General, " Mid. Hour," Capt. Battledore — Sir David Dunder — Jemmy Jumps — P. Vulcan — M. Doctor — Yo. Quaker — Clod — Autolycus — Sir Shenkin —Old Doiley. I am quite fatigued, and truly unable to proceed or write again, so very ill as I am. Therefore write to my son, or expect his ans^r, if you write to me.

I am, dear sir, yours, &c.
Tate Wilkinson.

---

* *Renault*, in " Venice Preserved," a part utterly unsuited to a comic actor, but which it was Mr. Wilkinson's pleasure to confide to his " low comedian ;" and therefore it had been represented by Mr. Mathews.—A. M.

TO MR. LISTON.

Dear Sir, York, March 24th, 1803.

Mr. S. Kemble has, in his usual breeze, laughed and perverted y^r engagement with me, as if you wanted to leave him in Oct_r last, and my saying I could not engage until May, entertained him much. But to real business. Here is a great opportunity for you, if you can enter on the comic singing, Irish characters, also *Denis Bulgruddery*, &c. all vacant with the unexpected departure of Mr. Denman. Now I should suppose by a very little attention you would soon attain a good brogue. In short, *Lump* is a line of acting much in that road. Therefore, wish you can be here all last week in April; act *Lump* before Mathews's departure,* which cannot be done until the end of Aug. when Fawcett comes. A line by the first post as to the Irish is material for me to know, after a few hours' consideration. I am in the same bad way, and indeed one third of the company in dreadful colds,

Am, sir, yours, &c.

Tate Wilkinson.

I say you never meant to leave Mr. S. Kemble till near Mr. Mathews's departure, but Mr. S. Kemble says you wanted to engage for Oct. Nov. Dec. Jan. Feb. and March. I say were I to betray the names of performers by return of post, no performers dare write to any manager. My visiter, Mr. Colman, has got Mr. Mathews, Miss Jackson, Mr. Denman, and Mrs. Ward, suddenly. I am not

---

* Mr. Liston made his first appearance in *Lump*, to Mr. Mathews's *Caleb Quotem*, in York.—A. M.

pleased, but such circumstances must occur. Garrick says—

> A year's alliance is with us an age,
> And where's the wonder? all surprise must cease,
> When we reflect that interest or caprice,
> Makes real kings break articles of peace.

The time now arrived when Mr. Mathews's feelings were to be put to a very severe trial. He was again about to quit the secure present for a doubtful future; the numerous warm friends which his private worth had drawn about him, an unprecedented range of professional business, and last, but not least, the kind, though eccentric Tate, to whom he found himself strongly attached, and to whom he was grateful for a thousand acts of kindness, which that good old man was so much in the habit of showing to the deserving.

Mr. Mathews's marriage was necessarily arranged to take place prior to his leaving York, since it could not with propriety be deferred till his arrival in London, his intended wife having no protector up to town but himself. On the 28th of March, therefore, the ceremony was solemnized by the Rev. Mr. Parker, at St. Helen's church, York.

On this occasion some incidents occurred of rather an unusual character. Mr. Denman, already mentioned, was requested to act the part of father, and, as it is called, to give the bride away. Unfortunately, he had been seized during the preceding night with a severe fit of gout; but, unwilling to disappoint his friend, he determined not to acquaint him with his illness, but to proceed to the church at the appointed hour, at whatever risk, in a sedan chair, the obtaining of which at such short notice occasioned a little delay. In the mean time, the bride and bridegroom had, as arranged, reached the spot by different roads, in order to give as little publicity to the occasion as possible; for the young lady had discovered, to her infinite annoyance, that instead of being married with a licence, she had been "asked" for three successive Sundays in the parish churches of her own and her future husband's respective dwellings—a process which was cautiously kept from her at the time. Being under age, her mother's approval was obtained, but this was rendered nugatory by the absence of her husband from England, whose permission the law also demanded. Thus, like Lydia Languish, the bride elect had "lived to be called *spinster*," and had been obliged to "ask the consent of every butcher and baker in the parish" to her marriage. It was settled that she should leave home with a female friend, in her usual walking dress, and enter at a private door of the church. Accordingly, when they arrived they found the intended husband waiting to receive them, with the bridesmaid,* " clad in robes of

---

* Miss Adelade De Camp, sister to Mrs. Charles Kemble.

virgin white," who absolutely started at the first view of her friend's *black* silk spencer and beaver hat. But the cause of this unusual dress was explained while they waited for the arrival of the "father" (Mr. Denman). The clergyman was already at the altar preparing for the ceremony, when the principal entrance-door was thrown open, the sedan admitted, and carried solemnly along the aisle of the church, by two grave-looking chairmen, straight up to the foot of the altar. The clergyman's looks expresed the amazement this apparition naturally created, and the bridal party were totally unable to account for it, until the vehicle was set down, and the head being thrown back, Mr. Denman, with flanneled ankles and black cloth shoes, was lifted up by the chairmen. His crutches, which had, as it were, been looking out of the side-windows of the sedan as it proceeded up the aisle, were carefully placed under his arms, and there he stood resting upon them, with a countenance of affected gaiety, and, as if unconscious of pain, his ample person dressed in a light-coloured coat, of a mixture then in fashion, called "pepper and salt." The rest of the party were beckoned up by the clerk, and Miss De Camp promptly advanced, the bridegroom hanging back with his intended upon his arm, in order to recover a little from the fit of laughter which he had vainly endeavoured to suppress, at the unexpected sight of his friend in the sedan-chair. The clergyman glanced from Miss De Camp's juvenile figure to that of Mr. Denman with great severity, as if he would have said, "in your state, I think it would have been more decent to have deferred the ceremony," for he evidently mistook the young lady "all in white" for the bride, she having previously placed herself close to the *pepper and salt* of the supposed bridegroom. He nevertheless prepared to commence the service, in order to unite the unmatched couple who stood forward, when Mr. Mathews thought it high time to assert his claim upon the reverend gentleman's office; and, after a little explanation and embarrassment on all sides, the white lady and he of the sedan took their proper positions, the destined couple stood forward, and the irrevocable knot was tied.

In the mean time, the defrauded "public," who had got an inkling of what was going on, resented their exclusion from the church by surrounding the doors just as the ceremony was concluded, determined to witness the exit of the parties. This determination the chairman communicated to their *fare*, when summoned by the clerk to remove Mr. Denman, who, though well seasoned, as he might be supposed to be from the united qualities of his dress, was nevertheless afraid of the coldness of the church in his precarious state of health, and suffered himself to be borne through the crowd in his sedan, having first undertaken to send a carriage for the quartette he left behind, who were too bashful to think of walking through the mob of gazers assembled to witness the first appearance of the young couple in their new characters, without paying. Mr. Denman was carried along amidst shouts of merriment from the people collected, which the poor gouty man was obliged to take in good part, affecting good-humour and unconcern. Shortly afterwards a chaise drew up to the church-door, and four "precious souls agog" scrambled into it as fast as they could, and were driven *one* door round the corner, to their destined shelter, the crowd from St. Helen's Square and the private entrance arriving at the same moment to see them alight.

Thus it seems as if one of the most serious events of Mr. Mathews's life must necessarily be attended by something comic.

TO CHARLES MATHEWS, ESQ. THEATRE ROYAL, YORK.

DEAR MATHEWS, London, April 30.

I send you a hasty scrawl to put your mind at ease. I am most fully sensible that you are anxious to be just to all parties; therefore, do not permit any qualms of conscience (on my account) to embarrass you, while you are making your public bow to the good folks at York on the 7th May. The sooner, however, you can be with me, after that period, the better for our mutual interests. Write me a line by return of post, to say if I may hope to see you on the 10th. We can settle nothing (relative to your *début*) till we meet; and be assured that I will press nothing upon you that is repugnant to your feelings. Make my compliments to Mrs. Mathews. George sends his remembrances to you, and begs me to assure you, spite of your calumnies, that he has not been *drunk* above seven nights in the week since we parted from you at Tadcaster. Adieu. Rely on my being warmly interested in your success in London; and believe me, sincerely yours,

G. COLMAN.

P.S.—Don't take off Suett again till we meet.

The time at length drew near for the departure of Mr. Mathews to London; and, amongst other preparations, a new coat was ordered of Johnny Winter, as a parting evidence of good-will, which Johnny was unusually pleased to undertake, facetiously observing that he was the first London actor who had ever carried to town one of his *habits*. On the appointed day, Winter appeared with the new " coit," and with many preliminary praises, he helped Mr. Mathews to try it on, when, oh! horror, it proved a mis-fit. Indeed, so tight and unlike all former specimens of Johnny's handiwork was it, that Mr. Mathews could not move his arms in it, when he had, by much ingenuity and perseverance, got them into the straitened sleeves.

Here there was a final opportunity for Winter to show his characteristic self-possession and provoking pertinacity. The insolent tradesman in the play who answers Lord Foppington, when showed the shoes which were too tight for him to walk in, that "if that shoe pinches, I'll be d—d," was not more impudent and exasperating than Johnny when he beheld his patron pinioned like a culprit, as he seemed, in the coat he had made for him. "Eh! hah! well! what's t' matter wi' t' coit, I wonder? It's vary pratty, I's sure," stroking and tugging in turn as he spoke, with the view to adjust and force it into a fit.

"Well," said Mr. Mathews, trying to bear with Winter for the last time, and affecting composure, "I suppose you can see that you have made it too tight for me?"

"Eh! nay, I see nought o' t' koind; it's a beautiful thing! I think I niver seed a prattier piece o' cloth in my loife! My spouse, who is a joodge o' cloth, admired it all the time I had it on my knee. 'Eh!' says she, 'I think Mr. Mathus will be pleased with this coit, if iver he was pleased wi' ony thing!'"

"And so I should," replied Mr. *Mathus*, "if it fitted me."

"Eh!" said John, affecting not to have heard this remark, and looking admiringly at the coat, "it fits sweetly, sweetly!" again pulling and smoothing down the objectionable and misfitting parts: "I think I niver seed a prattier fit!"

"Why," replied Mr. Mathews, "you cannot affect to believe that I can wear it?"

"Not wear it!" exclaimed the incorrigible fellow in an exaggerated tone of wonder,—" why, what wad ye dee wi' it? Eh, ha! it's a sweet coit indeed! What a colour! just see it i' th' light! Eh, I think I niver turned such a soft bit o' cloth o'er my finger as it is. Only feel it, that's all, and joodge for thyself, Mr. Mathus!"

In this way did Johnny persevere and argue about the coat, in the face of its absurd effect on Mr. Mathews's figure, and even during the cautious difficulty with which he peeled it off his arms again. My husband, becoming at length very much irritated, declared that he should return it upon his hands, if only to punish his offensive obstinacy in persisting in saying that it fitted. At this, Winter assumed a meek tone of resignation to his customer's injustice, making from time to time remarks and reflections, like the following:—

"Eh, ha!" sighing; "then, ye wain't keep the coit? Eh, ha! what maun I dee wi' it? Wha shall I foind ta tak' it?" (folding it together and sighing deeply.) "H—eh! I maun look out for soombody that oonderstonds what a good coit is; it woint dee for a poor tailor, wi' sixteen shillings a-week ta keep sooch a coat by him to look at." Then hanging the coat over his left arm, while with his right hand he smoothed and twitched it about in pretended admiration, and a pensive regret at its rejection, again sighing profoundly, asked, " Eh! then ye wain't tak' it, Mr. Mathus? Eh, ha! well, then, I maun put a loine i' t' newspaper, I reckon. I must advertise for some one to tak' t' coit off my hands. I maun try ta find soombody that it will fit; another sooch figure as yoursel', i' so *thin* a one is to be found ony where, which is unloikely. Eh! well, it's a sad disappointment ta me, I know. Eh, ha! wha wou'd be a tailor? It's bad to 'bide. Ah! eh! This coit, of all t' coits I iver made, was my favourite; I'd set my heart upon 't; and just now, when I finished it, I said ta my spouse as I folded it up to tak' home; well, said I, I look upon this to be the best coit I iver turned out o' hand; as pratty a bit o' work as iver tailor finished, I reckon. Eh, ha! says I ta my spouse, I suppose Mr. Mathus is ganging up ta Lunnon next week, and soom day or oother he'll be walking down Pall Mall wi' t' coit upon his back, and t' Prince o' Wales will go up to him, and say, ' I beg pardon for speaking ta you, Mr. Mathus, but pray, wha made your coit?'"

The parting interview between Tate and his young friends was affecting. The manager was exceedingly ill, scarcely able indeed to bear the presence of any one; and when Mr. Mathews expressed a hope that he would soon be better, he checked him, saying, " Do not hope it; is is unkind to wish me to live in pain, and unable to feel enjoyment. No, my children; I do not wish to live. I should like to stay over the August race-week to see my old friend Fawcett, and hear how the audience receive their former favourite, and then I shall be content to die." *

The dear old man then shook Mr. Mathews affectionately by the hand, calling back his "grandchild," as he often called me, to kiss him once more, and, as he prophetically said, " for the *last* time."

* It is remarkable, that his wish was granted exactly as he expressed it, as will be seen by a letter in its proper place.

CHAPTER XVIII.

Anecdotes of Tate Wilkinson.

IT would be quite unnatural, nay, impossible, to take leave of York without some concluding notice, some reminiscences of Tate Wilkinson — that excellent man and manager. His eccentricities were manifold, but not more numerous than his virtues. I will here record some of his oddities; but it should be borne in mind, while I set them down for the purpose of entertaining the reader, that I regard the memory of my dear old friend with the utmost reverence and affection.

One of Tate's whims of management, was always to cast the part of the *Lord Mayor* in Richard the Third to the principal " low comedian" of his company. Consequently, during the interval of Mr. Emery's departure and Mr. Hatton's arrival, the young " intermediate" was allowed the opportunity of giving ridicule to a scene in the tragedy, devoid of any intentional humour of the author, and of rendering a part utterly destitute of drollery, ridiculous and absurd.

Some of the wags of the theatre had told the inexperienced actor, upon his complaining of the sort of part given to him, that it was customary to heighten its effect, when bowing to *Buckingham's* artful report that *Richard* thought it " hard that the Mayor should lose his title with his office," to shake the powder from his wig as he acknowledged the compliment, assuring him that this was expected by the audience, and always made a great laugh for the comedian! The apt pupil, glad of any plea to make a comic point, used the precedent given him with great zeal and alacrity; and being determined that the effect should not be weakened by any half measure, he carefully placed a large quantity of hair powder, in one lump, upon the crown of his elaborate wig. This he contrived to keep steadily balanced, until the emphatic " Ah, my lord!" had received its cue, when his abrupt bow caused the powder to fall from his head upon the stage with a dull, heavy *pat*, which sent up such a cloud over the face of the amazed *Buckingham* that he was at first completely enveloped in it, and eventually blinded. Thus his appearance, when the audience caught a view of his face after he had partially cleared away the powder with his handkerchief, was so irresistibly ludicrous that not another word of the scene was heard; but a fearful voice proceeded from the gallery, which seemed more like that of an avenging demon than a god, exclaiming, " U—gh! shame! shame! Hiss him, hiss him, I say! Shame! Bartlemy Fair! His him! Why don't you hiss him?" But the good folks had not the faculty to laugh and hiss at the same time. In a minute after the *Lord Mayor* had left the stage, the same voice, " by distance made more sweet," was heard making its way gradually through the winding passages leading from the front of the theatre to the side scene, " Where is he? where is he? Let me get at him!" now loudly struck upon the ear; and immediately afterwards " the manager " was seen coming through the private door, trotting in the utmost haste to seek the perpetrator of the enormity we have mentioned, and shaking his cane as often as he could get on without its aid— " Where is he, I say? Where *is* he? Let me get at him! let me get at him!"

At this moment he caught a glimpse of the scarlet and ermined robe of the offender, and away he trotted after him, crying, " Stop him! stop him! Catch him for me! Somebody stop him, I say!" But the nimble-footed *Mayor* easily eluded his pursuer and all his attempts to " get at him," first running behind one scene, then before another, threading the needle of the stage-intricacies, so as utterly to prevent the immediate execution of the threats of the manager, who, out of breath, and baffled, uttered one long, despairing "U—gh!" which lasted all the way till he reached his rooms, which were in a passage near the side scenes: that night the "manager" was seen no more!

The trembling culprit scarcely knew what to expect: he feared his discharge on the following morning, but, to his surprise, no notice was taken of the circumstance. The next day, and the next, strengthened his hope that his fault had been forgotten or forgiven. On the Saturday morning, that day of days in the actor's calendar, he repaired to the treasury. Mr. Swalwell received him with unusual gravity and awfully-depressed eyelids. This deputy dispenser of Jove's thunder, with due solemnity of manner, placed a folded paper in one of the comedian's hands, and in the other his salary, evidently "robbed of its fair proportion," impressively desiring him to peruse the fatal missive, which mournfully explained the result of his mayoralty in one pithy line—"Mr. Mathews, debtor to Tate Wilkinson for *flour, five shillings!*"

On another occasion, when the same play was to be performed, for the purpose of bringing forward some new *Richard*, Tate was enjoying his afternoon nap, during which it had been the custom from time immemorial never to approach his room, or attempt to awaken him, but to wait until he rang his bell or voluntarily emerged from his retirement. Nay, had the theatre been on fire, those about it would have hesitated whether to disturb "the manager" with the intelligence until his usual waking hour. It had happened that on this evening, just before the play commenced, the *Queen* in Richard the Third had been taken ill at "short notice;" and in this dilemma her husband, who was the prompter of the theatre, instead of either changing the play or waking the manager — both hazardous experiments—had resorted to the only alternative left him. Mrs. Wood, an old actress, who had some years before settled down from Shakspeare into a chandler's shop, (never having been a very bright ornament to the drama,) had heard of the difficulty, and on the instant volunteered her services. The perplexity of the moment, and the brief space of time allowed for decision, induced Mr. Jarman to supply his wife's place in the only way that presented itself.

Mrs. Wood had arrived at the very pith and energy of the mother's woe at seeing her two children forcibly dragged from her to the Tower, when Tate, awaking long after his usual hour, and out of temper from his prolonged sleep, (not improbably roused from it by the startling tones of the agonized *Queen*,) came slowly hobbling behind the scenes, with wig ominously awry, and hat jerked upon it side foremost, winking his eyes, depressing the corners of his mouth, with divers twitchings of his nose, and lifting of his brows. For an instant he looked on the stage, and passed on till he stopped close to the prompter, (who trembled at this terrible apparition,) looked from him again upon the stage at the *Queen*, arrayed as she was in superannuated finery, and pumping out her wrongs in the true tragedy tone of her day. Words seemed wanting to express his amazement at the extraordinary novelty before him; and other means of ascertaining the cause of such effect were at once adopted. Taking Mr. Jarman by the arm, Tate slowly and quietly drew him forward from his prompting seat to the first entrance to the stage, pointed his fore-finger significantly at the resuscitated actress, and, with some expressive contortions of countenance, looked inquiringly in the prompter's face. Mr. Jarman, in great trepidation, began his explanation:—" Very sorry, sir: Mrs. Jarman taken suddenly ill. Couldn't disturb you, sir. Thought you would not like the play to be changed. Mrs. Wood kindly—"

This was enough. He was listened to no more by his master, who, in a tone made up of surprise, rage, and disgust, at such an arrangement, suddenly put his hand to the back of his head, forcibly thrust off his hat and wig, sending both forward to the very feet of the unfortunate *Queen*, who for a moment lost sight of her maternal sorrow in order to investigate the cause of such a windfall, when the sound of the well-known " U—gh!" explained it all, and proclaimed " The Manager!" Tate immediately trotted across the back of the scene as if for a wager, reached his room door, which he banged to, and then double-locked!

An awful silence ensued. The hat and wig were borne from the stage by the green-coat man, in a herald's dress, and respectfully sent after their revered owner, who tacitly refused to admit them or to open his door; and for several hours after, indeed for the rest of the evening, these mementoes of their owner's wrath were seen upon a chair placed at the side of the manager's room-door waiting his pleasure for their admittance. Doubtless the prompter, though he discreetly kept his own secret, suffered the penalty of his crime, and perhaps on the following Saturday was proclaimed a " debtor to Tate Wilkinson for *Wood*."

Whenever a performer proved perverse, and attempted to thwart the manager with regard to the production of a new piece, he would often print an explanation, in order to rescue his own judgment from an imputation of error, and to shame the actor who had forced him to resort to such a measure. The following announcement was drawn forth by the refusal of one of the principal performers to act a " walking gentleman."

Theatre Royal, Hull.

Mr. Wilkinson respectfully informs the public, that he feels himself at present much perplexed, and very unhappy, at being under the necessity of requesting their indulgence to Mr. Dunn, on Tuesday next, he having at a very short notice undertaken Mr. H. Johnson's very pleasing part of *Young Leonard*, in the new comedy of " Folly as it Flies:" it must be well known that Mr. H. Johnson is in possession of a principal range of characters at Covent Garden Theatre. Mr. W. truly laments he has it not in his power as manager to cast a play in the best manner for the public; but it is evidently the contrary, and he is very sorry for it.

Mr. Garrick, Mr. Barry, Mr. Quin, and Mr. Woodward, were certainly first rate-actors, but Mr. Wilkinson has seen the two first give up *Hamlet*, and act the *Ghost;* and Mr. Quin, *Justice Balance*, in " The Recruiting Officer ;" * and Mr. Woodward, *Gibbet*, in " The Beaux' Stratagem ;" and if a part is really good, allotted by the manager, and exactly suits the abilities of the actor, why certainly that constitutes a first part to the actor, sooner than any other for which his talents are not adequate.

* Mr. Garrick acted one of the recruits.

Tate was extremely jealous of any interference in his management, and resented in his peculiar way every attempt at dictation. If a performer pressed himself into any part that the manager's better judgment knew to be unfit for him, he would as a point of conscience object to the performance; but if the desire was persevered in, and in a manner distasteful to Tate, he would eventually give his consent, in order to convince the person of the folly of opposing his opinions. I remember his principal tragedian once wishing to play *Macheath*. Tate saw at once the mistake which this gentleman made, from the praises of private friends, to whom he played and sung with great taste, and refused him the opportunity of exhibiting his accomplishment in public. This rankled in the tragedian's mind, and he afterwards on some other account had a quarrel with the manager, during which he taunted him with his refusal to let him play in the opera. The next day " The Beggars' Opera" was mischievously announced to be in rehearsal, and Mr. ———'s first appearance in *Macheath*. Being ill on the night it was performed, Tate was so determined to see the result, that he insisted upon being helped up into the gallery to see Mr. ———, as he said " Make a fool of himself."

The attempt, as he anticipated, proved a failure; the small voice, which in a room was pleasing, proved totally ineffective in a theatre, and only the general respect for the performer's talents as a tragedian preserved him from open contempt as a singer. The manager's anger was appeased; and in order to atone for having been an accessary to Mr. ———'s mortification he immediately got up one of the actor's favourite tragedies with great strength. Tate liked to display his power; but having proved that it could not with impunity be interfered with, he would become as gentle and as kind as his generous nature was capable of being.

At one time Mr. John Wilkinson, Tate's eldest son, having a passion for the stage, his father was prevailed upon to allow him to perform; and at the period of Mr. Mathews's arrival, he was one of the company. "Mr. John," though a sensible man, and possessing much judgment in theatrical matters, was destitute of any personal talent for the profession. His mother, a Yorkshire lady, had an almost overweening fondness for this son, and would often urge her husband to put him into characters which even a father's partiality did not prevent him from feeling to be above his son's powers, and it was very amusing to hear their discussions, which sometimes would be carried on in the presence of a visiter. Mr. Mathews was one day sitting in the manager's room, when Mrs. Wilkinson entered, and first saluting Mr. M., observed in the dialect of her county, (from which few who have never lived out of it, whatever their education may be, are entirely free,) " Eh, Mr. Mathus, I want you to help me to persuade Mr. Wilki'son to let John play Rolli, in t' new play cooming out." Then turning to her husband—" Eh, my dear Mr. Wilki'son, do let John play Rolli."—" Ugh!" answered the manager, " I wish Mrs. *Wilki'son* you wouldn't interfere with matters you really don't understand. You know nothing of theatricals, and ought not to meddle with my management, Mr. John is a very bad actor, though he's my son; and as to his playing *Rolli*, as you call him, it's quite out of the question."—" Well, then, let him play Pizarri; I'm sure he ought to play one of the parts."—" Oh, for God's sake, madam, hold your tongue. Mister John has murdered many a hero, but he shan't murder either *Rolli* or *Pizarri*, as you call them. Ugh! Mrs. Wilkinson, you're a sensible woman, but you know nothing of acting."

When "Pizarro" was played, Tate, as usual, took his station in the back row of the gallery. At the end of the play he came round to the green-room in much ill-humour, at several things he had disliked in the performance; particularly the performers' manner of pronouncing the names of the characters. " Ugh! how you all differed in the name of *Rolla*. You, Mr. Burton, (giving a faithful imitation of the performer's voice and manner,) must forsooth call him Roll*er*, 'Oh, god-like Roll-*er*! where's the man who would not foll*er* Roll*er*!' Ugh! then you, Mistress Jarman, choose to call him Roll*o*. Then comes Mr. Toms with his Roll*a-a*; and Miss Cummins in the Boy, with her Roll*i*,—disgusting! Now pray remember, another night, that it is neither Rolli, nor Polly: and for God's sake be agreed — let it be Cato or Câto—Ugh!" and away he hobbled with his wig awry, that general evidence of his equanimity being disturbed.

One morning, Mr. Mathews called upon and found the manager " quite peart," as Yorkshire people say, that is, quite in spirits, and tolerably well for a confirmed invalid. " Oh, how do you do? Sit down. I'm much better than when you saw me last night, and spent a few hours very pleasantly, take them for all in all."—" I'm glad," said Mr. Mathews, " to find, sir, that you were well enough to enjoy society." — " Yes, sir, I was in very agreeable company, I assure you. Mrs. Wilkinson went to visit Mister John (his son, so called by everybody), so I got up a little amusement for Mr. Wilkinson, who was my guest. In fact, I gratified him, by performing *Macheath* in my best manner, with all the songs, in several of which I encored myself, and really was not much fatigued with my exertions." All this, there was no doubt, was literally the fact.

He then imitated some of the old actors and actresses, Garrick, (from which, I believe, Mr. Mathews took his imitation,) and others of his day, for he was an incomparable mimic, and his representations carried with them the same conviction of their truth that we feel when a fine portrait of a person we have never seen assures us (we do not know why,) of its faithful resemblance to the original. Like such paintings, Mr. Wilkinson's imitations of persons of the old school, satisfied the observer that they must be perfect likenesses.

Tate was, or rather had been, a great lover of good living: his table, even after he was debarred any participation in its luxuries, was elegantly and liberally supplied, and his house the seat of hospitality. His appetite had long forsaken him, and he was very capricious in his tastes, liking to be surprised into a desire for something uncommon and unexpected. It was his custom to sprinkle about his room, between his papers and behind his books, some ratafia cakes, or any other little refreshment of the kind not liable to be soon spoiled by keeping, in order to detect one when he was not thinking of such a thing. Mr. Mathews has seen the effect of this contrivance more than once, the old gentleman upon the discovery, exclaiming, " Oh, here's a cake!" as if its being there was a matter of wonder to him; he would then nibble it with childish avidity, after having resisted all Mrs. Wilkinson's attempts to invite his appetite, by proposing all sorts of delicacies.

His manly independence with his audience was as remarkable, as his generous feelings towards his performers, when he found them illiberally used by the public. When Mr. Kemble was a regular actor in the York company, he offended a leading family of York, who were in fact great supporters of the theatre. A great noise being made one night in Mr. ———'s box, which was on the stage, (two persons in it speaking much louder than the actors,) while Mr. Kemble was playing a scene with another performer; after several pauses and expressive glances at the box, Kemble thus addressed the person with whom he was playing the scene, in an altered but very distinct voice: " As those gentlemen evidently have business to talk upon, we will retire until they have settled it," and immediately made his exit with his companion.

A furious resentment from the great folks who had caused this notice ensued, and they imperiously called for Mr. Kemble to return and apologize. His answer was, a firm " Never!" The scene became alarming. The family were of great importance, and no one would venture to take part against them. At last the party left the box; and the next day a letter was addressed to Tate, demanding the discharge of Mr. Kemble on pain of their everlasting resentment, declaring that neither the family nor its immediate friends, nor any of their tradesmen, would again enter the theatre if he was allowed to remain. This was a threat of no small import to the interests of a provincial theatre. But Tate was not to be sundered from his principle of justice by any consideration of his interest. He thought Mr. Kemble had been insulted in the first instance while performing his duty to the public and his employer; and that his mode of reproving the act was fair and justifiable. His answer, therefore, to this demand was simply:—" Mr. Wilkinson begs to say, that he values Mr. Kemble more than all Mr. ———'s family and connexions put together." No further notice was taken on either side; and in a few weeks the offended party were seen occupying their favourite box, and listening with polite attention to Mr. Kemble and the rest of the performers.

What rendered the manager's conduct upon this occasion more praiseworthy was the fact that Mr. Kemble was not at this time at all distinguished as a first-rate performer, or of any striking professional importance to Mr. Wilkinson; but he was always a gentleman, and that was sufficient to ensure Tate's esteem and protection.

Just before Mr. Emery went to London he performed *Frank Oatland* in " A Cure for the Heartache." Mr. Mathews was that evening sitting near the manager at the back of the gallery, (Tate's usual seat, and the only part of the theatre to which he would go,) and upon one of those touches of nature, for which that great actor was remarkable in his " countrymen," the audience being dull, and appearing to Tate not fully to appreciate what they witnessed, he called out, (first giving an example with his own hands,) " Clap him! clap him! Ugh! you don't deserve good acting!" At the close of the performance he turned to Mr. Mathews, and said—" There!

sir; you may form some notion from the acting you have just seen, of what Mr. Garrick was."

Tate had a most extravagant, nay, childish fondness for spangled and embroidered clothes; and would purchase at any price rich court-suits, or anything else of the kind thrown in his way, without considering or caring whether they were suitable for the performers or applicable to any of the purposes of the theatre. When he had received a lot of these gauds from some London Jew, whom he was in the habit of encouraging to forward such things, he would order a line to be fixed across his room of audience, and cause the dresses to be displayed, reminding all who entered of Prospero's temptation to Stephano and Trinculo. He would then light them up with a parcel of wax candles, and walk before them to and fro, in order to catch and enjoy their glitter.

While we were with him in Yorkshire, he purchased a very splendid coat, which had been recently worn at court by the Prince of Wales. This coat and its accompaniments had crossed the line for several days and nights, to the admiration of all beholders that went to the manager's house. Suddenly, the unattractive, hackneyed comedy of "The Belle's Stratagem" was announced at the bottom of the bills to be produced on a certain night. Much surprise was elicited by this in the green-room, as there was no new performer at the time who seemed to give occasion for such a revival, and the prompter could give no information about it. The next morning the manager, during the rehearsal, requested to see one of the performers in his room; and lo! the heart of Tate's mystery was given up. Mr. Cummins, the "superannuated" *Charles Surface* noticed by Mr. Colman, was the person summoned, and requested with an air of triumph by his master "to try on *that* coat." The request was of course granted; and Tate condescended to assist diligently in the operation. Mr. Cummins was a short, but not a fat, man; on the contrary, he was thin and angular, so that when the coat was lifted upon his shoulders it looked as if it was hung upon a brushing-horse, the tale touching his ankles, and the extremity of the cuffs hiding by several inches the tips of his fingers! The manager pulled and smoothed it, and rebuked Mr. Cummins for want of management in not accommodating himself more dexterously to this beautiful garment, teaching him how to stretch out his arms so as to make the sleeves shorter in effect, &c. At last, Mr. Cummins inquired what was the manager's object in trying on this coat? which, "of course," he added, "I cannot attempt to wear." "Not wear!" thundered out Tate; "Not wear the most splendid coat that ever was seen! Is the man out of his senses? why, I've bought it purposely for you, and am going to get up 'The Belle's Stratagem,' in order that you may use it for *Doricourt!*"—

"Horrors on horrors accumulate!" thought and looked Cummins. "My *dear* sir!" said the old actor soothingly, after a breathless pause, "perhaps Winter, then, will alter it to fit me?"—" No, sir!" said Tate resolutely, " I won't have it altered: it shan't be touched! What! cut up this elegant velvet, and destroy the pattern of the embroidery. No, sir; you must wear it as it is; and wear it you shall!" And wear it he did!

Never shall I forget the effect. Poor Mr. Cummins (the elegant *Doricourt!*) put a good face upon what he found he could not avert; but really his appearance was so ridiculous, (especially as the rest of the play was performed in plain clothes,) that the actors upon the stage with him could not repress their smiles, while those not engaged in the scenes amused themselves behind them at his expense. The audience (fortunately a polite one) seemed not to know what it meant. The box-people smiled, and those in the other parts of the house stared; but Mr. Cummins looked more than usually earnest; and as he was a man much respected off as well as on the stage, he escaped the open ridicule which his appearance seemed to invite. Every time he moved, the lower part of the coat, influenced as it seemed by its independence of the wearer and intrinsic weight, swagged from side to side. The sleeves (which had been unknown to the manager pinned up in haste at a convenient moment, by Mrs.

Cummins when Tate turned his back to hasten to the gallery to gaze upon his glittering treasure,) being still many inches too long, the performer was prompted now and then impatiently to push them up out of the way of his hands. But it is impossible to give any just idea of the figure poor *Doricourt* made (fortunately for him) to the worst house of the season.

Some months after this, Tate had been tempted to buy a dress and ornaments that had really belonged to an Indian chief. This dress his eyes had gloated upon from day to day, yet without a hope that he could ever behold it exhibited on the stage. It was displayed upon his line, and commented upon to all visitors, and really much admired for its handsome and picturesque effect. One day a new piece from London was announced, under the title of " Paul and Virginia ;" and the performers were requested, " with the manager's compliments," to be ready as soon as possible in their respective characters. Mr. Mathews was sent for by Mr. Wilkinson, and informed that he need not order anything to be made for his character, *Dominique,* for that he had arranged for him to wear the beautiful Indian dress he had so often admired, which would be appropriate and striking. The comedian (not equally impressed with its appropriateness, though alive to its inconvenience,) was much confused and embarrassed, and with some difficulty convinced the manager, that as *Dominique* was a mere servant, though a man of colour, it would be out of character to wear so splendid a costume; which, he added, was too graceful for comic purposes, and moreover, that he had a dancing song, to which it would be impossible to do justice with so cumbrous a dress upon him.

Tate was out of humour; but recollecting that there were other coloured people in the piece, he consulted the manuscript, and found that the slave *Alambra* was a sentimental character, and that no objection on the score of requisite alacrity or humour could therefore be offered. Miss Adelaide De Camp, who had been cast the part alluded to, and who was delighted at the thought of the simple and becoming dress worn by the original performer at Covent Garden Theatre, (a fac-simile of which her sister had promised her,) was rehearsing the character, when she was also summoned to the manager's room. As she entered, the chief's dress was held up ostentatiously before her; and she was informed, that she was to wear it in the new piece! Independently of the circumstance that her figure was *petite*, and therefore unlikely to accommodate itself to a costume which had obviously belonged to a mountain of a man, poor Miss De Camp felt bow inappropriate and ridiculous it would prove for the dress of a mean slave, even were it possible to adjust it to her small person, which it must have totally obscured. She thought of her nice dress from town; and mortified and distressed at the preposterous expectations of the manager, burst into tears, declaring, that if he insisted upon *Alambra* wearing such a disguise, she would prefer giving up the part. It mattered not; no refusal would be taken: reason had for the time abdicated her throne. Tate's ruling passion would bear no further opposition. He declared that she *must* wear it. Accordingly, she left the room without offering further objections, awed by the violence of the manager and his determination to have his will obeyed.

In a few minutes afterwards a servant brought in the savage appendages, with a message from Mr. Wilkinson, that all possible care was to be taken not to injure or alter any part of them. Miss De Camp, and her young friends of the theatre, retired to the dressing-room in order to try whether anything could be done to render this elaborate and mortifying disguise wearable. We regretted that Miss De Camp should be obliged to spoil her appearance in her interesting new character, and assisted her to try on the Esquimaux finery, that is, we attempted to do so; but it was impossible. All declared that to appear before the public so absurd a figure as she then looked, was out of the question. In spite of her tears and our real sympathy in her distress, we could not repress our laughter. It was ultimately agreed amongst us, that the matter should rest until the night of performance; that, without any word as to her intention, Miss De Camp should wear the simple dress suitable to the character, and, when too late to exchange it for any other, declare the impossibility of adjusting that of the chief to her figure.

The dreaded moment arrived. *Alambra* was attired in a simple and most becoming costume; and the manager being pronounced too ill to leave his room, and therefore incapable of seeing the new piece, poor Miss De Camp was relieved from all apprehension of his anger. The overture was about to begin, when "the manager," waking from his nap, and being eager to ascertain the effect of his darling dress, sent a request to see Miss De Camp in his room. This was a shock. We gathered round the poor terrified victim; and, after some consultation, the messenger was sent back, and told to say, that in consequence of Betty Bearpark (the ladies' dresser, and Winter's coadjutor,) finding it impossible to make the dress fit Miss De Camp without alteration, the young lady had been compelled, at the last moment, to wear her own.

It would be necessary to find some word more expressive than any I ever knew to convey the effect of this information to the astounded Tate:—
" Not do! Who says it will not do? Who *dares* say so? It shall do! Betty Bearpark!" calling

in a voice that deafened all near him, and threatened the breaking of a blood-vessel in the invalid; " Betty Bearpark! Where's Betty Bearpark?" roared, in a distracted tone, her exasperated master. " Here! somebody find her, and d—n her for me!" But Betty knew better than to be forthcoming. He then ordered the cause of all this annoyance to be brought to him; and when it was placed in his arms, he rushed out of his room with the whole paraphernalia of the deceased chief, ran about the stage and greenroom, looking out for a new victim for his purpose. *Alambra* of course kept out of his sight. He ran up to Mr. Mathews:—" Mathews, you *must* wear it?"—" Impossible! sir; I told you I had to dance."—" Well, then," looking wildly round at the different characters assembled for the piece, and running up to one of the performers, " here, *you* shall wear it!" — " Oh, sir!" in a deprecating tone, " I am playing a Spanish officer; it would be quite unfit!" Again he scrutinized those about him. At last he seized upon a little man dressed for one of the chorus, with a copper complexion, and commanded him to go and put on the dress immediately. Mr. French retired with his arms full of savage finery, and Tate exultingly exclaimed, as he looked round at his disobedient people, " Somebody *shall* wear it!" He then hobbled, in a state of exhaustion, though at a quick pace, back to his sick room, unable to quit it the rest of the night. The encumbered chorus-singer was led into the presence of the manager before he went on the stage in full costume; and Tate's rage was thus appeased.

The consequence of his obstinacy was, that the really splendid ornaments of the dress and head, gave so distinguished an effect to the wearer, that, supposing he would turn out a character of importance in the piece, the attention of the audience was diverted from the main business to the back-ground, where he appeared; and this *illustrious anonymous* completely threw into shade the principal performers throughout the piece.

Previously to his getting up "Pizarro" in York, Tate had occasion to visit Birmingham, where he witnessed Mrs. Siddons's performance of *Elvira*, and in the afterpiece of "Obi," he saw Mr. Henry Johnston as *Three-fingered Jack*. These two performers delighted the York manager by their peculiar though different excellences, and he returned home with his mind full of both exhibitions. On his way from Birmingham to York he met with an adventure at an inn where he slept, which dwelt also on his memory. In the course of the night a rat had entered the old gentleman's room, and of that animal he had always entertained a more than ordinary horror. Murphy's Life of Garrick, by which he had been greatly disappointed, for he had detected many inaccuracies and anachronisms, had also shared his attention, with other novelties, during his absence. All these various matters, mingled with the excitement of a long journey, caused a confused mass of recollections, which rendered his conversation more intricate than it usually was.

Tate Wilkinson's extraordinary habit of wandering in conversation, with at the same time the faculty he possessed of making, to a patient and experienced listener, his meaning finally understood, has been already alluded to. He would bring forth, in whimsical alternation, the conflicting matter which pressed upon his brain at the moment, giving himself no time for thought or for regulation in its delivery. A craniologist would have perhaps said that the organ of consecutiveness was not developed in him, for he gave up his confused crowd of recollections and feelings to his hearer as a lapidary would at first exhibit the many-coloured particles required for the formation of a mosaic, rough and irregular, but capable of being put in order by a skilful and practised hand, and wrought into a smooth and significant substance.

Mr. Mathews never omitted an opportunity of visiting his revered though eccentric manager; and on the morning after his return from Birmingham, the actor presented himself to make inquiries after his health. He found the traveller, as might be expected, much fatigued after his journey, but at the same time highly excited by it, and brimful of his adventures. He was seated in his hall of audience in a great chair, in the same uncomfortable morning costume before described — wig awry, hat, &c. At his feet reclined a little spaniel puppy, an acquisition made on the road. On the table before him lay Murphy's Life of Garrick, recently published,* a phial of cough-drops, a spoon, and a wineglass, &c.

Enter Mr. Mathews. — "Good morning, sir; I'm glad to see you at home."

Tate, in a creaking tone. — "Oh! good morning! Sit down."

Mathews. — "I hope, sir, you've enjoyed your trip, and are not suffering from your exertions?"

Tate. — "Why, as for *that*,—not but I'm glad I went, for the weather was very fine; and,—if it hadn't been for the firing of the pistols, (which you know will never do for Mrs. Townend,) I should have enjoyed it very much; but," he continued with gathering animation, "to be sure, Mrs. Siddons was all in all! *not but* I have a great disgust of women with blacked faces;— it's never a pleasing sight;— and the Obi woman was hideous. But then her grandeur and dignity was indeed wonderful! and if you ask me, what is a queen? I should say, Mrs. Siddons! — Still, to come into one's room when

* See Mr. Mathews's letter of March 1801.

one's asleep, and run all over the bed and over one's face — ugh! — is more than anybody would like, I imagine; and I have a particular horror of rats! — At the same time, when they carry fire-arms about their persons, and let them off close to your ear, all through a piece, it makes your head ache;—and I've such a cough, that I can't get a moment's sleep when I'm upon my back; and—what with Murphy's Life of Garrick—I really have been a great sufferer all night. —I've been recommended this bottle of drops to cure me, but I've been greatly disappointed in it.—It's full of blunders and lies;—the book's shamefully incorrect.—I took three drops upon a lump of sugar, and it made me very sick. *Not but*—Henry Johnston,—who, by the by, is a remarkably fine young man;—but he doesn't know what he writes about when he asserts that Garrick had never played before the King. Now, at the time 'The Chinese Festival' came out, Johnston surprised me very much with his strength; for in the first place, he threw little *Lucky* (meaning *Tucky*) the black boy, over a high bank, and carried Mr. Orford, who performed Captain Halpin,"—(he meant to say, Mr. Halpin, who performed *Captain Orford*,)—" on his back into a cavern, lifting him up as easily as I lift this puppy,—so you may suppose that he must be pretty strong; — a very clever person indeed. — Oh! —

he's thorough-bred—he'll let you hold him up by the tail without squeaking, as you see;—but, then, he's a fine pantomime actor, sir! Still, as I said to Mrs. Wilkinson, where is there to be found such another as Mrs. Siddons? Her fine figure and majestic mien in *Elvira* exceeded anything I ever saw. And such a person is really requisite in the character, to give it effect. You, to be sure, might make yourself up to look like the old hag, and do it very well; but I doubt whether Henry Jackson's part could be done justice to by anybody but—. The ostler, indeed, proposed to shut the door upon him, and then try to catch the rat; but, as I said before, he came, and argued with myself previous to ringing the bell and giving the alarm, are you sure it *is* a rat? for, said I, Mr. Williamskin, or Mr. Devilskin, or whatever your cursed name may be, don't let your ridiculous whims, sir, drag people out of their warm beds and their sleep. Look again, said I,—are you sure that it's a rat, after all? Be certain of this before you call up the landlady. —At that moment in she came, dressed in black velvet, and a long veil thrown gracefully over her head; and I think a more impressive figure I never beheld! Well, at the same time I looked into the corner of the room, and there I saw her lover, *Pizarro!*—on his hinder legs, screwing his nose at me, and squeaking, as much as to say, am I a rat, or am I not?—Ugh! said I, you're a rat, sure enough!—upon which, *Elvira* went up to him with a dagger, and was going to kill him,—when I remonstrated with her upon the gross impropriety of putting anybody into the room to sleep, without first stopping up the holes in the floor; and,—as I said, while they bore Mrs. Siddons off,—why don't you keep a cat? but she seemed very indifferent, I thought, about the matter, and turned upon her heel. When up comes the ostler with a pitchfork in his hand,—and *Cora's* child all over blood,—and pursued the reptile all round the room, to my great horror, as you may suppose. Well,—where was I?—oh—In the last scene *Crook-fingered* (Three-fingered) Jack is taken, and his hand cut off, and brought on the stage, fastened upon a pole (which, I confess, had a disgusting effect to me,—for though I hate rats, I don't like cruelty). After this, came the young lady of the piece (I forget her name), who had rescued her lover,—a dirty looking fellow with a smock-frock on, and without more to do, ran the pitchfork through his back,—his screams were dreadful,—and as she rushed into his arms, the curtain dropped, and—and there was an end of Mr. Rat!"

In such manner would Tate ramble on, nor is this account at all an exaggeration of his general style. It required the most fixed attention, even with a knowledge of the subjects he so blended, to be able to separate the tangled web of his discourse. Well might he, in his amusing book, call himself " The *Wandering* Patentee!"

We all have our antipathies: " some men cannot abide a gaping pig." Tate, in addition to his dislike of rats, had an unconquerable aversion to that appendage to an unmarried young lady—an anxious, protecting mother;—one whose peculiar sense of duty keeps her ever at the side of her daughter, and whose quick and sensitive perception of what is due to " her child," holds her at all times prepared to struggle for and maintain her merits and her interests in the theatre. It must be confessed that these doubtless well-meaning persons are, theatrically considered, little better than nuisances, not only to managers, but to all about them, when they infest the dressing-room, green-room, and side-scenes. Their dragon-like watchfulness, their over-weening partiality, their excitable anxiety, all natural, and indeed amiable qualities to a certain extent, time and place agreeing, are otherwise very troublesome and disagreeable. At home, where all good principles are supposed to be implanted and matured, those feelings are proper and admirable; but once initiated into habits of decorum, and practised in virtuous conduct, it is hard if the so instructed cannot be trusted for a few hours out of the four-and-twenty in the midst of a multitude, in which, supposing there may be found one lurking to corrupt, there are numbers ready to defend.

That females in a public profession are exposed to more notice, and consequently to more temptation, than in private life, is manifest; and the greater merit, therefore, may be claimed by them when they preserve their reputation without blemish. I cannot however allow that actresses are more generally (certainly not necessarily) corrupt than others, as the illiberal part of the world affect to believe; but when they *are* corrupted, their errors, like their attractions, are more known to the public than the lapses of private individuals. No young female ever fell, however, because intrusted to her own guidance, behind the scenes of a theatre. It is from without that the spoiler comes. It is not from the professors, but from the followers of the profession, that any wrong is to be apprehended. A young lady of virtuous principles and correct behaviour, is less in danger in a theatre than in a private assembly, where she may be allowed to converse and dance with any well-bred rake who seeks her as his partner, and with whom her cautious parent fearlessly intrusts her.

Be all this, however, as it may, Tate abhorred such guardians from the bottom of his heart. He found no difficulty in regulating and controlling the most self-willed and vain of his youthful heroines; but let one of these only have a mother to assert her merits, and to fight for a due portion of her daughter's rights and immunities in the theatre, and there was an end to all peace and comfort. "Ugh! these *mammas!*" Tate would cry in tones of the deepest disgust. I really believe that two-thirds of the favouritism I enjoyed with the manager, arose from my having no one present to defend me, right or wrong. I remember his first question to me on the day I was presented to him, was, "Pray have you any *mamma?*" and when I reminded him of his kind promise of protection, he replied, "Oh, true; I forgot. It's a great comfort, Miss Johnson, to have one young lady without a *mamma.* Ugh! they make me sick. There's Mrs. D——n with *her* daughter, and Mrs. C——ms with her's. 'Sir, my daughter shan't do that part—my daughter ought to have the other—my daughter is so beautiful—my daughter is so clever—my daughter must sing this—my daughter should act that.' Ugh! common nuisances, Miss Thompson; I hate all mammas from first to last. I'm glad you have no *mamma.* I shall have one young lady that I can manage, Miss—Miss——"—"Jackson, sir."—"Ay, Jackson." Never was kinder management. We never had a difference, except indeed when he artfully picked a little quarrel with me, in order to have a fair pretext for declaring himself wrong, and then for making me a handsome present by way of compensation.

Tate once pretended that I had not sung a favourite song of his, in some old-fashioned piece, and when the explanation was given, he sent me a white silk dress, to play the lady scenes of *Rosetta* in, as an apology for his injustice, having previously (Mrs. Wilkinson told me,) ordered her to purchase it, because he knew I must want one on the occasion of Mr. Incledon coming from London to perform *Young Meadows*. It is true he ventured to suggest that it would please him to see the sleeves of said dress made to cover the elbow; and that a small ruffle would enhance his satisfaction;—barbarous propositions to a young girl who had never worn more of a sleeve than would suffice to cover the shoulder, and therefore not to be listened to. "I can tell you," he observed, "it would look much better than dressing as you all do now, like a parcel of washerwomen in the suds. Ugh! Woffy (Woffington) never showed her bare elbows; she knew better." Tate would have been gratified had he lived long enough to see his favourite style of dress revived in the present day,* to the confounding of all shapes and sizes, burying symmetry in a profusion of silk and lace, and destroying personal identity, to the delight of the ill-proportioned part of the community. It must, however, be added, that this has been beneficial to the general

* 1837.

effect in society, the grouping of which is certainly as much improved by plenty of drapery, as the mercer and lacemen are benefited by it. An old gentleman at a large party, two years ago, was heard to say to another who had inquired after his wife, and who asked whether she was present —" She is among that group of ladies. I know she is there, but I have not the remotest idea which to point out as my wife. You must wait till she emerges from that mass of silk and gauze, where she is undistinguishable."

After the instances given of Mr. Wilkinson's eccentric manners, which may seem coarse to the reader, I must conclude with some other anecdotes of the smoother and more benevolent part of his character, which outweighed in a great degree the former.

After all his prejudices against Mr. Mathews as an actor, and all the mortifications his ill-opinion of his talents had occasioned him, when he was becoming popular Tate went to see him perform *Frederic*, in " Of Age To-morrow," originally played by him in the York theatre. The piece was entirely successful, and Mr. Mathews's performance eminently so. At the close, the manager appeared upon the stage, and in the presence of the assembled performers addressed the comedian, making an elegant old school bow—" Sir, I beg to thank you publicly for your performance.

I owe to you something previously for your patient perseverance in showing me my unjust opinion and treatment when I first engaged you. Your acting to-night has finally convinced me of my error; and, by way of atonement, you must allow me to make that *Old Housekeeper** of yours a pensioner of mine while you remain in my company." On the next treasury-day Mr. Mathews found his salary raised to the highest sum given, being above one third more than the previous amount received by him.

Mr. Wilkinson was indeed a polished gentleman in private life; and even as a manager, when he could justly indulge in such instances as the last I have related, his liberality was conspicuous. In the course of the year certain removes occurred, such as a nine-mile journey from Pomfret to Wakefield, which many of the actors would walk, if the weather permitted, in summer. Tate, on such occasions, preceded them in his carriage, and on their arrival at a certain point of the road he would invite them to an excellent dinner, which he had ordered ready for their refreshment; and towards the whole of the performers, from the highest to the lowest, on these occasions, in manners and conduct he would be a Chesterfield in all he said and did.

* One of *Frederic's* assumptions to impose upon old Baron Piffleburg.

At the end of every unusually prosperous season also, the performers were sure to receive, on their last visit to the treasury, a present in addition to their salary, " With the manager's kind compliments."

CHAPTER XIX.

Arrival in London of Mr. Mathews and his young Wife.—Their reception at the paternal home.—Gloom of the house.—Removal to Manchester-street.—Old Mr. Mathews listening to his son's songs and stories.—Mr. Mathews's first appearance in London.—Anecdote of Mr. Cumberland.—Letter from Tate Wilkinson.—Letter from a York actor.—Mr. Liston.—Death of Tate Wilkinson.

ON our arrival in London in May, I entered the abode of my husband's *serious* relations with some trepidation, remembering their self-congratulations on their son's first marriage, that he had escaped falling into the dreaded fangs of one belonging to the proscribed class in which he had enrolled himself. This alarm was, however, speedily dissipated by my first encounter with my husband's family. His young sister, a well-educated and lively girl, immediately became attached to me. His mother also, a gentlewoman in ideas, deportment, and language, and the benevolent old man, who might have suggested to Goldsmith his "Vicar of Wakefield," treated me with great kindness. According to my idea of Parson Adams, Mr. Mathews's father was a personification of the character; guileless as sensible, he was an image of simplicity and goodness.

The house had a very sombre appearance. I recollect that my spirit quailed when I first entered the drawing-room. The wainscot everywhere was completely covered with small oval frames of ebony, surrounding engraved portraits of *saints*—" Great (indeed,) was the company of the preachers." All gloomy and dark, they seemed by their presence to forbid any approach to gaiety, and frowned disapprovingly upon all laughter. With the exception of the dado of the room, not an inch was spared by these worthies for anything besides. No sinful mirrors relieved the aching sight—no ornaments but those of the conventicle met the eye. Even the light summer attire of youth seemed unnatural, if not offensive, in such a place, and out of keeping, as a painter would have said, with the scene; yet these worthy people had no gloom in their hearts. I have often laughed since with Mr. Mathews at the recollection of his father's gallery of pulpit-performers, and amused myself to see the similar propensity in the son, to collect portraits of professional stars, though in another line.

As soon as the opening of the Haymarket drew near, Mr. Mathews removed to a pleasant lodging in Manchester-street, Manchester-square; for, of course, we could not then accommodate our hours to those of his father and mother. We could neither have eaten nor prayed at their time. During our stay with them we all knelt down together, before and after every meal, while old Mr. Mathews pronounced a lengthened prayer; and before bed-time of course all the household were present.

Although we removed from the Strand, I was almost daily with the family, and perfectly happy with them. This made my husband very comfortable; and his liberal father, although he would not see his son act, was most anxious, "since he had embraced such a profession," that he should prosecute it with as much credit and success as possible. He would allow—nay, invite—his son to give him "a taste of his quality," and complacently listen to his songs and stories, now and then laughing till tears poured down his face: his wife was equally delighted. My husband had once drawn from him his slow consent to go to a private box at the Haymarket, to see him represent *Mr. Wiggins*, in which character his face, when made up, so much resembled that of his father; but somehow at the eleventh hour he repented,—consistency triumphed over inclination,—so that he never saw his son perform. Mrs. Mathews would, I am sure, have gone; but, out of respect to her husband's opinion, she and her daughter abstained from visiting the theatre.

On the 15th May, Mr. Mathews made his first appearance in London at the Haymarket Theatre, in the characters of *Jabel,* in "The Jew," and *Lingo,* in "The Agreeable Surprise," with the most unqualified success.* The account of his acting, given in one of the newspapers of the following day, (all of which praised him highly,) stated that when he was encored in his songs, he produced a laughable alteration 'in the last verse on repetition, which caused much merriment. This was a novelty then, but every one will remember with what effect he made such variations in after years when encored. On the following night their Majesties George III. and Queen Charlotte, and the five Princesses and suite were present to a repetition (by command) of the first night's performances, which went off with increased effect.

The following is a characteristic anecdote of the author of "The Jew." Mr. Cumberland was always remarkable for his fastidious feelings about the performance of any of his characters; and at the same time for his courteous desire to compliment everybody as much as was possible. He had been attracted by the novelty of a play of his acted in London by a company made up entirely of provincial performers, and at the dropping of the curtain came round to the green-room, being desirous to express his approbation of what he had witnessed. Elliston received what was due to

* He took his farewell in York, in the character of *Proteus,* in "Family Quarrels," and *Ralph,* in "Lock and Key."

his really beautiful representation of *Sheva;* and the *Jabel* of the night entering the room, dressed for the after-piece, was by Mr. Cumberland's desire presented to him. He delighted the young comedian, by assuring him that the part had never been better played ; and that in figure, dress, and acting, he was the very thing he (the author) had intended. " I wrote the part, and ought to know —it was perfect. I assure you, sir, I never was more gratified ; but" (with irrepressible irritation) " you spoke so low, I couldn't hear a word you said."

Immediately after his appearance at the Haymarket Theatre, Mr. Mathews naturally made his old manager acquainted with the result; and, in the plenitude of his satisfaction, described his success exultingly, and probably in very animated language. In reply he received from Tate Wilkinson the following letter, the last he ever wrote to him.

MR. MATHEWS, HAYMARKET, LONDON.

DEAR SIR,

I am truly pleased at your success, and think it a feather in the cap of the York company. But you write to me as easily as if I was in a recovered state : instead of that, this is a violent fatigue. I had nearly 90*l.* Monday night, at Leeds; but I am not equal to be pleased, or to eat anything—am worse than ever. Your letter is now before me. I cannot get through it; yet you write to me as if I was as gay as yourself. I want not to see any July

Richards or *Octavians:* not but tell Mr. Elliston if he can come on the 7th Sunday of Trinity, I shall be glad to see him. Tell him to write by return. He can play in London on Monday, August 12. Have no strength or time for the comp^{ts}. Am wishing good health.

Yours in great pain,
TATE WILKINSON.

P.S.—This a great fatigue and pain to me.

The following letter from an actor in the York company, shows the interest for my husband's welfare entertained by his less fortunate brethren. I should not perhaps think it worth publication for that reason only, but that it also contains a curious account of Mr. Liston's progress after our departure.

TO MR. C. MATHEWS.

DEAR MATHEWS,   York, Sunday, 22d May, 1803.

Many thanks for the interesting particulars communicated in your letter. It was a source of much satisfaction not only to me, but apparently to every one of the company to whom I imparted it. I assure you, a great degree of anxiety prevailed throughout our body corporate for your success, and Thursday morning's papers were resorted to with avidity by most of us. The accounts they gave, and the warmth of commendation so liberally bestowed by some of them, has afforded me (as, I dare say, you will readily believe) the most sincere satisfaction and pleasure, and I heartily congratulate yourself, Mrs. Mathews, and your family, on an occasion so truly gratifying as this must be to you all. A reputation and fame that in its commencement seems founded on so firm a basis, must progressively gather increasing strength, which I sincerely hope will be productive of every advantage you can desire. Mrs. Mathews, I take it for granted, has not yet made her *début*.

Time has not yet matured anything in the nature of theatrical news from this quarter, that may be worth attention. Liston rather disagreed with the manager about having Denman's part in " The Tale of Mystery" sent to him, and a dissatisfaction arising in his mind, he sent in his discharge; but an interview with Tate accommodated matters, and the *mysterious* objection is removed. Mr. Gattie (the singer from Exeter) joined us yesterday, and is to open, we believe, in *Young Meadows*.* I write in much haste, as I am pushed to save the opportunity of sending this by a private hand.

I am, dear Mathews,
Your real well-wisher and friend,
G. C. CARR.

Duke-street, Manchester-square.

The character alluded to in " The Tale of Mystery," and naturally objected to by the " low comedian" of the theatre, was that of a serious, almost tragic, old man. It is a remarkable fact, that Liston had made but small impression upon the York audience. His humour, perhaps not then matured, had not been felt; and I, who, like others, have since found his acting so ex-

* Mr. Gattie since known in the London theatres as an actor of old men.

quisite and irresistibly droll, saw him on his first appearance there in *John Lump,* in " The Wags of Windsor," without a tendency to smile! We were introduced to him in private, and liked him so much as to feel deep regret at the probability of his not becoming a great favourite. In a short time after we heard of his departure, and saw his name in a Scarborough play-bill, for the part of *Capulet,* in " Romeo and Juliet!"

How it happened that managers entertained such *serious* impressions against Mr. Liston's talent for comedy, it is difficult now to understand; and certainly Mr. Mathews and myself were not then favourably struck with them. Indeed, when Mr. Colman, on negotiating with him for the Haymarket (I think, in 1806,) asked us what sort of a comedian Mr. Liston was, both Mr. Mathews and myself felt embarrassed, and we compromised the matter by commending him as a very " gentlemanlike young man, but we had not seen him act often enough to enable us to form any opinion of his powers!" What little we knew of Mr. Liston impressed us with the notion of his inveterate gravity, both on and off the stage.* On

* Since writing the above account, Mr. Liston has reminded me of a droll result of the earliest impression he made upon Mr. Mathews. On taking leave in the evening after his first dinner with us at York, my husband followed him to the head of the stairs, where Mr. Liston detained him with some grave remarks, and, upon receiving his visiter's last " adieu," as he

the night of his first appearance in London, therefore, when he played *Sheepface* to Mr. Mathews's *Scout*, in "The Village Lawyer," his acting in the first scene with him took my husband by surprise, and so convulsed him with laughter, that he was scarcely able to utter a word of his own character intelligibly, while they were on the stage together.

The "gentlemanlike young man" turned out also the inimitable actor; and we have often asked ourselves, while witnessing his exquisite humour, what could in the first instance have rendered us so unmoved by it. Since Mr. Liston came to London, where it might be imagined all agreed about him, we knew one man only with hardihood sufficient to confess that he never could laugh or be amused by his acting. Such a man was undoubtedly to be pitied; but I went further—"Let no such man be trusted," said I; and he ought *not* to have been trusted, as it was afterwards proved.

In the latter part of August 1803, intelligence reached us which, though not unexpected, gave us poignant grief. Tate Wilkinson was dead!

was quitting the house, Mr. Mathews thoughtlessly exclaimed, as he ran back to the room, "Adieu! *thou dreary pile!*" which Mr. Liston overheard, and was much amused at, perfectly comprehending the nature of the feeling that had unconsciously prompted the quotation; and aware that the evening had not been much enlivened by his presence, in his then anxious state of spirits.

The following letter will best give the interesting particulars.

TO MR. CHARLES MATHEWS.

DEAR MATHEWS, York, Saturday, 27th August 1803.

My last letter was addressed to our friend Denman; regularity requires that this should be addressed to you; though as you have both been silent so long, I should have followed your peaceful example till one of you chose to write, had not an occurrence taken place on Thursday that I should deem myself blameable if I did not immediately communicate it to you. The lamentable fact of which I have to inform you, is no other than the departure of our dear and truly esteemed old Tate; who, on Thursday afternoon a little after four, was relieved from the pain he had of late so severely endured, to receive the reward of his integrity, generosity, and solid virtues of heart.

But I shall not panegyrize a man whose good qualities were fully known to yourself. He was completely worn out, and though he did not expire till the taper of life had long blinked in the socket, his reason and the ruling spring of all his actions, his generosity and honesty, strongly evinced themselves even to his last moments; and I fear his dissolution, though inevitably at hand, was somewhat hastened by an honest warfare in the cause of justice. Mr. Fawcett, who performed with us a week at Pontefract, previously to his coming hither, had stipulated by letter, that if the receipts at Pontefract should reach a certain sum, he would receive a compensation, but if not, he begged his services might be *accepted* for that week. The receipts were but poor, and of course nothing was offered Mr. Fawcett by our acting manager. On Wednesday night, Tate sent for Mr. Fawcett, and inquired of him if they had paid him for Pontefract. The reply was " Lord bless you, as it was bad, I told you I should not take anything." The old man, however, fell into a bitter passion, exclaiming, " Not pay you! oh, if they don't pay you, they'll be robbers, cheats, plunderers; why should you not be paid?" Mrs. Wilkinson and John were accordingly summoned into his presence, and violently attacked. His passion was so extreme, that Fawcett left him in the midst of it: it continued however all night, and the next morning, Swalwell called Mr. Fawcett in, and insisted on his taking 25*l*. This, by the by, was the second agitation he underwent that night.

The farce on Wednesday was "The Wags of Windsor." Tate made many anxious inquiries how Mr. Fawcett was received, as he said he had his doubts of the farce doing well, on account of the great popularity you had gained in it. He was of course pleased to hear it went off well. At the conclusion, Mr. William Wilkinson[*] went in to him. An inquiry was made how he liked Mr. Fawcett. The answer was evasive: "Oh, I don't know, sir."—" Don't know, sir! and why don't you know?—how did you like Mr. Fawcett in the part?"— " Oh, sir, he was very well."—" Why, what the devil do you mean by very well? Why don't you give me your opinion why he was only very well?"—" Why, sir, I hope I may be allowed to give my opinion; I have seen Mr. Mathews in the part, and I give the preference to him."—" Ugh! here's a man! everybody tells me the farce has gone off with unbounded applause, and my son comes and says Mr. Fawcett was only very well." This was the first violent fit he underwent that night.

[*] Tate's youngest son.

As the event of his death was made public directly, everybody heard it as they came from the race-ground. The poor old soul had some persuasion of his departure, and desired that the theatre might not be shut up that night, if he should die. We accordingly played to upwards of a hundred pounds, though a general gloom overspread us all. Yesterday's bills were prefaced as follows. " York, 26th August, 1803. *In consequence of* (a ridiculous expression by the by) the death of Mr. Wilkinson, the trustees under his will most respectfully inform the public that they feel it to be their duty to continue the theatre open this evening, Saturday and Monday, when it will finally close until the winter season."

Of the purport of his will, I can only give you conjecture and report; the formal reading of it has been deferred till after the funeral. It is said that to all the children he has bequeathed equally, though everything is at the disposal of the old lady for her life. Four trustees are named: Mr. Wilson, Mr. Suttle, Mr. Wallis, and a fourth gentleman, whose name I do not recollect, in behalf of and as a particular friend to Frank Wilkinson, the lawyer. They say too, that he has enjoined either by will or verbally, that none of the performers shall be discharged without a sufficient reason being apparent. But all this is only vague as to its authority. The old man is to be buried to-morrow morning at seven o'clock at the Pavement church. Mr. Swalwell asked Mr. John whether it was wished that the gentlemen of the theatre should attend. A negative was given, and an intimation that there would be only two coaches, one for the four trustees, and the other for the three sons and Mr. Cummins. A general determination, however, prevails amongst us to see the last of our worthy old manager, every one being well convinced that " we shall not look upon his like again."

We understood that your benefit occurred last Monday. Fawcett said for twopence he would ensure you 250*l*. It is said that you are engaged for Liverpool at 4*l*. per week.* My theatrical *general* intelligence must be still reserved, and so shall remain till I hear from you or Denman. Yours, in sincerity,

G. C. CARR.

---

* 4*l*. per week was at that period considered a great salary in a provincial theatre.

CHAPTER XX.

Mr. Mathews's success in "Love Laughs at Locksmiths."—His *Mr. Wiggins.*—His engagement at Liverpool.—Letter from Mr. Lewis.—His prediction.—Letter from Mr. Mathews to Mr. Litchfield.—Serious accident to Mr. Mathews.—Mr. Young the actor.—His talent in mimicry.—Letter respecting him from Mr. Colman.—Birth of Mr. Mathews's son.—Letter from Mr. Colman.—Letter to Mr. Litchfield.—Letter from Mr. Emery.

MR. MATHEWS's success during the season continued evenly, until Arthur Griffinhoofe (alias George Colman) produced his "Love laughs at Locksmiths," in which Mr. Mathews, in his first original part, *Risk,* produced a very great effect. The song of "The Farm-yard" introduced to the notice of the town his imitative talents in one form, and the change of appearance in the second act, and his song of "Unfortunate Miss Bailey," at once established the dependence of the public upon his powers, and made him the favourite he never ceased to be. *Risk* may be recorded as his first great part, *written* for him; all characters besides, at least for many years, were in fact mere outlines left for him to fill up by dint of his genius by authors who felt it necessary to write *words* for others. One of his most popular characters, *Buskin,* in " Killing no Murder," was almost all his own, except the situations, and where he had to give cues to the good things set down for that pet with all comic authors, Mr. Liston.

His next new character of weight this season, was *Mr. Wiggins,* " a gross fat man," in the farce called " Mrs. Wiggins," which succeeded so far as his performance went, and was for his sake often represented, though the piece was certainly weak. His dress and face in this part were admirable, as well as his acting; and were introduced by Harlowe into his painting of Mr. Mathews in five characters, now in the collection of the Garrick Club, with the rest of Mr. Mathews's theatrical gallery.

At the close of the Haymarket season, Mr. Mathews entered into an engagement with Mr. Colman for the three following seasons; a conclusive evidence, it may be supposed, of his success in London. In the autumn, he proceeded to join the Liverpool company for the ensuing winter, at a large salary for a provincial theatre. It was then the property of Messrs. Lewis and Knight; the Lewis of merry memory, and Mr. Knight, (not " little Knight,") the then popular performer, also a principal actor at Covent Garden, and the original *Farmer Ashfield*, in " Speed the Plough." In this piece Mr. Knight introduced the Somersetshire dialect with great effect, which was, I believe, banished from the stage by the more humorous dialect of Yorkshire, which Emery made so popular, and left as a sort of legacy to all succeeding actors of countrymen.

The following letter from Mr. Lewis, will show the estimation in which Mr. Mathews's talent, even at this early period of his London reputation, was held, not only by the public, but by first-rate professors.

TO CHARLES MATHEWS, ESQ.

Dear Sir,   Liverpool, 17th August, 1803.

I had the favour of your letter, and am happy to be aided by such merit as yours. I have the book and music of " Love laughs at Locksmiths," but will certainly retain it till you come here. If " Mrs. Wiggins" is printed, I wish you would desire Mr. Hill, our copyist, to send a book down, and I will have it ready against your arrival.

The time in which you would be most desirable to me, would be on Friday the 9th of September, and the whole of the following week, but I fear there is little chance of so desirable an event. On the 19th of September, Braham and Storace make their first appearance, and I should very much wish you to be in most of their operas, " The Cabinet," " Castle of Andalusia," " Family Quarrels," " Siege of Belgrade," " Haunted Tower," &c. " No Song," &c. " Grandmother," " Prize," &c.

With good wishes, I am, dear sir,
your obedient servant,
W[m]. Tho[s]. Lewis.

It would be of essential consequence if you could play here (no matter in what) on Saturday, 17th of September; and perhaps Colman would for once indulge you by leaving you out a night, which would enable you to do so.

It is rather curious that Mr. Lewis predicted that Mr. Mathews would some day be a favourite in London, in the same line of characters which that great comedian then sustained in so unrivalled a manner. He was performing his original part of *Tom Shuffleton* in "John Bull," and observed to my husband, that it was a part *he* should undertake, adding, "It is my opinion that it is in your line, and when I am gone, you'll find it out, and be my successor in eccentric comedy." At the time this was said, Mr. Mathews had not an idea that he could possibly present himself in such a part, his acting being confined to old men, countrymen, and quaint low comedy; he was in fact exceedingly amused at such a prediction, and repeated it as a good jest. In a few years afterwards, however, he found himself sustaining with great effect *Goldfinch*, *Rover*, and other characters of the same cast, a line of acting which he probably would have pursued, had not a serious accident checked his efforts, and in his own opinion rendered him altogether unfit for the drama.

TO JOHN LITCHFIELD, ESQ.

Dear Jack, Liverpool, October 30th, 1803.

I opened here on the 24th, in *Pedrillo* and *Sir David Dunder.** My reception was the warmest, I think, I ever experienced. When I spoke behind the scenes in reply to *Fernando*'s call, the audience applauded, which applause was kept up for some time after my entrance. This, of course, gave me confidence, and I played up, and hit them very hard. I introduced the song of the " Old Bachelors," which was uproariously *encored.* Sir David was a good card: it has never been played here but by Bannister, many years ago. It was very well received, and I repeated it three nights after. My second night was *Yuseph* and *Sharpe;*† the third, *Baron Oakland* and *Endless;*‡ and I played *Lenitive*§ twice during Braham and Storace's stay. I was lucky in playing on their nights, as they were well attended, and I was of course seen by the better part of the Liverpool audience.

I find one line of Yorkshire worth a length ‖ of anything else. Emery was adored here; never was anything like the favour in which he stood with the audience: so I am told. The Lancashire bears a strong resemblance to the Yorkshire dialect. Young advised me,

---

* *Pedrillo*, in " The Castle of Andalusia,"— *Sir David Dunder*, in "Ways and Means," two characters of striking contrast, and which were ever after amongst his most perfect dramatic performances.—A.M.

† In " The Siege of Belgrade," and " The Lying Valet."
‡ In " The Haunted Tower," and " No Song no Supper."
§ In " The Prize."
‡ A length technically means forty-two manuscript lines of an actor's part.

notwithstanding this, to try them in that line, which I did, first in *Young Testy;* and finding it likely to take, I played *Robin Roughhead*, in which I hit them; and have, in consequence, chosen *Dan,* in " John Bull," which we play to-morrow night. *Job Thornberry,* Young; *Peregrine,* Cooper; * *Dennis,* Hamerton, (a good Irishman); *Mary,* Miss Grimani, who is a great favourite here. I have seen her in *Mrs. Haller* and *Juliet,* and like her much. She is a better actress than she appeared to be in London. † I am much pleased with Young; I think he is the best actor I have seen in the country. In *Rolla, Romeo,* and the *Stranger,* I have greatly admired him; he is particularly happy in the latter. His appearance is fine; and his face admirably suited to the expression of melancholy. I am told he is very happy in Lewis's line. Cooper (from America) joined us on Wednesday, and played *Richard the Third.* " Mrs. Wiggins" has been played three times, " Love laughs at Locksmiths" came out last Monday. Young is the *Beldare;* Mrs. Mathews the *Lydia.* It went off exceedingly well, was repeated on Wednesday, and is likely to be very attractive. " Miss Bailey" takes, and has been *encored* both nights.

The theatre is beautiful; and holds, at 4s. 6d. 2s. 6d. and 1s. 6d., nearly four hundred pounds. The prices are now lowered, and we play to houses of 90l. or 100l., which is thought to be bad: the pit is usually well attended. They have little opinion of any actor who has not played in London. Young is the only exception: he is a favourite, and is greatly respected in private; he has also better connections than any actor here, and visits the first people.

* American Cooper.
† Miss Grimani afterwards married Mr. Young.

I have found him a valuable acquaintance. There is one thing here which annoys me intolerably. The clerks decamp at the end of the play to devour veal pies, in consequence of which when the farce begins half the pit is deserted, and they come clattering in again with greasy mouths when the first act is nearly over. They are sometimes a dull audience, and I have not much respect (from report) of their judgment. I am told they accuse Munden of copying Simmons — *risum tene!* I have, however, not much reason to complain, and expect to be a favourite. The town I like; the situation is beautiful. I have ridden seven miles on the sands; the sea on one side, the town and harbour on the other. The opposite Cheshire coast and distant Welsh mountains form altogether a most enchanting prospect. Prince William * is here, and will remain, it is supposed, for the winter. He has bespoken plays three times: the boxes promise well, by the by, for " John Bull" and " Love Laughs." Adieu, dear Jack, and be assured that I am, and must be, yours unalterably, CHARLES MATHEWS.

During this season Mr. Mathews had a very serious accident while attending a review at Liverpool. He was seated carelessly upon a horse lent to him by a friend, when the animal took fright at the first fire, and his rider being totally unprepared for the effect, was thrown off with great violence upon his head, which, from the force of the fall, thrust out the crown of his hat. Prince William, who had previously recognised

* The late Duke of Gloucester.—A. M.

the actor who almost nightly entertained him at the theatre, perceiving on the instant what had happened, descended from his own horse with the most humane alacrity, and assisted to raise up the senseless body of my husband, who was conveyed home in a short time, where he suffered a severe though brief illness, which established a local complaint of a very dangerous tendency, and which more or less must have distressed him ever afterwards; but its extent was only revealed after his death. Except to his surgeon, he never spoke of his suffering from this accident, which, like all other serious calamities that befel him, he bore with great fortitude in silence.

On Mr. Mathews's first arrival in Liverpool, he was presented to Mr. Charles Young, the "acting manager" of the theatre, with whom he had previously a slight acquaintance, Mr. Young having been one of the boy-men who amused themselves with private theatricals in the building described by Mr. Mathews in his account of Short's Gardens. Mr. Young was then a general performer, and the best "either for tragedy, comedy, history, pastoral, pastoral-comical," &c. that could be found, inasmuch as he might be seen in turn enacting *Rolla* and *Captain Beldare, Job Thornberry* and *Richmond, Alexander the Great* and *Dick* in "The Apprentice," *Leopold* in "The Siege of Belgrade," *Romeo, Doricourt,* and *Whim-*

siculo in "The Cabinet." In short, there was " nought too high and nought too low" for him to show his ability in. From the moment these friends met, they were inseparable.

Everybody who knows Mr. Young at the present moment, may imagine what he was so long back as the period to which I allude, for he has lost none of his buoyancy of character or fine intellect. The charm of his manner, his sweetness of temper, and invariable goodness of heart, remain, and are acknowledged by a large circle of distinguished friends, with whom he is enjoying that independence which his public merits and private worth have so richly deserved. Such a manager and friend, it may be well imagined, proved very valuable to the new performer. Soon after their acquaintance, Mr. Young related a ludicrous description given to him of Mr. Mathews previously to his arrival, by Mr. Lewis, in consequence of his inquiry as to the sort of person Mathews was in his exterior. Mr. Lewis, after noddling his head about in his peculiar way, and tapping the side of his boot with his slender cane, replied, in his hesitating but quick manner, " Why—a—a—a— he — e's the tallest man in the world, and the funniest. He has no regular mouth, but speaks from a little hole in his cheek." It is singular that throughout the life of Mr. Mathews his excessive height should have been so insisted upon by everybody, for he was not more than five feet ten—a height much under many actors then and now before the public, who are unnoticed for such excess.

Mr. Young was a very first-rate mimic*—I use the favourite word, though one " unmusical to Volscian ears," to express a quick perception of manner and character in others, with talent to embody what is perceived. He had moreover a particular faculty of entering fully into the mind and manner of a person he had never seen, from another's imitation. All my husband's store was opened to this charming companion, who lent an eager ear to his descriptions; but of all others Mr. Young became enamoured of the style and character of Wynne, the Welsh musician already mentioned. Having become perfectly intimate with that amiable but peculiar person through Mr. Mathews's faithful portrait, he was thenceforth nothing but Wynne, and his own features being favourable for the representation, the resemblance was as good as the one from which it was so faithfully copied; indeed it was difficult to say which was the original portrait, so completely were both agreeing. Mr. Young would walk about as Wynne, his left eye shut, stumbling over everybody and everything in the

* Mr. Mathews's reluctance to acknowledge this term, when applied to *mental* as well as *personal* representation, is well known.

theatre; speaking and thinking like Wynne; on foot, or on horseback, everywhere in fact, he was Wynne, nothing but Wynne, except when on the stage. With this mania upon him, he and Mr. Mathews would ride out together as twin brothers, two Wynnes with but two eyes between them. At turnpikes one would stop, and in characteristic manner ask questions *à la* Wynne, and excite the man's wonder, which of course would be increased when another succeeded him with the same face, the same voice, the same gestures, the same questions and remarks. On such occasions the first Wynne took care not to lessen the surprise by riding out of sight, so that the puzzled and perplexed dupe would look after him just gone on, and then at the duplicate before him, as if he was almost in doubt whether he was sleeping or awake. It would take up more time than could be spared from the subject of these pages, to tell the many merry conceits which arose out of this Wynne-fever.

At this time my husband received a short letter from Mr. Colman upon the subject of Mr. Young's first engagement in London, which, as it will be seen, was negotiated by his friend.

TO CHARLES MATHEWS, ESQ.

My dear Mathews,   23rd December, 1803.

If I were to disclaim my antipathy to pen, ink, and paper, nobody would believe me. Heaven help all Epistolaries, from St. Paul to the Corinthians down to Lord Chesterfield to his son. Could anything make me write, your very pleasant letter would goad me. But,

"This is no answer, thou unfeeling man!"

In short, I cannot answer you in less than a week, for your question relative to Mr. Young involves a point which circumstances will not permit me yet to explain. Beg Mr. Young to allow me a week or ten days before he concludes an engagement; at the end of which time, my dear Mathews, you shall hear from me most fully, and then, "Were I as tedious as a prince, I could find it in my heart to bestow it all on your worship."

With great regard, yours, most sincerely,
G. Colman.

Soon after this period, a letter from my husband to his friend Mr. Litchfield announced an event which it will be seen gave him at the time a new delight, and continued ever after, without a single drawback, to afford him the greatest happiness.

TO JOHN LITCHFIELD, ESQ.

Dear Jack,   Liverpool, December 27th, 1803.

It is with the most exquisite pleasure I inform you that I am the father of a fine boy, at least so says the nurse, who would fain persuade me he is something uncommon. However, both mother and child, thank God, are extremely well, and, to go beyond the usual phrase, better than could be expected. My feelings on this occasion you may judge of, for as my fear and anxiety during the suspense of yesterday were severe, so is the joy I feel at the sight of my child, and safety of my beloved wife, infinitely more delightful than any other sensation I ever experienced.

I am happy beyond measure,—"who would not be a father?" You will perceive by the size of the paper, that I did mean to write a long letter, but I am sure you will excuse me. I have several letters to write to-day, you may suppose; think of my parental feelings! You will allow that this letter is written in a happy style. I am much gratified by your account of "Love laughs;" it is another proof of the great value of original parts. Remember me most kindly to Mrs. Litchfield.

Yours, ever,
CHARLES MATHEWS.

Mr. Mathews's father and mother were highly delighted at the birth of their first grandchild, and heartily welcomed the little stranger. As a postcript to his daughter's congratulations, the grandfather added the following lines.

MY DEAR CHARLES,

Give my love to dear Anne, and tell her I am happy at her safety. I wish, but not dictate, that you would name the child either by your own name or mine, or both, but not *William*, lest it might excite your mother's grief.

Yours, dear Charles,
J. Mathews.

Without hesitation " Charles James" was decided upon, and the tiny possessor of these names was promised to the church, if he inclined to that profession on attaining an age to choose for himself. The announcement of this intention was received by my husband's parents with gratified feeling, but with no rigid dependence upon an event which rested with the young man himself, who was enjoined, through us, not to enter upon such a profession unwillingly; his grandfather adding, " That he might be a good man without being a clergyman; but to force him to be a clergyman might tend to make him a bad man."

TO CHARLES MATHEWS, ESQ.

Suffolk Street, Charing Cross,
9th January 1804.

My dear Mathews,

You have chosen a curious correspondent in me, to gratify your passion for letter-reading. 'Tis like a drunkard inviting himself to a Mussulman's dinner, where there is no wine. I now write some days later than my promise. Indolence, however, has not swayed me in this instance; I have been incapable of answering a main point in your letter sooner. It is with much regret that I answer it now, by saying I must (for the present at least) relinquish Mr. Young's offer of assistance. Elliston's engagement with me, still extends to two seasons. This circumstance, and the limited scale of both business and expenses in the Haymarket, (and since the receipt of your letter, I have been looking minutely into expenses for next summer,) form a bar to my wish of treating with him. Pray present my best thanks to him for his proposal; and if, in the engagements he may immediately form, he should keep the Haymarket in view, and not bind himself for a long time elsewhere, it may ultimately, perhaps, tend to our mutual advantage. You are by no means the only " Ghost, whose word I would take for a thousand pounds," from whom I have heard of his merit.

I begin a little to doubt the good taste of your Liverpool managers. I hear they brought you out in *Pedrillo*, a vile part, surely, for the *début* of a man who is to make a *splash*. All actors call it an *up-hill part*, but I think it is *up mountain*. If, however, our " Love and Locksmiths" pleased them, it is more than it did the good folks at Covent Garden. I did not see it, but I am told it was almost marred, except Emery's *Solomon Lob*, which they tell me was excellent. Almost all the rest was " filthy dowlas;" even my friend Fawcett, I hear, (excellent actor as he is,) was not so happy as usual. They who had seen the piece in the Haymarket, attributed its want of effect to the bungling mode of getting it up; and we triumph most decidedly by the comparison.

You ask me if I am writing. I am like the puppet-show-man, " Just a-going to begin!" a comedy. Alas, alas! with my antipathy to pen and ink, what have I to endure, before I have the pleasure of meeting you. For my own sake, if not for yours, I shall endeavour at something which may please you, and be effective in your hands.

Whenever you are at leisure (if it be not too imprudent a request for a professed bad answer,) scribble a few lines to me. I shall always be happy to hear from you; any intelligence of your proceedings and welfare will be interesting, my dear Mathews, to yours, very truly,

G. COLMAN.

TO JOHN LITCHFIELD, ESQ.

DEAR JACK, Liverpool, February 2nd, 1804.

Why don't you write, you villain? I have the pleasure to tell you that my benefit last Wednesday produced 238*l.*, which is the best house of the winter season; that is, since the reduced prices.

The pit and boxes overflowed considerably more than any night since the theatre opened; the gallery was bad, only 21*l.*, and will hold above 50*l.* It was a box bill, " Clandestine Marriage," " Turnpike Gate," " Imitations." The gallery folks are used every night to pantomimes, and dances, by Cross, &c. I did not expect them, nor lament their loss, for they are a most riotous set. This house is what I call a "circumstance!" I have now found out that I am a prodigious favourite, as they are rather cold in their treatment of performers, in the theatre. I confess I doubted it till lately. All my lower boxes were taken, and many up-stairs. The imitations were of considerable service to me.

I have heard from Colman lately, who swears he will

write for the opening. Elliston has some novelties ready, I don't know by whom. He talks of a comedy the first week; if so, we shall go on swimmingly. I was in a dangerous state for four days. Prince William bespoke the play last night. Write, you villain.

Yours, ever,
CHARLES MATHEWS.

TO CHARLES MATHEWS, ESQ.

DEAR CHARLES, London, February 29th, 1804.

I received yours yestermorning, and have to thank you very sincerely for your kind attention.

I don't know the account you may have seen respecting Holman's comedy, but if you had been in the house, you would not have put the question as to its being done again. That there was a strong party against poor Holman, is beyond a doubt; for they showed themselves at the end of the first act, — a most unprecedented procedure in London, and which does not (as you know) accord with the usual liberality of this audience. I can safely say not one of the actors expected such would be the fate of the piece. We have a new afterpiece coming out, by P. Hoare; should it hit, I think Fawcett's part will be a good card for you.

I give you joy of your little one. Hope Mrs. Mathews and it are everything your earnest wishes could suggest. Mr. Harris and self have settled again for five years: the terms very advantageous. My mother is included in the treaty. They have behaved shockingly to me respecting her at Drury-Lane. She was engaged last season by Mr.

Richardson,* and because, poor fellow, he died in the interim, the remaining proprietors (after bringing her and father a journey of nearly two hundred miles) refused to ratify the engagement. " Dom it, this can't be justice!" The consequence is, that the old people have been thrown on my shoulders all the season : the burthen is a pleasant one, I grant ; but, d— it, why need I carry a pack-saddle, when I ought to be on the turf?

I have enlarged a little on this subject, to put you on your guard in the event of your having to do with them. " Remember whom you have to cope withal—a scum of managers."

It is needless to say, I am proud of the approbation of the Liverpool audience, and shall ever gratefully acknowledge it. Of your panegyric, Charles, I am also vain, but cannot admit it at your own expense. Your success has caused you equally to share their favours. We are hard at work here, soldiering. I suspect our regiment† (very generally considered among the best appointed in London) will be one of the first to take the field when Boney comes. "I'd rather be your third or fourth,‡" but as the song goes, " God defend the right." Our beloved sovereign still continues the same. The bulletins are so cold and evasive in their accounts, that I fear he is worse than he is represented. If the prayers of a loyal people

* One of the proprietors.
† Mr. Emery was a volunteer.
‡ A quotation from the farce of " The Poor Soldier," in which, when *Darby* is requested by *Bagatelle* to be his *second* in a duel, he replies, under an impression that he will be further removed from personal danger—" If it's the same to you, *mounseer*, I'd rather be your third or fourth."—A.M.

can save him, then he is safe; for the theatres resound with the coronation anthem every night, amongst thunders of applause.

Well, with kind regards to Mrs. Mathews (in which Mrs. Emery begs most heartily to join me) believe me, dear Charles,

Yours truly,
J. EMERY.

(Errors excepted.)

END OF THE FIRST VOLUME.

LONDON:
PRINTED BY SAMUEL BENTLEY.
Bangor House, Shoe Lane.

Lightning Source UK Ltd.
Milton Keynes UK
UKHW02n0702260618
324798UK00017B/42/P